Authoritarians in the Academy

Authoritarians in the Academy

How the Internationalization
of Higher Education
and Borderless Censorship
Threaten Free Speech

Sarah McLaughlin

JOHNS HOPKINS UNIVERSITY PRESS
Baltimore

© 2025 Sarah McLaughlin
All rights reserved. Published 2025
Printed in the United States of America on acid-free paper
9 8 7 6 5 4 3 2 1

Johns Hopkins University Press
2715 North Charles Street
Baltimore, Maryland 21218
www.press.jhu.edu

Library of Congress Cataloging-in-Publication Data is available.

A catalog record for this book is available from the British Library.

ISBN 978-1-4214-5280-7 (hardcover)
ISBN 978-1-4214-5281-4 (ebook)

Special discounts are available for bulk purchases of this book. For more information, please contact Special Sales at specialsales@jh.edu.

EU GPSR Authorized Representative
LOGOS EUROPE, 9 rue Nicolas Poussin, 17000, La Rochelle, France
E-mail: Contact@logoseurope.eu

For Trudi and Shawn

Contents

Introduction	1
1. American Campuses, Red Lines	7
2. The Censorship Bureaucracy and Its Victims	49
3. How Did We Get Here?	82
4. The Global Threat of Authoritarian Censorship in Academia	111
5. Compromised Campuses	152
6. The Surveilled Classroom	198
7. A Free World Needs Free Campuses	229
Acknowledgments	*257*
Notes	*259*
Index	*311*

Introduction

You might not always see them, but there are red lines around what can be said in higher education. And every day they seem to multiply.

Administrators weigh their commitments to free expression against the cost of offending foreign governments and losing out on lucrative partnerships. International students fear that speaking out will result in consequences that await them or their families at home. Professors worry they will face professional repercussions, or that their students will face legal trouble, if they discuss sensitive topics in the classroom. The red lines are not always explicit or visible—and sometimes that makes them even more daunting.

Universities are meant to be among the most open places in the world for both research and unfettered debate. So why is it getting harder to speak freely on campuses about the state of authoritarianism in the world today?

For over a decade, I have aided students and professors facing censorship on American campuses, whether due to their political artwork, controversial tweets, or criticism of their university's leadership. In my work at the Foundation for Individual Rights and Expression (FIRE), I have defended the rights of people across the ideological spectrum, from students accusing their universities of perpetuating racial injustice, to professors weighing in on Israel and Palestine, and to student groups wishing to advocate for conservative political beliefs on campus—sometimes all on the same day.

And over the years, I began to notice something troubling: My interest in global censorship and my work defending free speech at American universities were converging with growing frequency.

Increasingly, challenges to the right to speak on campus now involve not just the familiar flash points in US politics—like abortion, race, or guns—but also external and internal pressure on universities to conform with the censorship policies of authoritarian countries. As college campuses have grown into global institutions—with international student bodies, campuses, and research agreements—they have benefited from the opportunities and relationships gained by expanding across borders. But they have also discovered that expansion can bring with it certain pressures and incentives that result in universities with larger global footprints, but with diminished rights.

In this book, I will address this confluence between campus speech issues in the United States and authoritarians' censorship overtures on a global scale. Foreign interference in higher education, particularly regarding China and other powers' access to scientific research, is a concern in the halls of Congress and the pages of newspapers. But too little attention has been paid to the ramifications for expressive freedom—free speech, academic freedom, and dissent—engendered by relationships with states that do not value, or are actively hostile to, these baseline needs of the academic community. Here, I seek to shine a light not just on the ways that unfree countries like China and the United Arab Emirates limit the rights of students and academics, along with the scholarship they produce, but also on the methods they use to pressure universities themselves to conform with authoritarian speech restrictions.

Two particular trends of note have emerged in this space. First is the "censors without borders": speech policing extending far beyond a country's traditional borders and into populations around the world. Think of Russia abusing Interpol red notices to target critics, agents from Saudi Arabia slaughtering a journalist in their Istanbul consulate, or China threatening its citizens for their relatives' surveilled activism abroad. Efforts to intimidate exiled critics are nothing new, but today's technology allows authoritarians to get targets in their sights more quickly and effectively. In March 2022, in what is just one of many recent examples of such repression in the United States, federal prosecutors unsealed complaints revealing that individuals acting on behalf of the Chinese government orchestrated efforts to stalk, censor, and spy on dissidents and critics, including a Tiananmen student leader who fled to the United States and later planned to run for Congress.[1] Much of this book will focus on international censorship efforts coordinated by the Chinese government simply because of the outsize role China plays in higher education. But readers should understand that the threat of borderless censorship is posed by a number of governments around the world.

Readers in mostly free nations might understandably ask, "Why should I worry about censorship in a country thousands of miles away?" People, of course, rightly tend to be more concerned by what is taking place in their same state, region, country, or postal code, than by what is happening somewhere thousands of miles away. You are more likely to be affected by, and able to change, something happening next door. But those who ascribe too stridently to this worldview risk missing the full picture of how censorship operates in today's extensively interconnected world.

You may not be interested in authoritarianism abroad, but that does not mean it is not interested in you.

Censorship imposed by foreign countries is a problem that exists in institutions across society, but it is especially dangerous on college campuses. International students, who sometimes make up a significant portion of a university's student body, can risk severe consequences at home with just a single political statement abroad—even in a country like the United States where the First Amendment is intended to protect them, and even on campuses that are supposed to host the unrestricted exchange of views. The First Amendment is constrained by borders, and university administrators by conflicting interests. The censors targeting students do not share those same limitations. Censorship laws that may seem so distant to readers may nevertheless be influencing what is and is not said on a campus down the street.

And while universities have increasingly turned to international students to staunch financial bleeding as other funding sources have dried out, their enthusiasm for seeking out pupils to pay full-freight tuition has not coincided with a desire to protect those same students' basic expressive rights. Far from it. This reliance on international students' tuition has also offered a powerful lever for well-populated authoritarian countries to pull against noncompliant universities. These nations have the power to deny universities millions in tuition payments, a fact university administrations, pressed by dwindling domestic investment, no doubt know.

The second trend is what I will call "sensitivity exploitation," which describes appeals to cultural sensitivity to justify or demand censorship of political speech critical of authoritarian governments. Critics of the Chinese government especially face increasing censorship attempts on campus under this guise, from both consular officials and hypernationalistic students. It is not just on campus either. For example, after a sporting event

Introduction

mix-up where a protest anthem was played for Hong Kong's team instead of the Chinese national anthem, Hong Kong security chief Chris Tang claimed that Google "hurt the feelings of Hong Kong people" by refusing to alter search results to prioritize the Chinese anthem.[2]

Chapters 1 through 3 will focus on sensitivity exploitation and censors without borders in the United States, how they manifest at universities, and how existing campus speech restrictions are ripe for such exploitation, while chapter 4 will look at these issues on a global scale.

In later chapters, I will also look at developments taking place at campuses in the United States, as well around the world, detailing how universities' international reach has expanded, sometimes at the cost of what should be the most important institutional values: academic freedom and freedom of expression. While the discussion is largely focused on higher education—like the plight of international students, government officials' interference efforts, or satellite campuses in significantly unfree countries—it should be understood as part of a much larger challenge to free expression.

The problem is this: We do not fully understand or appreciate the way speech suppression operates today. It does not always bear the traditional and blunt signs we may expect. As authoritarians around the world become savvier at finding ways to silence individuals and institutions far beyond their borders, citizens of countries accustomed to generally advanced speech protections must recognize that those legal protections may not be enough to truly shield them or preserve their rights in their communities today. Demarcation lines on maps mean little when it comes to the actual reach or secondary effects of censorship regimes.

The COVID-19 pandemic illustrated how oppressive laws that silence dissent and debate in one country can have far-reaching effects on a global scale. If, before COVID-19, you thought that censorship in countries apart from your own was a regrettable reality, but one that would not affect you, it should be clear now that this is not the case. While many countries, like the United States, grievously mishandled the COVID-19 pandemic in its early stages and would have likely done so regardless of how much advance warning they had been given, it is indisputable that the censorship efforts led by the Chinese government stole valuable time and opportunities from the world's pandemic response.[3] Global, mass-scale repercussions can result from localized censorship.

The pandemic crystallized the dangers we incur when we ignore the broad reach of censorship and its downstream effects. I fear we are insufficiently cognizant of how authoritarian censorship is embedding itself within higher education, and what that means for at-risk individuals in our universities and for the knowledge production broader society relies on from our academic institutions. Even as avenues for expression expand through technological innovation, human freedom is on the decline around the world, and we should be deeply concerned by the role industries and institutions *outside* of authoritarian countries play in the state of declining global freedom.

Authoritarianism does not act alone. It relies upon the willingness of institutions to comply, silence, and self-censor, sometimes even in the absence of orders to do so. So, we must ask: Are our universities ignoring the strain put upon them by authoritarianism?

Or, even worse, are some aiding its spread?

CHAPTER 1

American Campuses, Red Lines

In February 2022, human rights advocates watched uneasily as the Chinese government used the Beijing Winter Olympics to mask the country's human rights violations with a veneer of pageantry. Despite its lofty ideals, the International Olympic Committee embraced political neutrality—a stance it adopts and abandons at its convenience—while dismissing valid ethical concerns about hosting these games in China. Officials from the Beijing organizing committee openly threatened to punish anyone engaging in "speech that is against the Olympic spirit, especially against the Chinese laws and regulations."[1] Teams warned their athletes against political expression that could endanger their safety.

Almost uniformly, sponsors, officials, athletes, and advertisers fell into line. They knew there were Uyghur internment camps in Xinjiang and democracy activists imprisoned in Hong Kong. But, until after the games, they would not be saying a word about it—if they ever chose to say anything at all.

These Olympics were the latest example in an alarming trend. Countries—often China, but not always—are getting better at exploiting the interests of foreign businesses and global institutions while threatening individuals and communities outside their borders. The result is an exported form of censorship, one that is tough to track and even harder to combat. Discussing authoritarian governments, even thousands of miles away, is becoming more difficult. I observed this "censors without borders" trend and began working on this book about authoritarianism seeping into academic communities.

And then an all-too-timely controversy erupted at George Washington University (GW).

Sensitivity Exploitation and China's Critics

Before the games began, anonymous GW students posted artwork on campus satirizing the Olympics and China's human rights record. The art was created by Badiucao, an Australia-based Chinese artist, activist, and frequent target of censorship. The stylized depictions of faceless, anonymous athletes representing China's curling, figure skating, skiing, and hockey squads might look, from a distance, like promotional posters. Up close, not so much. The art, which CBS News called "a provocative visual argument for why China is unfit to host the games,"[2] depicted images with allusions to violence against Tibetan monks and Uyghurs, China's initial cover up of COVID-19, and the country's extensive surveillance regime.

The posters sparked a debate that has become increasingly common at universities worldwide: What *can* be said about China on campus? And perhaps an even more contested question: What *should* be said? This debate is not just about what students and professors can say about China without punishment, though that right is under attack. It is also about the shifting social boundaries of this political discussion.

At GW, some student groups made it explicitly clear that they believed the Olympics artwork had crossed both the line of appropriate debate and the limits of university protections for free speech. The George Washington University Chinese Students and Scholars Association (CSSA) chapter, which called on the university to "severely" punish those responsible for the images, claimed the posters "insulted China" and were "not only trampling on the Olympic spirit," but also constituted an "extremely vicious" act against all Asian students and "a naked attack on the Chinese nation!"

Then another student group chimed in. The university's Chinese Cultural Association said the posters "may incite Asian Hate sentiment and pose a potential risk to the personal safety of all Chinese and Asian students" and were outside the "scope" of free expression. I reached out to both groups after the incident, asking which university policies had been violated and what punishment would be appropriate. Neither group responded.

Initially, the demands of the two student groups were granted. In a private email, then–University President Mark S. Wrighton shared that he was "personally offended by the posters," which he had directed staff to remove, and would "undertake an effort to determine who is responsible" for this "terrible event."[3] For the students who demanded punishment and censorship, this was quite a victory: Not only did the university's leader agree to investigate those involved for policy violations, but he also concurred that the artwork was offensive and unacceptable.

Years earlier, as chancellor, Wrighton helped to make Washington University in St. Louis the first North American member of the University Alliance of the Silk Road. Wrighton praised the program, saying it would "contribute significantly to a brighter future,"[4] while accepting membership on behalf of his institution at an event at Xi'an Jiaotong University in 2016. The University Alliance of the Silk Road launched the year before as an academia-focused entry into China's large-scale infrastructure project, the Belt and Road Initiative, a global government program linking China with dozens of countries in Africa, Europe, and Latin America for local development projects. These projects, though, often come with rising costs, debt, transparency issues, and troubling strings, leading some critics to call it "a Trojan horse for China-led regional development and military expansion."[5]

No evidence suggests Wrighton's involvement in the alliance had any bearing on his decision-making during the controversy at GW. But given his background and experience, Wrighton surely knew how unwelcome the political dissent displayed in Badiucao's posters is among Chinese government officials, and that he was agreeing to punish political expression protected by the First Amendment in the United States, while that same expression could land activists behind bars in China.

A GW associate vice provost focusing on diversity initiatives confirmed that the university police had indeed launched an investigation. Jordan S. West, said administrator, wrote in response to a bias incident report that she had "immediately contacted" campus police, who were "checking all surveillance cameras to try and determine who entered the building and posted the images." West then offered university counseling services while police sought "to identify any individuals involved and responsible."[6] For students upset by the artwork, counseling was offered. For students who had posted it, punishment was ordered.

I contacted campus police for more information about their investigation. A spokesperson sent me an already public statement made by Wrighton, writing it was "all I have to share with you on this topic."

Zach Blackburn, a student journalist who initially reported on the story at the GW Hatchet, told me this was the most complex story he had covered on campus. It combined disputed allegations of bigotry, criticism of the Chinese government, and potential employment of university resources to punish expression. Blackburn told me that some students opposed the content of the posters, but also questioned the wisdom of punishing those responsible for them. "From what I've seen, even Chinese and Asian students on campus are divided as to whether the posters were inappropriate," Blackburn said.

As Wrighton's email spread among angry commentators on social media, the problems with GW's response should have been obvious to university leadership. For one, GW promises to protect its students' free speech, but was quick to violate that commitment to censor artwork criticizing a major world power's human rights record. More troublingly, if the responsible students were *from* China or Hong Kong and their involvement became known, the university could be placing them in genuine legal peril. As I will discuss more in this chapter and book, documented cases show Chinese students facing threats, police inquiries, and imprisonment for what they have said while abroad. A disciplinary incident that might inconvenience American students could genuinely imperil international students and their families.

What was not widely known at the time was that Wrighton was putting the students in exactly that danger: Dissident students *from* China were involved in the protests against China at GW. The students I spoke to, including three from mainland China, one from Taiwan, and an American student ally, told me that their anonymity, which the university's leadership treated so carelessly, was vital. "It's obvious. You have families in China," one of the students said. Should they be uncovered, their futures, and their families, could pay the price. Two of them said they could not even tell their families about their activities. One student, whose father participated in the 1989 student movement in China, thought his family would be proud if they knew. But, for their protection, he did not tell them.

They said the demands for their punishment were no surprise. The CSSA, which called for their punishment, "thinks they are the leaders of mainland Chinese, Hong Kongers, and Taiwanese. This is not exclusive to George Washington University, but at all CSSAs in postsecondary education," one student said. These hypernationalistic views, they said, do not represent all Chinese students—no matter how much chapter leaders pretend they do.

Even worse, Wrighton appeared to take the offended students' word for it when they complained about the posters. Why did he not look closer at the artwork and form his own conclusions? What he probably hoped to broadcast was a swift response to alleged bigotry. Instead, it looked like he saw students battling over China's human rights violations—and picked the Chinese government's side.

FIRE, GW students, alumni, national commentators, and politicians including Senator Marco Rubio spoke out against the investigation. To his credit, Wrighton announced it would be ending just days after promising it. "I want to be very clear: I support freedom of speech—even when it offends people—and creative art is a valued way to communicate on important societal issues," he wrote.[7] Wrighton also confirmed the university would take no further action against the students.

It is rarely easy to acknowledge mistakes, and Wrighton deserves praise for publicly admitting his errors and altering course. Nevertheless, it remains troubling that Wrighton's first instinct, one shared by many university leaders, was to promise censorship rather than examine what he was being asked to censor, especially when the stakes for the speakers were so serious. Indeed, Wrighton had even said that he *himself* found the posters offensive. Were those his actual feelings, or simply something said to appease the artwork's critics? Neither answer is particularly reassuring.

While the incident resolved as well as could be expected, it remains disturbing. That multiple people in authority at a prestigious American university so quickly and carelessly directed their police force to seek out critics of a foreign government is, to put it mildly, a warning sign. Authoritarians need no assistance with hunting down their critics.

The day after Wrighton's announcement, members of the Chinese government broadcaster CCTV were seen on GW's campus, presumably to interview students about the posters. Who the CCTV employees spoke to or what information they sought is unclear, but their presence would likely reaffirm to involved students that Chinese authorities were interested in unmasking them. Chinese state-run outlets have grown increasingly pugilistic in recent years and serve as a tool in the information wars both within China and the rest of the world. Another state outlet, *Global Times*, followed up with an op-ed from GW alumni Zhang Sheng and Bao Haining, who wrote that "the last refuge of [the] racist hater" is free expression. "The sudden and fundamental flip of Wrighton's attitude toward the posters also clearly demonstrates that much of American society today is so indulged in launching a witch-hunt against the Chinese," they wrote, "that it cannot even tolerate a university president granting the minimum degree of protection to save students from racist demonization."[8] Consider this: People need protection not from an authoritarian government, but from its peaceful critics.

Later that year, when some of these dissident students took part in global protests surrounding the 20th National Congress of the Chinese Communist Party (CCP), they feared being surveilled once again. While putting up copies of more protest posters in October 2022, a man they suspected to be a Chinese nationalist stopped to stare at their signs. He demanded, in Chinese, that they tell him what organization they were from. Then he pulled out his phone and began to record them. "It was a pretty scary moment," one of the students told me. "It's like the person has power over you," another added.

The events surrounding the Beijing Olympics protest at GW illustrate "sensitivity exploitation." This occurs when an appeal to an institution's status as a welcoming, diverse place is used to demand censorship of political speech about a government, by claiming it targeted that country's *citizens*. To many observers, the story was shocking. How could an American university, intended to be the pinnacle of institutions devoted to freedom of expression, even temporarily promise to censor critics of the Chinese government, especially during the country's widely discussed Olympic games? But to those paying attention, it was less surprising. After all, this tendency has been a growing problem in academia and other institutions and corporations in America and abroad. Global brands are deeply unwilling to cross lines when it comes to China's sensitive subjects, including Tibet, Taiwan, Tiananmen, Xinjiang, Falun Gong, or the democracy movement in Hong Kong. We need only look back a few years earlier for another incident involving criticism of China, a backlash, and internationally famous sporting events.

In 2019, a single tweet sparked a very public meltdown within the National Basketball Association, illustrating these dynamics to the general public. When then–Houston Rockets General Manager Daryl Morey tweeted an image with just seven words, "Fight for Freedom Stand with Hong Kong," he intended to share a simple message of support for Hong Kongers protesting increasing encroachment from Beijing in the form of a proposed extradition law. Instead, he set off an international chain reaction that resulted in ugly feuds within the National Basketball Association, demands from the Chinese government that Morey be fired, and the likely loss of hundreds of millions of dollars.

Many well-known names in and outside the league, including LeBron James, responded to Morey's tweet by distancing themselves, criticizing his behavior, and seeking to make amends. James said the tweet could have harmed people "not only financially, but physically, emotionally, spiritually." Joe Tsai, cofounder of Chinese tech company Alibaba Group and governor of the NBA's Brooklyn Nets, wrote an open letter on Facebook denouncing Morey. He criticized Morey for touching on a "third-rail" issue for the Chinese government and "all citizens in China," saying "1.4 billion Chinese citizens stand united when it comes to the territorial integrity of China." Tsai lamented that "the hurt that this incident has caused will take a long time to repair."[9] Once again, expression about an authoritarian government is discussed not as political speech, but as a form of insensitivity against its citizens. In 2016, Tsai donated $30 million to Yale Law School for its China Center, which was then renamed the Paul Tsai China Center in recognition of his father.[10]

The Chinese consulate in Houston shared its anger as well: "We have lodged representations and expressed strong dissatisfaction with the Houston Rockets, and urged the latter to correct the error and take immediate concrete measures to eliminate the adverse impact."[11]

One of the most interesting reactions was the initial response from the NBA itself, which shared an English statement calling Morey's tweet "regrettable," but noting that league members had the ability to share their views. On the other hand, their statement in Chinese took a different tone, announcing that the NBA's administration was "extremely disappointed in the inappropriate comment" by Morey and that "he has undoubtedly seriously hurt the feelings of Chinese basketball fans."[12] (Keep an eye out for Chinese-language apology statements that take a different tone than English-language ones, a theme which will come up again.)

The takeaway was clear: China's backlash was expected and unsurprising. Morey, not the Chinese officials that sought to penalize the NBA, was seen as the one who transgressed norms. The heavy implication within the league, sometimes stated outright, was that Morey's vocal support of human rights was a direct attack on the business interests of his colleagues. Even in a deeply activist athletic league, some activism is simply too costly.

An institution known for its commitments to certain values, whether those values are activism in athletics or truth-seeking in academia, may struggle to stick with them when the controversy centers on China.

After the initial storm over Morey's tweet subsided, questions about the relationship between the NBA and China remained. Months after the controversy, a report from ESPN found that "the league faced complaints from its own employees over human rights concerns inside an NBA youth-development program" in China.[13] The programs were located in Xinjiang, where "re-education camps," detentions, forced labor, sterilizations, mass surveillance, and disappearances of members of China's Uyghur population have taken place in recent years.[14]

The NBA ultimately ended its programs in Xinjiang, but the league remained vague about the reasons for the closure in the face of questions about its potential knowledge of the treatment of China's Uyghurs. "My job, our job is not to take a position on every single human rights violation, and I'm not an expert in every human rights situation or violation," NBA deputy commissioner and chief operating officer Mark Tatum told ESPN. "I'll tell you what the NBA stands for: The values of the NBA are about respect, are about inclusion, are about diversity. That is what we stand for." It is not difficult to imagine the same arguments coming from the head of a university facing a similar controversy.

The incident revealed an uncomfortable truth that had previously been easier to ignore: When faced with a conflict between freedom of expression, human rights, and their bottom line, institutions rarely side with critics of authoritarianism. That is troubling in professional sports, but it can be even worse in other contexts. When these conflicts arise in higher education, it is students who are at risk of losing the most, students like those who dared to speak their minds about the Beijing Olympics at George Washington University. Whether you are a high-ranking employee in an international sporting league or a 19-year-old with access to a campus bulletin board—there can be consequences for criticizing the powerful.

International students have left China for school overseas, but have they truly escaped Chinese authorities? In the rest of this chapter, I will discuss how students at US colleges face significant barriers when it comes to talking freely about China. No space is guaranteed to be safe for student dissenters—not the classroom, the quad, the internet, or even their college president's office. The consequences extend beyond the campus walls as well. A tweet, essay, protest, or debate can have implications thousands of miles away, years later. It is no surprise that the Chinese government is trying to silence its critics, but it is perhaps unexpected that some students themselves have joined the campaign for censorship.

Students Censoring Students

Before COVID-19, more than one million international students enrolled at US universities, with Chinese students making up nearly 35 percent of the total, vastly outnumbering those from other countries like South Korea, Saudi Arabia, and Canada, though students from India may soon match or outpace them.

US campuses are, of course, no stranger to contentious, and often headline-grabbing, disputes among students about sensitive issues like race, gender, and politics. The Israeli-Palestinian conflict, for example, is a frequent source of discord among students, the focus of blistering media and congressional attention in late 2023, and the impetus behind campus encampments that led to sometimes shocking arrests.

And over the past two decades, China has increasingly emerged as another source of contention on campuses. What has changed during that time is that these disputes about what can be said about China now often take the form of public demands and disagreements by and among students themselves, rather than primarily at the hands of private pressure by consular officials, which I will discuss in the next chapter.

Two recent incidents at Cornell University and Carnegie Mellon University (CMU) provide insight into how these disputes around "sensitivity exploitation" among students play out. At a March 2022 Cornell colloquium, student Rizwangul NurMuhammad asked Michigan Rep. Elissa Slotkin about the disparity between the international response to Russia's invasion of Ukraine and China's oppression of Uyghurs in Xinjiang, where her brother was arrested in 2017. Her question resulted in boos and a walkout by about forty students.[15] That is troubling on its own. But what happened next gives insight into how haphazardly university leaders handle these disputes, and how their desire to protect the feelings of some students leaves others, like NurMuhammad, out in the cold.

Matt Hall, director of the Cornell Institute for Public Affairs, wrote in an email the next day that the public administration program and the colloquium series "are spaces where difficult conversations can and should take place," but "we must also respect that walkouts are a legitimate form of protest and an appropriate expression of disapproval."

William Wang, then–president of the Cornell Public Affairs Society, coordinated a response to Hall from over eighty fellow international students from China explaining the walkout "was not orchestrated in any way whatsoever," though Slotkin suggested it was "coordinated" in a statement after the incident.[16] Wang also decried "that our restraint directly resulted in us being called a cult, Nazis, and brainwashed CCP worshipers," presumably referencing a classmate's tweet critical of Hall's suggestion to "respect" the walkout.

Wang's sign-on letter claimed that NurMuhammad was not the "sole reason" students were upset, though her question launched the walkout. They also reported being angered by a fellow student who pointed out that students from China make up a significant portion of the incoming class, and by Rep. Slotkin's response that she disapproved of the Chinese government and hoped the students from the country would help change its policy when they returned home. "We were not sitting in a classroom," they wrote, "we were crucified in a courtroom for crimes that we did not commit. Thus, we hope the school could formally respond to our email so that we know we made the right decision of choosing CIPA and Cornell." The letter concluded that the classroom environment was "hostile" not to NurMuhammad, but to the students who walked out.

Their complaints were apparently heard. Hall's next email took a different tone, writing in part that some "have expressed worry that Chinese students are not welcome at Cornell" and that the events showed "how harmful it is when conversation devolves into derogatory anti-Asian expression."

"Please know, we have reached out to the students directly involved to offer assistance, and we are mobilizing university resources to support student well-being," Hall wrote. The incident highlighted Cornell's seeming preference for the concerns of the students who walked out over those of the student walked out on. Did the administrators genuinely believe the classroom was hostile to students from China or were they simply appeasing tuition-paying customers? Like the potential motivations in play during the GW controversy, neither option is particularly encouraging.

Magnus Fiskesjö, an associate professor at Cornell, suggests that the university, while trying to appease a large tuition-paying contingent, was likely acting out of ignorance. Fiskesjö told me when we spoke shortly after the incident that he was told at the time that after NurMuhammad spoke, there was an instruction given by one of the students to the others in the room. "He said something like 'If you're a patriot, you'll leave now.' That was seen as a command to fellow students."

What Cornell's administration may have seen only as an act of student protest via walkout could very well have obscured an uglier reality: Some students may have walked out while NurMuhammad spoke not because they particularly wanted to, but because they felt their peers would notice if they stayed. "They should know what is going on, that the Chinese students are not enjoying free speech because they're being monitored on campus," Fiskesjö says. When it comes to recognition of the unique position these students are in, "administrators have been kicking the can down the road for a long time." Fiskesjö mentioned other incidents at Cornell in previous years, including theft of posters supporting Tibet, vicious messages to a professor who organized a documentary screening about Tibet, and a warning from the Chinese consulate directed to a Chinese student who intended to start a student group without the consulate's involvement.

Just weeks after this incident, a recent graduate was attacked on campus while posting Free Hong Kong and Free Uyghurs posters. The student, Kinen Kao, said his assailant left him with cuts on his hand and tried to steal his phone when he began filming the attack.[17]

At Carnegie Mellon, a year before the incidents at Cornell, administrators also seemed unwilling to grapple with the complexities surrounding criticism of China and discussion of its human rights record. CMU is a popular destination for international study, with students from abroad comprising 35 percent of the student body.[18] In March 2021, CMU's Graduate Student Assembly (GSA) Executive Committee released a statement objecting to "the spike of hate crimes being perpetrated against our Asian community" during the pandemic. The statement acknowledged that "various events—often traumatic—are happening in different Asian countries" that could "add to the stress our peers are feeling during this time." Those events listed included protests in India, encroachments against Hong Kong, and internment camps and forced labor in Xinjiang.

Overall, the statement focused on the spike of discrimination and harassment against Asian communities in the United States. But that singular mention of Xinjiang and Hong Kong provoked a wide-ranging backlash against GSA members. Divyansh Kaushik, a vice president in the graduate student assembly at the time of the statement and president the following year, told me in a 2022 interview that the assembly had long been politically vocal, including against the Trump administration's proclamations against Chinese students. But when the criticism of China was released, "suddenly people had issues with GSA taking political stances."

Almost immediately, furious emails and social media messages began rolling in to members of the committee, some of them demanding resignations and apologies. Students painted "GSA MUST APOLOGIZE, RISE UP AGAINST RACISM, GSA RACIST RESIGN" on a campus fence open to student artwork. Then a petition created by a group calling itself the Asian Student Stop-Asian-Hate Petition Organizing Committee was shared on Change.org, demanding the GSA "acknowledge the harm that has been caused by this inappropriate and insensitive language," "retract this objectionable language and apologize for its inclusion and the hurt that it has caused," and "revisit the process in place to prevent such a statement from being published and disseminated" again.[19] In just a few days, the petition gained thousands of signatures, as well as comments calling for resignations and revoked alumni donations. The statement's authors were taken aback. All they had done was mention human rights abuses in China as part of a broader statement recognizing suffering among Asian communities in the United States. Why were thousands of people, including some of their peers on campus, now accusing them of racism?

In an attempt at damage control, CMU's administrators worked with the assembly to issue an apology, which stated that the writers of the statement "acknowledge and regret that some of the topics we chose to address at that moment distracted from our core message, and we apologize for causing pain in the communities we were trying to support." CMU's administration privately suggested that the GSA members paint an apology on the campus fence. Dacen Waters, a previous leader of the GSA, told me he was "disappointed that the admin's advice wasn't: 'You did nothing wrong, continue to stand up for what you believe is right. You have the right to say what you did and we have your back.'"

In retrospect, Kaushik says that while he regretted some wording in the initial statement, he also regretted the decision to rescind it. A Uyghur student told the GSA that the statement acknowledging what is occurring in Xinjiang was the first time he felt recognized at CMU. "We failed him by issuing that apology," Kaushik said.

Sulaiman Gu, a former University of Georgia graduate student and member of China's mostly Muslim Hui minority, told ProPublica that American university communities' preoccupation with sensitivity and avoiding offense is far too easy to exploit for those wishing to deflect conversations about China, as happened at CMU. "American universities tend to treat these issues as issues of racism and diversity," Gu explained, and lose sight of another important goal: protecting students against oppression from authoritarian governments.[20]

Gu has some experience with dissenting as an international student. In 2018, he and a fellow dissident entrapped a Chinese public security officer using known activist Gu as bait. "We said as dissidents we knew we were in trouble, and we wanted to come home to work," according to Gu. He recorded and publicized the officer's attempts to enlist him as an overseas spy, which he was told would be his only opportunity to redeem himself for his transgressive activism. When officials learned they had been embarrassed, Gu's family in China suffered retaliatory harassment.

In a 2018 Woodrow Wilson International Center for Scholars report about China's political interference on campus, author Anastasya Lloyd-Damnjanovic noted this conflation between criticism of the country of China and racism against Chinese people. "Many faculty expressed anxiety about being publicly identified in this study for fear that the PRC government might retaliate or that some social progressives in the United States might perceive criticisms of the PRC as 'racist.' This was true even among respondents who claimed they do *not* self-censor," she wrote.[21]

Incidents of anti-Asian racism and hate crimes like those decried by CMU's GSA have indeed been a worrying trend alongside the pandemic, and some public rhetoric—including from US government officials—fueled insinuations that Chinese citizens should be personally blamed.[22] But this push and pull among students about criticism of China does not all stem from the years of the pandemic. Since at least the early 2000s, students have pressed on administrators and their peers to downplay or censor negative commentary about China, sometimes under the justification that such commentary is hurtful or offensive. In recent years, those incidents have multiplied.

The University of Rochester, for example, experienced weeks of turmoil over a series of incidents taking place on campus in 2019, and it offers a useful example of what this push and pull looks like. Early in the fall semester, the university's College Republicans held an event about democracy in Tibet that was protested by students holding posters showing a self-immolating Tibetan monk with the caption "Freedom or Terrorism?"[23] Around the same time, a group of visiting Tibetan monks left a campus Starbucks when a student put a sign near them asserting that "Tibet is part of China." After the Tibet event, the president of the campus Chinese Students' Association made a request to the student government's judicial council asking for the cancellation of an upcoming College Republicans event on the mass incarceration of Uyghurs, followed by a letter from the College Republicans calling for an investigation of the Chinese Students' Association.

That November, the conflict moved into the university's painted tunnel, where students added artwork as a response to the events taking place on campus in previous weeks. The messages included "Free Hong Kong," "Free Tibet," "I♥Dalai Lama," and praise for Hong Kong's protesters. Soon, other students arrived to cover these messages.[24] The editorial board of the student newspaper specifically accused the campus Chinese Students and Scholars Association chapter of engaging in "regressive, suppressive" behavior. "We go to a university, an institution for learning. To learn, we must challenge our perspectives by exploring those different than our own. To obscure an opposing view by painting over it rejects such exploration," the board wrote.[25]

Chinese Students and Scholars Associations

These censorship or sensitivity exploitation incidents taking place at various American universities are not all the same. Some feature students attempting to take efforts into their own hands. Others involve appeals to administrators to do the censorship for them. But one actor shows up in many cases: the Chinese Students and Scholars Association. Since the 1980s, CSSAs have formed as student-run groups at campuses nationwide as a resource for Chinese students. Wanting to organize with peers who may be able to provide a support system for international students in a foreign country makes complete sense. After all, that is the purpose of most campus groups: to provide a space for like-minded people to associate over shared culture, beliefs, language, values, backgrounds, passions, or experiences. Increasingly though, CSSA chapters have been involved in efforts to directly censor or surveil what their peers say about China, rather than just serving as a forum for students from China.

Some of these students are no doubt demanding censorship of their own volition, and critics should be careful not to assume Chinese government interference without cause. Students from China, as those from any other nation, should not be treated as representatives of their government or assumed, without evidence, to work with them. But at some universities, direct relationships between the student chapters and party officials have been documented.

A report from the U.S.-China Economic and Security Review Commission found that "CSSAs often attempt to conceal or obscure their ties to the Chinese government, frequently omitting incriminating language from the English-language versions of their websites—the ones typically reviewed by university administrators." The report found some concerning language on campus CSSA websites, including Southwestern College's CSSA instructing that the Chinese Consulate in Los Angeles would approve presidential candidates, as well as the Harvard Medical School CSSA chapter's Chinese-language page mentioning consular support, while the English page said nothing about the consulate, and claimed the group was apolitical.[26]

In a 2018 investigation for *Foreign Policy*, journalist Bethany Allen-Ebrahimian wrote about these chapters and "China's long arm" reaching into US campuses.[27] "Although the extent of Chinese government funding and oversight of these organizations is not entirely clear and appears to vary from group to group, it seems to be more significant than previously known—and growing," Allen-Ebrahimian explained.

Her report found evidence that a "few CSSAs explicitly vet their members along ideological lines, excluding those whose views do not align with Communist Party core interests." *Foreign Policy*'s look into internal and public documents and interviews with CSSA members found that the chapters sometimes accept funding and "guidance" from regional consular officials, who offer "the occasional political directive." Some student members even complained about the "growing ideological pressure from the embassy and consulates."

Consular officials commonly use WeChat to create group chats with local chapter presidents and an official assigned to work with them. That WeChat, the most popular messaging app in China from Chinese tech conglomerate TenCent, has been used by consular officials to pressure students is fitting. The app exists as a censorship tool in the first place; messages sent to and from users who create accounts with numbers from mainland China are reviewed for blacklisted words and topics. Neither the sender nor the receiver is notified if a message has been censored.[28] Even WeChat users with accounts created in the United States and Canada have alleged censorship of their political messages on the app.[29]

When these chapters do receive financial support, they do not always make it known. "CSSAs regularly accept funds" from consulates and at some schools, consulates sent money directly to a treasurer, other group member, or separate unofficial account created to receive the funds—and, Allen-Ebrahimian wrote, "In either case, the university administration may be unaware that the organization is receiving funding from a foreign government." The chapter at George Washington University, for example, coordinated payments to students who took part in public displays of patriotism on at least two occasions, in 2012 and 2015. In 2015, the Chinese Embassy reportedly worked with CSSA chapters in Washington, D.C. to organize hundreds of students to wave banners and flags during Xi Jinping's visit to the city. Months after the visit, the GW chapter distributed about $20 each to student participants.

CSSAs, Censorship Attempts, and Sensitivity Exploitation

Like the chapter at George Washington University, CSSAs across the country have been involved in efforts to censor speech about China on their campuses. In November 2020, Brandeis University hosted a virtual panel titled "Cultural Genocide: An Overview of Uyghurs in Xinjiang, China." Rayhan Asat, an attorney, advocate, and sister of an imprisoned Uyghur businessman, was one of the panelists. The event was interrupted repeatedly by attendees who played China's national anthem over speakers. Attendees also scribbled "FAKE NEWS," "Bullshit," and "hypocritical" over Asat's online slides. Another panelist, Professor James Millward, called it a "coordinated disruption."[30]

But if students had their way, the event would never have happened in the first place. Brandeis's CSSA chapter created and shared on WeChat a template letter that students were encouraged to send to university officials, which stated: "I do support freedom of speech in this community. However, concerns are raised about the negative influence this panel will bring to the

Chinese community in Brandeis, since the information in the panel may be based on false or unconfirmed information."

The letter then called for "all future panels about topics related [to] China to be established on impartial standpoints" and for Brandeis to "respect my country and not treat it as a target for condemnation."[31] In this case, the students suggested that by *allowing* discussions critical of China to go forth, Brandeis was targeting China and the international students from there. Failure to censor is a sign of disrespect to students offended by the speech.

Facing these complaints, Brandeis's administration did not cancel the panel, but it also failed to speak up when the event was disrupted—and professors noticed the silence. More than a year after the incident, President Ron Liebowitz finally sent an email to faculty, noting that a number of them had reached out to "express concern about the lack of an institutional statement in response" to the Zoombombing incident. Liebowitz admitted that he should have responded sooner, but some professors were still troubled by the response. Unlike other statements sent from the Office of the President, this one was not made publicly available online.[32]

Another prestigious university faced a similar incident soon after. Nathan Law was a pro-democracy student leader in Hong Kong and later an elected politician there, before being jailed for his political activism. Law now lives in the United Kingdom, exiled from his home in Hong Kong, where he remains on the city's wanted list. And at the University of Chicago (UChicago), the CSSA chapter wanted to make sure he was not welcome on their campus either. In May 2021, Law announced that the executive board of the campus CSSA tried to interfere with his invitation to take part in a speaking series at the university's Harris School of Public Policy. They wrote that the invitation to Law "not only falls outside the purviews of free speech, but also has been widely perceived as exposing the insensitivities and disrespect the Harris administration shows toward Chinese students and scholars." The board "firmly" requested that UChicago "seriously address" the group's opposition to Law's invitation and "internalize the current and future demands" from the chapter.

"This incident is only adding onto the trauma of discrimination that has befallen the Chinese international student community at the University especially during COVID-19," the CSSA board wrote. "Many Chinese students at Harris have already expressed regret coming to this institution, or have advised incoming students not to attend."[33] When faced with a petition from other students calling for an investigation into the UChicago CSSA's relationship to the Chinese government, the group—which, remember, had *just* called for censorship of political speech—replied, "we are greatly saddened that somehow we've become a target, and that some people are trying to intentionally politicize us."[34]

Law told me after the disinvitation attempt that this was not the first time he had faced such demands. Similar attempts took place at NYU, Johns Hopkins, and the University of Pennsylvania (Penn). While he was optimistic that public awareness regarding China's human rights record was increasing, Law said "there are still extended arms of CCP trying to silence democratic activists even though they are abroad."

Prior to a 2020 symposium at Johns Hopkins University, Law and fellow activist Joshua Wong, now imprisoned under Hong Kong's national security law, were met with an online petition that gained nearly 2,500 signatures. Wong and Law's presence "on our campus is a blatant insult to our feelings and evokes our deep fear of our personal security," signatories wrote.[35] The petition to cancel the speech was unsuccessful, and the event went forward, but not without protests. Around 100 students gathered to oppose Law and Wong's speeches, met by a small group of counterprotesters. One protesting student told the campus newspaper: "There are a lot of Chinese people in this school, so by inviting those two people, who are considered criminals, the school is really not caring about our feelings at this point."[36] Students were arguing that it was an act of *insensitivity* to allow a speaker on campus whose political views on China offended them.

University administrations do not grant all calls for censorship of China's critics, but the demands alone can signify to student dissidents that their speech rights are under attack and their peers will use the means available to silence them. Students do not always hit an administrative wall when it comes to speaking about China on campus—but that is not necessarily for their fellow students' lack of effort.

Administrators Censoring Students

While demands for censorship were ultimately rejected at Brandeis, the University of Chicago, and some other schools, these disputes have not always ended with administrators professing their support for free speech. In some cases, students have found themselves called into student conduct offices because of their speech about China. Sometimes that wall is built—and it is administrators who are laying down the bricks.

Fordham University student Austin Tong, for example, found himself at the center of controversy in 2020 when he shared two posts on Instagram. One showed a photo of a retired St. Louis police captain, who was killed during the unrest after George Floyd's murder, with Tong's criticism of what he deemed "the nonchalant societal reaction" to the officer's death. The second post depicted Tong, who emigrated from China as a child, off campus with a legally obtained gun along with the caption "Don't tread on me" and #198964, a hashtag referencing the Tiananmen

Square massacre. Tong posted the photo on the massacre's thirty-first anniversary.

The post quickly amassed comments from students demanding Fordham punish Tong.[37] Fordham did take action, finding Tong guilty of violating policies on "bias and/or hate crimes" and "threats/intimidation."[38] Tong sued Fordham, which has a history of trampling student rights. Previously, a group of students had sued the university for rejecting recognition of a pro-Palestinian student group because it might lead to "polarization."[39] Fordham ultimately prevailed in both cases, because New York state courts refused to hold Fordham to its policy commitments to students' freedom of expression.

The following year, Emerson College suspended and investigated conservative student group Turning Point USA after members distributed stickers that said "China Kinda Sus"—"sus" being slang for suspicious and a reference to the online game "Among Us"—and depicted a hammer and sickle emblem, alluding to the Chinese Communist Party. Campus groups, including the Emerson Chinese Student Association, accused Turning Point USA of anti-Asian bias, and the college promised to investigate the "anti-China hate." In a message to the entire student body, William Gilligan, the interim president, implied the group engaged in "anti-Asian bigotry and hate."[40] The conservative group's vice president, KJ Lynum, said she found being called anti-Asian very strange, given that she "was born in Singapore."[41]

The group was found guilty of a bias violation by Emerson's conduct board, even though it conceded that the students "did not intend to target anyone other than China's government."[42] Equally baffling, the college's Twitter account hid from view replies mentioning its censorship of the student group and even ones that simply contained pictures of Winnie the Pooh—a mocking reference to Chinese President Xi Jinping.[43] Doing so gave the impression that the college was uncomfortable being associated with any criticism or mockery of Chinese officials. But Emerson earned itself a swift lesson in the Streisand Effect, as its decision to hide replies only encouraged more users to send them photos of the cartoon.[44]

It is important that we understand how and why student demands for censorship are made, and how universities handle those demands in public and private. Put simply, college campuses should be one of the freest places for students from around the world to discuss and learn about thorny international political issues, including China, Tibet, and Hong Kong. If those issues cannot be discussed on a campus, it should raise alarm bells about the freedom to discuss them *anywhere*.

Administrators, in an effort to respond to student complaints about their campus experience and take seriously allegations of discrimination or harassment, have been too careless. In some cases, through their desire to show sensitivity and react aggressively to bias, they have allowed themselves to fall prey to exploitation from bad faith actors. If administrative handling of bias reports results in the initiation of an investigation of students criticizing human rights violations or government officials, something has gone awry.

International Students, International Repercussions

In too many ways, students are finding it more and more difficult to openly discuss authoritarianism, especially the Chinese government, on campus. Perhaps they struggle with administrators who would rather silence a student protest than deal with the controversy. Alternatively, fellow students may be eager to shut them up under the guise of fighting hate. But in some cases, it is not the on-campus repercussions that they fear. Instead, it is what happens *off* campus that concerns them.

American Campuses, Red Lines

What happens inside university walls does not stay there and can follow you for the rest of your life, and perhaps your family too. More than ever, this is the chilling environment in which international students from China must operate. But this is not a phenomenon that appeared overnight—just look back to the case of Grace Wang.

In 2008, a public apology letter from the father of Duke University international student Grace Wang was widely shared online. "On behalf of Wang Qianyuan, we beg the forgiveness of the people of China, the forgiveness of all the Chinese in the world. We beg the entire nation to forgive her ignorance and give her an opportunity to rectify her mistake," he lamented.

There was just one problem. The letter was fake. Her father never wrote it.[45] But the controversies over Grace Wang, and the fallout she experienced from it, were very real.

In April of that year, Duke students were at odds during a vigil supporting Tibet. The disputes and arguments were fueled by the political environment surrounding the 2008 Summer Olympics in Beijing. A group of students supporting Tibet were met by a larger group of hundreds demonstrating in support of China. Wang, torn between friends on both sides, intervened. She attempted to facilitate a dialogue between the groups and even offered to write a "Free Tibet" message on the vigil organizer's back if he agreed to have a conversation with the other camp. She maintained that she "was not advocating Tibetan independence," but "did not think twice about doing this, because I believe that Tibetans should be free, Han Chinese should be free; all citizens of the People's Republic of China should be free to act according to their conscience, within the limitations of the Chinese constitution and law."[46]

Wang found herself the subject of widespread media coverage, including from *The New York Times*, BBC, NPR, and many Chinese-language outlets. But, far more troublingly, she became the target of threats, first at the vigil, and then online, where her and her family's personal information was spread—including on the Duke Chinese Students and Scholars Association listserv.[47] Wang's picture was shared with captions calling her a traitor, and she received threats of death and violence. Her parents in China had to go into hiding for a time after their home was attacked; their windows were smashed, and "Kill the Traitors!" and "Kill the Whole Family" were spray-painted onto the door. All because a student on a US campus attempted to peacefully mediate between pro-Tibet and pro-China factions at a protest. "I never imagined that the act of writing the words 'Free Tibet' would come back to haunt me so powerfully," Wang wrote weeks later.[48] Wang's story showed that encroaching upon China's sensitive topics can be dangerous, even on campuses thousands of miles away.

University of Maryland student Yang Shuping learned a similar lesson in 2017 after footage of her graduation speech praising "the fresh air of free speech" went viral among Chinese state-run outlets and government-aligned social media accounts. Yang spoke glowingly of the benefits of free expression and her amazement that her classmates could protest and discuss history critically. "I was shocked, I never thought such topics could be discussed openly . . . I have always had a burning desire to tell these kinds of stories, but I was convinced that only authorities owned the narrative, only authorities could define the truth," Yang explained. She went on to say that "the right to freely express oneself is sacred in America" and that "democracy and freedom are the fresh air that is worth fighting for."

Yang's detractors quickly proved her right, and that fresh air soon turned stale. State outlet *Global Times* tweeted a collection of insults and declarations against Yang. One was from Zhu Lihan, identified as a former president of the University of Maryland's CSSA, who said "not only is the UMD's lack of consideration questionable in this incident, but it is also suspected that there are other motives behind the school's support for such groundless opinions to be heard in a commencement speech. I hope Yang can behave herself." A comment from a Weibo user said "freedom of speech does not allow you to twist the facts in public. An adult should be responsible for what she says. Shame on you. I don't want you as my fellow alumni."[49]

A wave of abusive and threatening comments rolled in, along with campaigns to find her family.[50] In an attempt to minimize the backlash, Yang posted an apology on Weibo, writing, "I love my country and home town and I'm proud of its prosperity." She went on, "I hope to make contributions to it using what I have learned overseas. The speech was just to share my experiences overseas, and I had no intentions of belittling my country and home town. . . . I am deeply sorry and hope for forgiveness."[51] The apology was apparently not enough damage control. A University of Maryland faculty member suggested that the institution was later "subject to a Ministry of Education directive ordering PRC partner institutions to cease cooperation with the university."[52]

Two years later, University of Minnesota international student Luo Daiqing suffered a swift punishment too. He was arrested when he returned to Wuhan, China after the end of the spring semester in 2019 and was sentenced to six months in prison for "provocation." Luo's criminal offense? Some online posts critical of China's government, expression most students in the United States would not even think twice about.

Axios reported that Luo's "court document says that 'in September and October 2018, while he was studying at the University of Minnesota,' Luo 'used his Twitter account to post more than 40 comments denigrating a national leader's image and indecent pictures,' which 'created a negative social impact.'"[53] The "denigrating" images included memes mocking Xi Jinping, including multiple retweets of Winnie the Pooh memes. Luo's experience served as a warning to his fellow international students that authorities are watching what they say abroad, and that the freedom of speech they are offered overseas is not really theirs to enjoy. Sometimes the consequences for speaking out are immediate: threats, harassment, censorship, or worse. And sometimes, they lie in wait.

For Jinrey Zhang, a Georgetown University law student, it was his family who faced the most serious repercussions for what he said in the United States. Zhang, no longer hiding his identity, name, and face, came forward in 2023 to share that he was suffering the fate so often feared by dissident students: Security forces in China were investigating his activism and his alleged involvement with political groups in the D.C. area. And his family was in the crosshairs.

Zhang began to speak out in earnest against excessive COVID zero policies after being inspired by the White Paper movement, protests that swept China in 2022 challenging local COVID rules. He had hoped to use his relative freedom in the United States to reach members of the expat community who did not understand the extent of human rights abuses in China.

His words did not go unnoticed. In June 2023, state security forces contacted his sister in China about his activism, took his father in for questioning about Zhang's involvement with student activists in D.C., and warned that such activism must end. When I interviewed him later that year, he told me his father received another visit, months after the first, from a local Communist party official who issued a second warning about Zhang's behavior.

Zhang worried not just about what his family was experiencing, but about the personal consequences that may await him too. If he returns to China again, he expects, at minimum, for his passport to be revoked and for minders to watch where he goes and what he does. That would be the best-case scenario. He knows forced confessions and prison are a possibility too. To avoid those risks, he may have to commit to never seeing his family in person again. For self-exiled dissidents, there is no way to win. The only option is to weigh one painful possibility against another. How do you fight an opponent that will exact a terrible price no matter what you do?

When I asked Zhang if he had any reason to hope for the future of China, human rights, and activists like himself, he offered a surprising answer. "Actually, the suppression that's being done by the Chinese regime really gives me hope," he told me. Students fear the consequences of truly expressing themselves but, Zhang argued, Chinese officials fear student activism too.

"It shows that they're really afraid of all these kinds of activism, even trivial ones. They're really afraid, and they are trying to shut down any kind of dissent that's coming from inside of the country. And I think that shows, really, a kind of fear that the country is going to be not stable if many people have heard of the stories of the dissidents," Zhang said. "When maintaining order and stability is at the top of the pile for the Chinese government, it's natural to think that it's going to be really unstable if people know a lot about the opinion of the dissidents in China. So, their fear gives me hope."

Zhihao Kong, a Purdue University student, shared a similar experience. Kong, who had already begun questioning authorities as a teen in China, underwent a "political awakening" when he began his studies at Purdue. There, he converted to Christianity and began posting on social media at the outset of the pandemic, alleging that China's cover-ups of the virus had endangered the world. He followed up with an open letter praising the protesters killed during the Tiananmen massacre.

"We are young Chinese students who share the values of democracy and freedom, and we are fortunate to learn the message of the free world thanks to God. Thirty-one years ago, students who fell at the gun of [the People's Liberation Army] on the streets of Beijing became a topic that China could not mention," he wrote. "We refuse to be silent."[54] Just days later, police visited his parents and threatened trouble for his family if he did not stop speaking out, the first of multiple visits.

In 2020, Kong began attending rehearsals on Zoom for a Tiananmen memorial with dissidents and survivors of the massacre. Curiously, police—and through them, his parents—seemed to know that he was planning to take part in memorial events. What Kong did not know at the time was that a Zoom official secretly working for Chinese authorities may have been tracking his attendance from thousands of miles away.

Around that year's anniversary, Humanitarian China, a US-based nonprofit led by Zhou Fengsuo that promotes the development of human rights in China, held an online memorial attended by hundreds of people. Then the account was suddenly closed by Zoom. Another pro-democracy account based out of Hong Kong shared the same fate. Zhou was understandably outraged about the shutdown: "As the most commercially popular meeting software worldwide, Zoom is essential as an unbanned outreach to Chinese audiences remembering and commemorating Tiananmen Massacre during the coronavirus pandemic."[55] Zoom was temporarily defensive about applying China's "local laws" to users located outside China, stating that "like any global company, we must comply with applicable laws in the jurisdictions where we operate."

After widespread criticism, Zoom announced an update to company policies, including a commitment that Zoom would no longer "allow requests from the Chinese government to impact anyone outside of mainland China"[56] But months later, troubling details emerged about Zoom from a complaint unsealed by US federal prosecutors, who accused Xinjiang Jin, a Zoom executive based in China, of following Chinese officials' directives to shut down the accounts of users outside of China to silence their activism about Tiananmen. Jin was also accused of coordinating "with others to create fake email accounts to falsify evidence that meeting participants were supporting terrorism and distributing child pornography."[57] Even thousands of miles from home, students like Kong are closely watched—and they may not even be able to trust that companies operating outside China are not the ones surveilling them.

The threats were not only from overseas though. When Kong shared his letter about Tiananmen with Purdue's CSSA chapter, its "members went after him with a vengeance." On WeChat, CSSA members openly discussed reporting Kong to the authorities for "suspicion of participating in espionage organization that aims at overthrowing the government" and violating anti-secession laws[58]—an example of restrictive overseas speech laws weaponized to threaten students in America into silence. In response to ProPublica's investigation of Kong's treatment, Purdue President Mitch Daniels issued a statement to the Purdue community warning that students have the right to disagree with one another, but "any student found to have reported another student to any foreign entity for their freedom of speech or belief will be subject to significant sanction."[59] He continued, "Those seeking to deny those rights to others, let alone to collude with foreign governments in repressing them, will need to pursue their education elsewhere."

What does this mean for international students? The unfortunate reality is that while students might have the freedom to speak at US campuses, the consequences of their words may follow them longer than the freedom to say them does. In Kazakhstan, for example, it is made quite clear to students that their speech will be monitored closely. Since 2013, Kazakh students who qualify for a state-run foreign study scholarship program must agree not to violate any Kazakh laws while abroad and must provide officials with their university account information so their academic work and communications can be monitored. Violations of the contract could lead to the forfeit of property belonging to the students' parents.[60]

But for Chinese students, this fear is especially real. Timothy Grose, a professor of China Studies at Rose-Hulman Institute of Technology, told me that he heard from one of the school's advisers that a student from China was looking to avoid taking Grose's class to fulfill a degree requirement for a worrying reason: The class, Islam in China, could raise eyebrows on the student's transcript when he returned home.

A few years earlier, when Grose first taught the class, six of the thirteen students were international students from China. But that number rapidly declined. When we spoke in May 2022, the popularity of his Islam in China class had grown, with twenty-five students attending, but the number of Chinese international students in it had dropped to zero. Enrollment of Chinese students in his classes has declined significantly in the past few years, Grose said. "I'm starting to believe students from China are reluctant to take my classes because of how I'm speaking out about the Uyghur crisis or the general changing political crisis in China."

The Fraught History of Student Exchange

To fully understand the environment international students operate in today, we must briefly look to the past. In recent decades, Chinese students have grown into the most populous international student community in the United States (the top destination globally for international students today), but even when their numbers were small, their speech rights were contested. The plight they find themselves in today, and the fear Zhang identified from government officials against student activists, has its roots in history.

The first Chinese government-organized group of students, composed of 120 teenage boys, came to the United States in 1872 amid a period of growing xenophobia against the Chinese population. Nine years later, China recalled the students, who were also treated with suspicion and viewed as a "threat" upon their return home because of the different ideas they were exposed to abroad.[61] In the following decades, waves of Chinese students would come and go in waning and waxing numbers as shifting global events, varying levels of discrimination, and political changes occurring in both China and the United States adjusted how willing the former was to send its students abroad, and how eager the latter was to accept them. To some extent, students from China have always been in a bind, often treated with suspicion when they arrive in the United States *and* when they return home.

American interest in using higher education as an arrow in its foreign policy quiver grew during the late 1930s. It served as a means to pursue specific policy aims and combat efforts by the Nazi government and other Axis powers to expand their cultural outreach to foreign nations, especially in Latin America. In the 1940s, China served as the first country outside the Western Hemisphere that the US government targeted with its cultural outreach. At the time, public opinion in the United States heavily favored China, as Japan was waging war against the country.

Alongside cultural and academic exports sent to China, the Bureau of Educational and Cultural Affairs focused its energy on bringing select Chinese academics to the United States and aiding Chinese students at American campuses. Wilma Fairbank, who served in this program as a cultural relations officer, noted in a 1976 volume compiled by the International Educational and Cultural Exchange Program of the US Department of State that it was "ironical that, of these well-meant attempts to develop talented leaders for China, we should ourselves have become the major beneficiaries."[62]

During the time of the program, as World War II raged on, special opportunities existed for Chinese students and scholars, given that millions of Americans of military age were involved in the war effort and "American universities were functioning but, aside from special courses for the military services, were underpopulated in the war years." When the program began, about 1,500 Chinese students were in the United States, unable to return to their war-torn home, but also without financial support, as their assets had been frozen as a wartime measure. American officials coordinated support for these students and found them positions in government agencies, private businesses, war industries, medical programs, and schools. Universities, too, sought to provide assistance matching that offered by Chinese and American government officials.

Scholars and students wishing to travel to the United States, though, were met with suspicion and surveillance by China's dominant ruling party. Ministry of Education regulations published in China in 1944 directed that "all the thoughts and deeds of self-supporting students residing abroad must absolutely be subject to the direction and control of the Superintendent of Students and the Embassy." Students conveying "irregular" words or acts would "be summarily recalled to China."

"The Kuomintang Party for its part had an interest in having large numbers of young men take advantage of advanced education and training in the United States so long as it could be certain that such a move would strengthen the Party in its future grip on the country," Fairbank wrote. "Any left-wing deviation or even individualistic self-betterment by students studying abroad would be therefore regarded as evidences of dangerous defiance."

These regulations quickly reached American shores through media reports in late winter 1944—and ruffled feathers among an audience concerned about the implications for free expression in the United States. A collection of politically active Harvard professors—the American Defense, Harvard Group—issued a well-publicized resolution to colleges across the country calling on the US government to threaten to revoke permission to study to Chinese students "who accept the conditions" imposed by the Ministry of Education and for colleges "to refuse to continue the instruction of those students who submit to the control."

Ralph Barton Perry, chairman of the Harvard Group, wrote in a 1944 memorandum that "if students from abroad are to profit by the opportunity of study in the United States they should be allowed to enjoy and to imbibe this atmosphere of intellectual liberty, without fear and without the sense of constant official scrutiny." Eighty years later, those words could just as accurately be said about the struggles faced by Chinese students on American campuses today.

Widespread rejection of Chinese students—who would have had no real ability to simply reject the party's oppressive conditions in the first place—ultimately did not materialize among universities, despite the boycott suggested by some academics. But the political damage was done. "A boycott such as was urged by the Harvard Group in its resolution and for the reasons given was a direct insult to the Ministry of Education," Fairbank wrote. "Harvard's prestige made the slap more insulting." In retaliation, the Ministry instituted a monthslong ban, interrupting the education plans of hundreds of students. After Chinese students eventually received permission to resume their travel to the United States, the Ministry's regulations controlling student thought were "quietly dropped," and near the end of the 1940s, the number of Chinese students in the United States climbed into the low thousands.

Student transfers, though, stopped entirely upon the victory of the Chinese Communist Party in 1949, and some of those students who remained behind in the United States were treated with suspicion, surveillance, and arrest as the McCarthy-era fever swept the country. When diplomatic relations were restored between the two countries three decades later in 1979, a small group of students departed to study in the United States. The massacre at Tiananmen Square ten years later would encourage vastly more students to look abroad, especially to the United States, for their academic futures. By the early 2000s, journalist Eric Fish wrote, "Chinese parents were happy to pony up for a prestigious American degree. Unlike the previous waves, which had been mostly government-funded, Chinese families were now largely self-funding their children's foreign study."[63]

The reasons why Chinese students traveled to the United States for an education, and the numbers of students in transit, have varied over the past 150 years. What has frequently not changed for these students is that government officials have treated them with suspicion for the new ideas they encounter abroad, as if those ideas could be a fundamental threat to their power. What has changed, though, is the ease with which their political expression can be catalogued and surveilled, and how widely the Chinese government can cast its net around students. Today, a digital trail, online and on phones, follows them everywhere they go.

While educational exchange with China is a primary focus of this book, given its weight in American higher education today, it is far from the only country with which such exchanges have played a notable foreign policy role. As part of its policy in occupied post–World War II Germany, for example, the United States included in its efforts extensive educational measures between both countries, as well as student and scholar exchanges, meant to democratize the German people. The transfer of German students—excluding members of the Nazi Party, SS, and Communist Party, to name a few—to the United States was intended "to give a maximum number of young Germans on the secondary school, undergraduate, and graduate level the chance to study at an institution in a democratic country" and "receive a first hand demonstration of democracy at work."[64]

Most notable, perhaps, are the educational exchanges conducted during the Cold War and what they tell us about American perception of higher education at the time. In his recounting of this era, long-term Foreign Service Officer Yale Richmond asserted that the cultural agreements signed between the US and Soviet leaders years after Stalin's death stand out from others created in the post-World War II era. Soviet leaders, "believing that they lent legitimacy to their regime and implied equality between the superpowers," specified bilateral conditions that other partners, like Germany, did not have the political capital to demand.[65] Rather than primarily one-sided exchanges that brought foreign students to America, both countries were sending thousands of students and scholars abroad to each other over the years. And the exchanges spurred greater cost and responsibility sharing between the US government and the private sector to facilitate the program, with over 110 academic institutions participating.

Ultimately, Richmond argued, the time Russian students, scholars, and intellectuals spent in the United States helped spread ideas for democratic and civil reform among members of the Soviet elite. Without this exchange, such reforms may have taken longer. And according to Sergei Markov, a Russian political analyst, the political reforms that developed over the Soviet era can be linked to the programs: "The exchange of scholars and other exchanges played a very important role in Soviet politics because through these exchanges Russian intellectuals were westernized."

Richmond relayed the stories of some of these intellectuals and figures who came to the United States during the period. Oleg Kaulin, who would reach high ranks in Soviet intelligence and eventually became a critic of it, joked that he was "undoubtedly the first KGB officer" and "the last" to serve in Columbia University's Student Council. He later wrote that his time in America taught him to "speak his mind."

Boris Yuzhin came to the University of California as a KGB agent, left it as a double agent for the FBI, and eventually spent five years in the gulag for treason before being released. He said studying in the United States helped him abandon his "internal censor." According to Yuzhin, the exchange students who came to the United States were comparatively privileged and therefore less inclined to find fault with the Russian society they benefited from, but their time in the United States nevertheless showed them the "need for change and reform." Some Russian students specifically cited the importance of their time reading books they could not access at home, like *Darkness at Noon* or *The Gulag Archipelago*. This may be what Chinese officials fear may happen among China's students in the United States—that they will encounter and engage with material banned in their own country and carry those ideas with them after they leave American shores.

In the aftermath of World War II, the United States directed a good deal of political and cultural clout to the idea that educational exchanges, and the movement of students among countries, would act as a democratizing force in the world. Readers now will likely debate the moral authority of the United States to direct this force and the ultimate success of such efforts, but at the time, many believed this would change the world for the better.

As educational exchanges now occur at much greater numbers, it is worth considering the modern purpose of these exchanges. Questions about the wisdom and soundness of American education as a democratizing force aside, other goals now seem to outweigh liberal values as a byproduct of global higher education. Universities that carelessly operate on a global stage, without a clear understanding of their purpose in it, will inevitably find those values challenged. Universities want to reap the financial and reputational rewards exchange offers, and grow international and lucrative tuition-paying communities in the process. But can they accept the responsibilities to free expression and academic freedom that accompany it?

The state of higher education suggests they have failed to do so—and it is students who pay the price. For students from China, they know that their words and deeds may be watched closely, perhaps by consular officials, perhaps even by fellow students. What they do not know, however, is if university leaders will stand by them when their rights are threatened, or if they will ignore or even *participate in* that censorship.

Decades ago, American higher education was seen as a force to make an authoritarian world more free. Today that idea falls flat, and the situation has reversed. Now it is higher education that is experiencing the effects of authoritarianism, rather than challenging it. Not only does higher education appear uninterested in considering its role in an unfree world, but it also appears unwilling to even acknowledge that it operates in one.

Students from authoritarian countries have always faced barriers to free expression, even while at campuses in freer societies. But today, those barriers and walls seem higher and more impenetrable than ever, and it is not just repressive governments laying down the bricks.

CHAPTER 2

The Censorship Bureaucracy and Its Victims

> With a view to maintaining the Sino-U.S. friendship and cultural exchanges between our countries, we both should be on our guard against any political scheme under the cloak of religious or cultural activities. . . . Anyway, I hope that you would kindly use your influence to handle this matter properly.
> —Song Youming, New York Chinese Consulate deputy consul general

In early 1991, the presidents of Harvard University, the Massachusetts Institute of Technology (MIT), and Cornell University, among others, received letters from the Chinese consul general's office in New York. The letters were sent ahead of scheduled speaking engagements by the Dalai Lama, the Tibetan spiritual leader whom the consul general called "an exile who engages in political activities aimed at splitting the motherland." The consul general called for the cancellation of the speaking events, part of a broader campaign by Chinese officials at the time to disrupt the Dalai Lama's tour of multiple countries, and asked university presidents to "kindly use your influence to handle this matter properly."

The current Dalai Lama first came to the United States in 1979 at age forty-four, "making his visit as a Buddhist religious leader, not as an exiled Tibetan head of state."[1] During that trip, he spoke at interfaith events and some colleges and universities, including Georgetown University. His trip to Washington, D.C. did not, however, include an invitation to the White House. A visit with President Jimmy Carter "would have proved too politically embarrassing" for the president, who was working at the time to "solidify ties with Peking since normalisation of relations."[2]

Since then, American presidents have met with the Dalai Lama with varying degrees of willingness. President Barack Obama rejected a meeting with the Dalai Lama in his first year in office,[3] though he agreed to later meetings, despite warnings from Chinese officials.[4] Former National Security Advisor John Bolton alleged that President Donald Trump rejected a bid from Nikki Haley, US ambassador to the United Nations at the time, to meet with the Dalai Lama during a trip to India out of concern for Chinese officials' reaction. Though decades and many visits have passed since his first trip to the United States, the Dalai Lama's presence in the United States continues to be a sore spot for Chinese authorities, to the point that they have issued frequent warnings and complaints to those inviting him, whether it is the president of the United States or the president of a university.

MIT President Charles M. Vest replied to the consul general's letter regarding the visit in 1991, writing that the purpose of a university is to "encourage the exploration and discussion of different, often divergent ideas" and that he "cannot therefore, agree with you that the participation of the Dalai Lama in this program is inappropriate."[5] The effort reportedly failed, with no universities agreeing to cancel their events with the spiritual leader. That failure, however, did not signal the end of such censorship attempts, nor did MIT's sterling response set a standard that universities would always follow in the years after. Although American universities have some of the strongest speech protections in the world, those protections do not mean that these rights are never challenged or disputed—sometimes by foreign governments.

As international education and exchange between the United States and China have grown increasingly intertwined, efforts to interfere with campus conversations about China have grown, too, from Chinese officials, but sometimes from their partners in US universities as well. In the previous chapter, I looked at how the disputes over China's "sensitive topics"—Tibet, Taiwan, Tiananmen, Falun Gong, and increasingly Xinjiang and Hong Kong—have played out among students, who are finding it more difficult to talk about China. These students do not just encounter threats or limitations to their education, but sometimes to their very freedom and safety.

In this chapter, I will move away from the student experience to focus on the bureaucrats, both those on campus and those employed by the Chinese government, who play a role in harming open discussion about China, as well as the academics who have become collateral damage. As we now shift to look at faculty and administrators, it becomes increasingly clear that the ties between American universities and China have benefited both officials employed by the Chinese government, who seek to influence what is said and taught on overseas campuses, and university administrations, who pursue financial benefits or expansion opportunities such relationships can offer. And all the while, academics suffer as they are caught among these plots and pursuits.

Confucius Institutes

Confucius Institutes (CIs) have become symbols of the troubling relationship between universities and China. While it would be a mistake to assume that CIs represent the entirety—or even the majority—of the speech challenges posed around discussions of China on campus, they are an integral part of the story since their launch in the United States in 2004. If you know anything about China's role on campus, you have probably heard of Confucius Institutes.

Confucius Institutes are Chinese government-funded educational centers that are advertised as providers of language and cultural programming at host schools around the world. What the institutes actually accomplish, though, is not as virtuous as their advertisements promise. As early as 2014, the American Association of University Professors recommended that universities ensure their partnerships with CIs prioritize academic freedom, or that they be eliminated.[6]

In the early 2000s, universities were proud to launch Confucius Institutes and lauded the opportunity to grow relationships with China. "It is essential that higher education reflects the increasing global prominence of China. I am extremely proud that the Confucius Institute will enable San Diego State to take a leadership role in this critical area," Provost Nancy Marlin stated in 2009.[7] "This award is the latest confirmation of KSU's role as a national and global leader in international education," Kennesaw State University Vice Provost Barry Morris said when accepting the "Confucius Institutes of the Year" award at a 2012 ceremony in Beijing. "It speaks loudly to the higher education imperative of preparing students for the world that they live in today." And when the University of Texas at Dallas launched its CI in 2007, Dean of the School of Arts & Humanities Dennis Kratz called the Chinese government's decision to select UT Dallas "an honor and an opportunity—for the University and our region."[8]

Yet by 2020, Marco Rubio and other senators were pushing for the closure of the Institutes, arguing that "the Communist Chinese government has attempted to infiltrate American universities through the disguise of the government-run Confucius Institute."[9] Rubio was not alone in his vocal opposition to the centers. What happened over the course of a decade to shift the conversation? How did these programs change from proof of internationalism, opportunity, and positive influence to symbols of American universities' improper relationship with China?

At their peak popularity in US institutions, over 100 campuses hosted Institutes and hundreds of K–12 schools worked with "Confucius Classrooms." Confucius Institutes are formed by a partnership between a foreign host university and a partner university in China. This relationship was historically coordinated by the Chinese Language Council International, known as Hanban. Hanban provided start-up funding—often grants of $100,000 to $200,000—as well as employees and their salaries, teaching materials, and annual funds, which were usually matched by the US host university, which offered support staff and physical space.[10]

In 2020, China's Ministry of Education created the Center for Language Education and Cooperation to take over education and culture programs previously managed by Hanban. The Chinese International Education Foundation (CIEF), "a nominally independent organization registered with the Civil Affairs Ministry," was assigned the Confucius Institute brand. But "this rebranding is unlikely to relieve suspicions about the role of CIs in China's 'soft power' projection," according to Jamie P. Horsley, senior fellow at Yale Law's Paul Tsai China Center, given that "Chinese universities that participate in CIEF and serve as CI partners are mostly state-funded and, like everything in China, under CCP leadership."[11]

A 2018 *Politico* investigation into how Confucius Institutes had spread into American campuses across the country suggested that, despite how openly Chinese officials discussed the propagandistic goals of the institutes, "at a time when universities are as willing as ever to shield their charges from controversial viewpoints, some nonetheless welcome foreign, communist propaganda—if the price is right."[12]

For those willing to look beyond the promotional language used to sell Confucius Institutes to overseas universities and into the ways officials described the institutes within China, it is clear that the purpose was not simply a cross-border educational exchange. Indeed, a 2010 *People's Daily* article by Chinese Minister of Propaganda Liu Yunshan openly bragged about the purpose of CIs. "Coordinate the efforts of overseas and domestic propaganda, [and] further create a favorable international environment for us," he wrote. "With regard to key issues that influence our sovereignty and safety, we should actively carry out international propaganda battles against issuers such as Tibet, Xinjiang, Taiwan, human rights and Falun Gong. . . . We should do well in establishing and operating overseas cultural centers and Confucius Institutes."

A major motivation behind the Institutes was to establish footholds where government-approved educational materials would be distributed to universities around the world. Even more importantly, those footholds would come alongside friendly relationships with universities, who would be more likely to think well of the government body offering them money, educational materials, and a helping hand. Perhaps they would even be less inclined to host or seek out viewpoints considered inappropriate by the Chinese government.

A Financial "Black Hole"

The National Association of Scholars (NAS) released a troubling investigation in 2017 examining CI contracts and policies at eleven colleges and universities in New York and New Jersey (nine public and two private). NAS found that "every Confucius Institute contract we saw included some reference to either Chinese law, or the Confucius Institute Constitution, which itself includes respect for Chinese law among its requirements. Some

CI directors dismissed these texts as technical details that carry little weight in day-to-day affairs." While it may be true that this language does not cause frequent disruption in CI operations, NAS points out that "neither the contracts nor the Hanban's website offers explicit guidance" for when there are conflicts between American and Chinese legal systems, creating "a legally ambiguous structure that encourages American universities to defer to Chinese law."[13]

And a study of global Confucius Institutes released by researchers at Stanford and Princeton suggested that "teachers receive minimal training on political topics and encounter very little day-to-day monitoring while teaching abroad"—but the institutes nevertheless parrot CCP political positions absent direct instruction from officials.[14] Their survey of 284 CI teachers working in more than seventy host countries found that, in hypothetical discussions about Taiwan, a majority of teachers would either only present the official government stance on Taiwan's status, or would shut down the discussion entirely. "Interview data from CI teachers also suggest that even those teachers who foster open discussion on controversial topics such as Taiwan do so in order to persuade others that the CCP's position is correct, not to stimulate genuine debate."

Amid heightened scrutiny of China's influence on campus, both the Government Accountability Office (GAO), a congressional watchdog agency, and a Senate subcommittee[15] issued reports on Confucius Institutes in February 2018. In their findings, both reports stressed the need for transparency and academic freedom protections at universities hosting Institutes. The GAO wrote that their campus interviewees agreed that "schools should remove the confidentiality section of their agreements and make the agreements publicly available online" and the Senate subcommittee advised that "absent full transparency regarding how Confucius Institutes operate and full reciprocity for US cultural outreach efforts on college campuses in China, Confucius Institutes should not continue in the United States."

The GAO reviewed ninety agreements between US universities and Hanban and made some troubling discoveries. Of those ninety, forty-two included language "indicating that the document was confidential," likely borrowed from the template offered online by Hanban, a disconcerting finding to anyone who believes universities should be transparent about their financial dealings with foreign governments. Even worse, the GAO found only *one* contract asserting that "nothing in the agreement shall be construed to limit the academic freedom of faculty or academic programs at the school," suggesting at best that universities coordinating these agreements were ignorant of or careless toward the strains such partnerships could put on campus speech rights.

GAO's interviews with academics and administrators resulted in mixed reviews about the threat posed by Confucius Institutes. Some respondents asserted that US faculty members retain programming control and disputed suggestions that their CIs inappropriately rejected events. Some reported blatant episodes of interference from the Institutes. Others, though, worried that the presence of a CI on campus would limit what events the university would be willing to host anywhere, even separately from the CI, out of fear that it would jeopardize the relationship as a whole.

Lack of transparency and the potential for academic freedom violations have been major concerns not just with Confucius Institutes, but around foreign funding generally. Universities' foreign financial ties are immense, especially at big-name institutions. Between 2013 and 2019, approximately 115 US universities received around one billion dollars in gifts and contracts from sources in China (and that is assuming all gifts were properly reported, which is unlikely).[16] Harvard led the pack, taking in $93.7 million, followed by the University of Southern California, the University of Pennsylvania, Stanford University, and NYU. But again, institutions' reporting of their gifts and contracts has at times been woefully incomplete.

In 2020, the US Department of Education announced the launch of an investigation into Harvard and Yale, as part of a broader scrutinization of foreign academic funding, claiming both universities "potentially failed to report hundreds of millions of dollars in foreign gifts and contracts." The Department also claimed that its recent funding enforcement efforts "triggered the reporting of approximately $6.5 billion in previously undisclosed foreign money" from countries like China, Saudi Arabia, Qatar, and the United Arab Emirates.[17] Indeed, the Senate subcommittee report on Confucius Institutes went so far as to call foreign government funding at American universities "effectively a black hole."

"Academic Malware"

Marshall Sahlins, an anthropologist at the University of Chicago prior to his death in 2021 and leader of a successful campaign against the CI at his campus, was a frequent critic of the Institutes and deemed them a form of "academic malware" that "implement policy directives of the Party." Sahlins disputed arguments that the Institutes should be viewed similarly to other countries' international language or culture learning centers, like the British Council or Germany's Goethe-Institut. "Not only are the CIs unlike these other cultural exports by their existence within and as elements of host universities, they are also distinct for functioning there as elements of a foreign government," he wrote.[18]

Sahlins argued that CIs should not just be judged on whether they are involved in acts of campus censorship, but for what conditions they come with by nature. After all, politically disfavored viewpoints will be excluded from the institute's programming, staff, and materials, and self-censorship would occur at the start.[19]

Administrators' denial of academic freedom violations from CIs "ignores that a great deal of it had already occurred before teachers, lecturers and other Chinese personnel of the institutes even got there. Hanban politically vets and trains the teachers. And in many cases, the whole curriculum of Chinese language or culture courses is shipped from China, textbooks, videos and all," Sahlins writes. "Then again, much of the censorship in the classroom or Confucius Institute programs is not manifest, insofar as it consists of what cannot be said. It is self-censorship."

In one example of such self-censorship, the director at Portland State University, Meiru Liu, asserted in response to critics that her Institute actually *had* held events about Taiwan—but "with an emphasis on the beautiful scenery, customs, and tourist interest." She went on to admit that "we try not to organize and host lectures on certain issues related to Falun Gong, dissidents and 1989 Tiananmen Square protests." Confucius Institutes would not want these events organized, she argued, and anyway, "they are not [of] major interest and concerns now by the general public at large here in the US."[20] One cannot exactly censor viewpoints they are never willing to discuss in the first place.

Known incidents of censorship may not be the best metric to measure the Institutes' influence on campus, given the preexisting state of self-censorship—but that does not mean that such incidents have not been documented. In 2009, North Carolina State University demonstrated exactly how these relationships can go awry, both on the part of the Institute and the university hosting it. That year, the university had intended to invite the Dalai Lama for a speaking appearance, but the director of the Confucius Institute at the campus reportedly objected and warned that the event could harm the "strong relationships we were developing with China."[21] The university agreed. As administrators often do when axing controversial speaking events, NC State claimed other reasons for the cancellation, but the university's provost admitted, "I don't want to say we didn't think about whether there were implications. Of course you do. China is a major trading partner for North Carolina."[22] Though their reasonings and motivations were varied, ultimately bureaucrats in both the Confucius Institute and the institution hosting it worked together to achieve the common goal of tailoring university decision-making to the Chinese government's political preferences.

Troubling incidents occurred at other campuses too. Rachelle Peterson, author of the NAS report on Confucius Institutes, found herself personally escorted off Alfred University's campus in 2016 by a university provost and Confucius Institute employee while doing research on the Institutes. Peterson, who was sitting in on an Institute's class at the teacher's invitation, was told by the provost that she had to leave the class and the campus immediately.[23] That same year, professors at the University of Albany discovered that some Chinese-language materials and a banner for National Taiwan University had been removed— by the Institute's director, according to one of the affected professors—from their office doors directly before a scheduled campus visit from Chinese officials.

And in 2018, journalist Bethany Allen-Ebrahimian found out that the mention of her reporting experience in Taiwan had been removed from her biography in the printed materials provided at a Savannah State University Department of Journalism and Mass Communications event at which she had been asked to keynote and receive an award. Allen-Ebrahimian learned that the co-director of Savannah State's Confucius Institute,

Luo Qijuan, had personally told administrators to remove the mention of Taiwan and threatened a boycott if her demands were not met. She had also chastised Allen-Ebrahimian for her criticism of China after the event. An administrator admitted that this was not the first time Luo used her position to interfere with educational events about Taiwan. Previously, she "had tried, unsuccessfully, to block a teacher of Taiwanese heritage from participating in a Confucius Institute-affiliated program for local public school teachers."[24]

While Confucius Institutes do offer some resources for universities looking to expand their offerings without a severe financial burden, they ultimately exist as physical footholds for the Chinese government to directly access college populations with government-approved materials, programming, and messaging—at best, seeking to set parameters for campus conversations about China, and at worst, directly censoring them. Most worryingly, their presence alone could serve as a warning to students from China getting too comfortable with speaking critically of their country while studying abroad. Students may be far from home, but that does not mean they are far from government institutions. One might be stationed just down the hall. And, perhaps even worse, students may not be able to trust university administrators should they ever feel as if they are at odds with their government and facing repercussions. Can they trust that their speech rights will be prioritized over current and future lucrative partnerships?

It is likely that the Chinese government ultimately gained more from Confucius Institutes' campus relationships than the universities involved—but the returns for all have swiftly diminished. As of this writing, there are only ten remaining Institutes at American campuses, with more likely to close.[25] The widespread closures of Confucius Institutes in the United States can generally be attributed to a number of factors: heightened media scrutiny, on-campus pushback, demands for transparency, and legislative and governmental pressure.

Along with dozens of proposed bills regarding CIs, funding, and transparency in state houses across the country in recent years, individual legislators have called for the closures of Confucius Institutes in their states. In 2018, Marco Rubio wrote to four colleges and a high school in his state who had partnerships with CIs, urging their closures and citing China's campaign to "stifle free inquiry, and subvert free expression both at home and abroad."[26] By 2019, all four colleges' Institutes had closed or announced their closure was forthcoming.[27] Shortly after Rubio's letter, Texas congressmen Michael McCaul and Henry Cuellar sent a bipartisan letter to Texas universities hosting CIs to urge their termination "in light of China's subversive behavior and malicious intent to suppress our American values of free expression, speech and debate."[28] Within days, the chancellor of the Texas A&M system announced the closure of CIs at two Texas A&M campuses.[29]

The 2019 National Defense Authorization Act, a massive defense spending bill signed by President Trump, served as another form of pressure on universities still maintaining these programs.[30] The bill denied the allocation of Department of Defense Chinese language education funding to universities that hosted an Institute. And in August 2020, the Department of State announced that "the de facto headquarters of the Confucius Institute network," the DC-based Confucius Institute US Center (CIUS), would be designated as a foreign mission of the People's Republic of China, with the "opacity of this organization and its state-directed nature" as "the driving reasons behind this designation."[31] The designation would not force the closure of the CIUS or campus Institutes, but CIUS would be required to "regularly provide information to the State Department about PRC citizen personnel, recruiting, funding, and operations in the United States."

None of these acts alone would likely be so damaging to a university that its administration would be compelled to cast out its Confucius Institute. But together, alongside scrutiny from faculty bodies, activist groups, media, and the general public, the majority of Institutes in the United States have closed in the past few years. By this point, universities likely concluded that the benefits of hosting Institutes are not worth the reputational cost of keeping them. The lingering question is why it took so long for them to see the ethical concerns they posed.

Their decline has not gone unnoticed by Taiwan's government, which has launched language education programs between Taiwanese and foreign universities, including the University of California, Los Angeles, the University of Southern California, and Pennsylvania State University.[32]

While Confucius Institute closures may signify a partial victory for activists concerned about CCP influence on campus, the challenges about what can be said about China in international higher education have remained and, in many ways, grown thornier. Notably, a 2022 NAS report found that, while closures were widespread, "many once-defunct Confucius Institutes have since reappeared in other forms," with dozens of universities replacing the closed institute with a similar program, keeping the original relationship with their CI partner, or moving the institute to a new host. "The single most popular reason institutions give when they close a CI is to replace it with a new Chinese partnership program," NAS wrote.[33] The ties between university administrations and partners in China—and the associated risks to academic freedom—still remain.

It is possible the closures of Confucius Institutes may ultimately prove to be a pyrrhic victory, as institutes close but universities maintain or strengthen the underlying relationship they created through the program. But this time, they will be without the well-known Confucius Institute name to alert watchdogs about potential interference on campus. Confucius Institutes served as a useful red flag about the potential risks posed by partnerships with authoritarian governments but, as I will discuss more in this chapter, the threats run much deeper, entangling officials within both the Chinese government and American universities—with academics sometimes caught in between.

Consular Demands for Censorship

Universities do not need a Confucius Institute on campus to come face-to-face with the expectations of the Chinese government. Over the past two decades, representatives of the CCP have made appeals to the bureaucrats, and sometimes the faculty, of American higher education—with the occasional warning or threat of retaliation making an appearance too. The calls to cancel the Dalai Lama's 1991 campus tours were not isolated incidents.

In her 2018 Woodrow Wilson International Center for Scholars report, Anastasya Lloyd-Damnjanovic investigated interference attempts by Chinese officials. From interviews with over 100 faculty members, as well as students and administrators, Lloyd-Damnjanovic found "a worrisome trend in which faculty, students, administrators, and staff across a range of disciplines within American universities are encountering pressure to align their academic activities with PRC political preferences."[34]

In 2007, Smith College faculty member Jay Garfield invited the Dalai Lama for a campus speech. He then received a call from a Chinese consular official warning him to cancel the speech because it would "hurt the feelings of the Chinese people," to which Garfield replied that "the government might consider investing more in mental health resources for its people if their feelings were so easily hurt." Unsurprisingly, the official was offended and threatened consequences—including a ban on Chinese students attending Smith and visa restrictions for faculty—but Garfield said he went forward with the event anyway and the official's threats were not followed through.

That same year, Chicago consulate officials filed complaints with the University of Wisconsin-Madison's chancellor over an invitation to the Dalai Lama. At a meeting with the officials, administrators explained that it was not the role of the chancellor to police faculty members' speech invitations. Chicago consulate officials attempted this again at the University of Wisconsin-Madison years later. This time they complained that "the university was hosting too many Taiwan-related events and too many high-profile people from Taiwan" and "emphasized that Taiwan was part of China and that they regarded the university's actions as akin to having diplomatic relations with the island."

Then in 2009, the San Francisco consul general hand-delivered a letter to UC Berkeley calling for the Dalai Lama to be disinvited from a campus speech and stating the Chinese government's objection to the event. The consul general was not successful. Yet again, Chinese embassy officials attempted to interfere with a talk by a Taiwanese representative at George Washington University in 2013. In "a number of phone calls," embassy officials warned faculty and administrators that they should cancel the event, with the message: "You must not realize Taiwan's not a country, surely you don't want someone illegitimate speaking here." Three years later, George Washington University's chapter of Global China Connection, a nonprofit geared toward students, received an email from the Chinese embassy scolding them for holding an event about infrastructure in Xinjiang, and warning them not to hold similar talks again.

The Censorship Bureaucracy and Its Victims

In 2017, the pressure moved beyond veiled threats. That year, the University of California, San Diego (UCSD) invited the Dalai Lama to serve as commencement speaker, setting off a public and lengthy controversy about the presence of China's disfavored political figures on campus. In an op-ed at the campus paper, a UCSD student wrote that she "cannot represent all Chinese students' thoughts, but most of us share the same disappointment about the university's invitation of the 14th Dalai Lama to speak at this year's commencement." The Dalai Lama's "selection to be a presenter is inappropriate in such a situation, considering how many Chinese students and their families are going to attend this commencement," she went on.[35]

The invitation prompted a backlash from the Chinese Students and Scholars Association at the campus, who initially claimed they were in contact with the Chinese consulate in Los Angeles for "guidance" on how to respond to the event and were "engaged in negotiations" with the university.[36] Curiously, the CSSA then issued a follow-up statement asserting that they did not actually speak to the consulate about the event. Because of "sudden incident and haste, there is some inappropriate wording in the prior statement," they wrote. "We apologize for that. Especially the part about the group getting in touch with the Chinese Consulate lacks fidelity."[37]

Ultimately, it is unclear exactly what role the consulate played in the backlash at UCSD, but that controversy was only the beginning of the story. The consequences soon extended far past consular interference and into a more extensive series of retaliatory acts in the aftermath of the speech. Months later, a leaked notice from the Ministry of Education's China Scholarship Council revealed that the Chinese government would no longer accept applications from Chinese scholars intending to go to UCSD, and some scholars did end up losing their funding. UCSD faculty also reported being warned by colleagues in China that a "government entity, thought to be the Ministry of Education, had issued an oral directive ordering domestic universities to cease cooperating with UCSD." Though relations appeared to have resumed, at least unofficially, at some point in the following months, faculty at East China Normal University apprised their counterparts among UCSD's history faculty that they were under orders to cease partnerships with UCSD, including an annual conference. The Chinese partners for the Fudan-UC Center on Contemporary China, a center connecting Fudan University in Shanghai with all ten campuses in the UC system, also let the deadline for the renewal of the memorandum of understanding pass in December 2017 without promising new funding.[38]

The message was clear: If a university simply invites a speaker disfavored by the Chinese government, officials are willing to exact pain through termination of funding, elimination of scholarly collaboration, and endless red tape—for both the offending university and the Chinese scholars associating with it. Other university administrators who witnessed the fallout at UCSD might conclude that such invitations are simply not worth the trouble. What is the upside of bringing on a politically disfavored speaker when it could result in extensive disruption to university programs and partnerships?

Chinese diplomats are not the only ones attempting to interfere with US campus events. In 2019, Council on Foreign Relations Senior Fellow Steven Cook shared that he was disappointed to learn that Columbia's provost "effectively canceled" a panel two days before it was set to take place, adding that it set a "terrible precedent" given the likely interference of the Turkish government or its supporters.[39] The panel was supposed to discuss the rule of law in Turkey. PEN America, which also was scheduled to take part, issued a statement about the cancellation, sharing that "participants and organizers began to have serious reservations about the composition of the panel for the event, believing that it reflected an insufficient breadth of Turkish voices," so the event was postponed for reorganization purposes. But PEN America noted that "Columbia was approached by a representative of the Turkish government who expressed objections to the planned event and the views that would be reflected in the discussion."[40] A "senior Turkish diplomat" openly admitted to *The Washington Post* that he had intervened because he found one of the panelists "quite unacceptable to us, categorically," but he rejected the suggestion that he had made any financial or other threats to the university.[41]

Israel's Minister of Diaspora Affairs and Combating Antisemitism attempted interference as well. In an August 2023 letter, Amichai Chikli pressed Princeton president Christopher Eisgruber to intervene and remove a book from Assistant Professor Satyel Larson's course reading list. The book, *The Right to Maim: Debility, Capacity, Disability*, is "antisemitic propaganda" that implies "Israel uses a deliberate strategy of maiming Palestinians," Chikli claimed.[42] Princeton, for its part, did not grant the calls to force Larson to remove the book.[43]

These efforts by embassies and government representatives, most often from the Chinese government, mirror a spate of similar attempts occurring in civil society off campus. Fortunately, at least some have been publicly rejected. In 2021, the Museo di Santa Giulia in the Italian city of Brescia, after coordinating with Badiucao (the creator of the Beijing Olympics posters discussed in the last chapter) to host a solo exhibition of his work, received what the artist called "a direct order" to cancel the show. The Chinese Embassy in Rome wrote to Brescia Mayor Emilio Del Bono demanding the show's cancellation, calling it "full of anti-Chinese lies" with works that "distort the facts, spread false information, mislead the understanding of the Italian people and seriously injure the feelings of the Chinese people" and claiming it could hurt diplomatic relations between Italy and China.[44] It was sensitivity exploitation, deployed off campus. But these demands did not get far. "Art should never be censured," said Del Bono, who rejected the demands along with the museum's leadership. "In democracies, it often denounces, and even mocks, those who are in power. It's part of the rules of democracy."[45] Could the head of an American university be counted on to issue such a strong response while facing a similar demand? The available evidence from Badiucao's previous art censorship controversy in the United States suggests this is not always the case.

Blacklists

Individual scholars experience pressure from officials too. While consequences for universities, like terminated partnerships or financial agreements, can affect faculty members, professors can experience fear of much more personal ramifications, like restrictions on their ability to travel to China or obtain visas. For specialized scholars, this could be career poison. Academics must operate knowing that Chinese government officials can devastate their careers, and even their personal lives, with ease.

Professor Robert Barnett, who founded Columbia University's Modern Tibetan Studies Program, reported being contacted by New York consular officials in 2004 and 2007 with requests that he "lean more in our direction" in his discussions and research of Tibet. An official from the same consulate reached out to City University of New York professor Ming Xia in 2009 with an order that he abandon his work on an HBO documentary about the 2008 earthquake in Sichuan. The official reportedly told him that "this movie may give you financial rewards but we can give you much more" and threatened he "would pay the price"

The Censorship Bureaucracy and Its Victims

if he continued on with the documentary. "They thought that I am from China, [so] I should have some understanding of the red line," Dr. Xia explained.[46] Nevertheless, he denied their demands, and was blacklisted.

A 2004 collection of academic essays, *Xinjiang: China's Muslim Borderland*, led to the blacklisting of over a dozen scholars in the early 2000s. "I have been denied a visa to China since 2005, following the publication of the book on Xinjiang. I have applied each year and been turned down. The Chinese government has not given a specific reason: It said only, 'You are not welcome in China. You should know why,'" Yale professor and author Peter C. Perdue explained in 2008.[47] Another blacklisted professor, Calla Wiemer, who became "uprooted academically" after leaving her job in 1997, said "the problem with my visa has made it very difficult to land again. Because I'm a career Sinologist and I haven't been able to get into China for five years now." They joined a small group of scholars, the exact number of which is not known, who in recent decades have experienced visa denials because their work or words crossed an invisible red line.

In 2014, Elliot Sperling, a professor of Tibetan history at Indiana University, found himself immediately pulled into an interrogation room at Beijing's airport upon landing, and subsequently placed right back on the plane he landed in. Sperling's offense? Likely his support of Uyghur economics professor Ilham Tohti, who was facing accusations of "separatism" by the Chinese government. Sperling admitted he did not know if he could or would be removed from the blacklist, but that he would not do anything different. "I have done nothing wrong except to dissent—vociferously, I admit, but still I use only words—and have no intention of conforming to authoritarian norms for the sake of a visa," he said.[48]

James Millward, one of the blacklisted essayists from *Xinjiang: China's Muslim Borderland* and a historian who was finally granted short term visas years later, wrote a retrospective piece about the incident, asserting that the "context" of the book, not the "content," is what caused the trouble.[49] That context, according to Millward, included the editor's decision to reach out to the Chinese embassy about the book before it was published, the ongoing war in Afghanistan, and the likelihood that the book was leaked to authorities and accused of having a "separatist" stance. Millward wrote that, while some of the authors were able to get visas again, they usually had to go through interviews and meetings with embassy officials, a process he called "cumbersome, time-consuming, and occasionally humiliating and frightening." He asserted that he and the other authors were likely still on a "gray-list," despite some visa approvals, but that scholars "have an obligation—to our Chinese colleagues and friends as well as to our profession—not to be 'chilled' by such episodes as the blacklisting of contributors to the Starr volume."

In an update six years later in 2017, Millward wrote that while he "stand[s] by most of my conclusions and my final assessment that scholars should not worry about what they write or say in scholarly settings," it was clear that "Chinese authorities seem more interested in policing narratives outside of the confines of China and the Chinese language" as the "sensitive subjects have become more sensitive." Dr. Grose, whose Islam in China class I discussed in the previous chapter, told me his visa should be valid until 2025, but he has not been in China since 2017—and "for the foreseeable future" does not intend to try his luck. "Legally speaking, I could get there," Grose said, but because of the potential for retaliation for his commentary on Xinjiang, "in all honesty I fear going there."

Research-related repression or retaliation is "a rare but real phenomenon,"[50] according to a 2018 survey conducted by Sheena Chestnut Greitens, assistant professor of Political Science at the University of Missouri, and Rory Truex, assistant professor of

Politics and International Affairs at Princeton University. The survey received responses from 562 China-focused scholars in various social science fields about their experiences with backlash for their scholarship. Scholars' most cited problem was access to materials, with over a fourth experiencing denial of access, but visa issues occurred too, with around 5 percent reporting difficulty obtaining visas in the prior ten years, and six of the respondents said their visa requests have been denied.

Professor Perry Link discussed the challenge of studying and speaking about China in his influential 2002 essay, "The Anaconda in the Chandelier," an analogy he used to describe censorship pressure from the Chinese government. Link is personally familiar with blacklisting, given that he has experienced it since the 1990s along with his *The Tiananmen Papers* co-editor, Professor Andrew J. Nathan. "Normally the great snake doesn't move," he wrote. "It doesn't have to. It feels no need to be clear about its prohibitions. Its constant silent message is 'You yourself decide,' after which, more often than not, everyone in its shadow makes his or her large and small adjustments—all quite 'naturally.'"[51] What results is an environment where academics operate against intentionally vague speech rules, unsure exactly what will provoke personal or professional consequences. The self-censorship that flourishes in response is uniquely difficult to track. "The effects are hard to measure not only because people are reluctant to speak about them (no scholar likes to acknowledge self-censorship), but because the crucial functions are psychological and sometimes highly subtle," Link explains. "They happen within the recesses of private minds, where even the scholar him- or her-self may not notice exactly what is happening."

How do you track not only what scholars stop themselves from saying, but what they may not even recognize they are unwilling to voice in the first place? The fear of the *potential* for visa denials could also be enough to influence scholars early in their studies, guiding them away from career-damaging controversial paths into safer ones less likely to offend officials and keep them out of their country of research. Beyond the harms caused by self-censorship in academia today, there is also the threats of what the future will bring. How will our understanding of the world change if the academics we rely on to analyze it fear speaking openly? And how will future scholars operate in a field where the risks of certain topics and ideas are so damaging?

It is not only China that has "red lines" scholars may be punished for crossing. Though the Chinese government has been more willing than many to enforce its censorship on scholars well beyond its borders, and more effectively than most, this is a symptom of authoritarianism, not just of any one government or country. It is important that we understand these tactics, when unchallenged, will gain ground among other governments. If one country gets its way using illiberal methods and faces no consequences, others will surely follow. It seems increasingly the case that these methods are being adopted in defense of the Indian government too.

Rutgers University professor Audrey Truschke is one of a group of scholars facing repercussions for their advocacy, research, and writing about Hindu nationalism and Indian politics. In 2021, the Hindu American Foundation (HAF) filed a lawsuit against five defendants, including Truschke, for defamation. According to Truschke, HAF was founded in the early 2000s to promote the interests of Hindu Americans, but "ideologically they align with the Hindu right and Hindu nationalism and promote Hindu nationalism abroad." At issue in HAF's lawsuit was a tweet from Truschke asserting that "Indian Americans of diverse backgrounds call for [a] probe of US-based Hindu nationalist groups. As a scholar of South Asia, I can at-

The Censorship Bureaucracy and Its Victims

test that some of these groups spread hate & use intimidation tactics. These things are dangerous and unwelcome on US soil."[52]

"There have been Hindu right attacks on me in a systematic fashion for over 5 years," Truschke told me in a February 2022 interview. "These attacks culminated in a lawsuit against me and others." Members of the South Asia Scholar Activist Collective have tracked these attacks on scholars going back to 1995. The incidents include death threats against professors, campaigns to remove material from college syllabi, book bans, and a 2021 Title VI complaint filed by HAF against the University of Pennsylvania after it held a conference on Hindu nationalism.[53] Truschke noted that the lawsuit against her was filed after she had made it publicly known that she was conducting research into HAF. Christina Neitzey, an attorney with Cornell's First Amendment Clinic representing Professor Truschke in the defamation suit, told me that the lawsuit also followed an unsuccessful campaign to have the professor removed from her teaching position at Rutgers. "With respect to Truschke, the case is about academic freedom and whether an organization that dislikes the content of a professor's publication and research and advocacy connected to that research" can "use U.S. courts to silence her."

But it is not just US courts. In early 2022, media outlets reported that an Indian court issued a ruling limiting what Truschke and two other US-based professors could say about an Indian scholar they had publicly accused of extensive plagiarism.[54] Truschke told me she received no notice from any courts or attorneys and had seen no filing against her and the other scholars. I asked Truschke if she worried the lawsuit, which was clearly intended to chill her speech in the *United States*, could impact her ability to travel to India for research, but she told me the issue was moot.

"I can't return to India anyway," Truschke explained, citing the possibility that her scholarship would lead to her arrest there, and "I don't think the Indian government would give me a visa." She had made peace with likely being barred from revisiting her country of research, but added that it may not be as easy for other scholars. "I have no family in India but that's not true for most of the field," Truschke said. For others, "not being able to go back to India is a personal sacrifice." These sacrifices—and the associated balancing act between professors' careers, safety, and freedom to research and speak openly—are increasingly a concern for scholars in a growing number of fields. As China continues to face few consequences for targeting scholars, it is no surprise that other countries will show interest in adopting these methods. Today it may be China or India. Who will it be tomorrow?

Fears about blacklisting against scholars have only grown more valid as time has passed, and China's list of "sensitive" topics has grown. After the passage of the national security law, a *globally* applied and deeply repressive law foisted upon Hong Kong in 2020 (which will be discussed at length in chapter 6), it seems easier not only for academics to offend the Chinese government, but to actually violate its laws too. Academics increasingly must navigate threats to their livelihoods—and perhaps their safety as well.

Administrators Doing the Embassies' Work

Harvard Law School is famed for producing many members of America's legal and political elites—senators, attorneys general, governors, Supreme Court justices, and presidents. It is one of the most prestigious legal academic institutions in the world. But, when it comes to China, Harvard Law has made headlines for less distinguished reasons. Not because of a campus Confucius Institute bureaucrat or a diplomat seeking to protect the Chinese government's interests, but because of an administrator within Harvard's own leadership.

The Censorship Bureaucracy and Its Victims

In 2013, human rights lawyer Teng Biao accepted an offer to join Harvard Law as a visiting fellow and part of the Scholars at Risk program for academics in legal or physical danger. Teng, who was initially inspired by the protesters in the Tiananmen Square movement, suffered multiple disappearances and house arrests at the hands of Chinese authorities because of his legal work and government criticism. But his move to the United States did not mean an end to censorship of his advocacy for human rights in China.

In 2015, Teng coordinated with Harvard graduates to host an event featuring himself and fellow dissident Chen Guangcheng. There was just one problem: It was scheduled to occur during then–Harvard president Drew Faust's trip to China. *The Harvard Crimson* reported that a "powerful person"—who Teng did not identify, "citing fears of potential employment retaliation"—called Teng and told him to "postpone" the event, but never attempted to reschedule it.[55]

This "powerful person" was Harvard Law's vice dean for International Legal Studies, Professor William P. Alford, who reportedly told Teng that it would "embarrass" Harvard if the university held an event with Chinese dissidents just days after Faust met Xi Jinping in person. In a second call, Alford, who asked that news of the cancellation be kept private, again told Teng to cancel the event in order to protect the university's collaborations and reputation in China. Left without other options, Teng agreed. Alford later confirmed the reporting, admitting that he contacted Teng about the event because he "thought that timing might have an impact on university activity there (regarding academic, scientific, humanitarian and rights matters)." Alford told the Free Beacon, "as the person who first invited Mr. Teng to spend a year here, I felt some responsibility for whatever impact his undertakings might have for others at the university."[56]

Even though Teng left China, he was not free from the bureaucracy that dictated when and how he should talk about China and its governance. At Harvard, an administrator weighed university values of free expression and dialogue against its operations and opportunities in China. Harvard's espoused values did not win out.

Such censorship could easily happen again, Teng said. "It happens all the time at Ivy League universities and other colleges and think tanks. It happens all the time. They self-censor, they don't want to anger the Chinese government and they don't want their visas denied or to lose the chance to go to China or cooperate with the Chinese government and Chinese universities."

Teng alleges that it did not take long for him to experience a similar issue again at another Ivy League school, this time at Columbia University in 2019. Teng planned to join the executive directors of Campaign for Uyghurs and Students for a Free Tibet, Tiananmen survivor Rose Tang, and Hong Kong activist Roxanne Chang for a panel on "Panopticism with Chinese Characteristics" that was co-hosted by Columbia, NYU's Amnesty International chapters, and a group of students from Hong Kong.[57] The event was scheduled to take place shortly after heated arguments broke out about Hong Kong among students outside of a human rights event at NYU Law.[58]

But Teng's event was canceled. Officials at Columbia University asserted that the organizers failed to follow protocol for reserving event space and did not use "proper channels." *The Chronicle of Higher Education* reported, however, that "Columbia officials told the [Columbia Amnesty] board that a Chinese-student organization had told its adviser it would protest the panel. Because campus security was not scheduled to staff the panel, the Amnesty group decided to reschedule the event for next semester, with the same speakers."[59] Teng blames this protest threat as the reason for the event cancellation. "The Chinese Students and Scholars Association there protested against that panel and they wrote a letter to the university leader to threaten to protest in front of our venue," he explained. "And then that event was canceled."

Three years later, Columbia's Chinese Students and Scholars Association would host a campus event attended by Senior Vice Provost Soulaymane Kachani, David Austell, executive director of the International Students and Scholars Office, and New York acting consul general Jiang Jianjun. According to the consulate's report of the event, the consul general advised the more than 500 Chinese students in the audience "to love the motherland" and "to always maintain a clear understanding and correct judgment on issues involving national sovereignty and territorial integrity."[60] In short, a Chinese government official told hundreds of students in the United States, in front of Columbia leadership, that they are expected to follow the party line even while abroad. The consulate added that Columbia's Kachani was "eager" to strengthen university ties with China.

After the event, I emailed Columbia's media relations team to ask them about the event, and whether Kachani and Austell offered any response to the consul general's reminder to students about maintaining the "correct" opinions about Chinese politics. They did not respond.

What Teng experienced at Harvard—an official limiting criticism of China in an effort to avoid upset or offense—is an example of tacit censorship, where an institution censors or self-censors not because it is told to do so, but because it believes that is what is expected of it. Government officials do not always have to demand that an industry avoid certain topics, words, or ideas. It very well might self-regulate out of fear of upsetting its prospects or financial relationships. Sometimes bureaucrats follow orders that are never issued.

How often does this happen in higher education? At campuses across the country, universities with relationships with Chinese universities or government partners likely feel such pressure, even if they have never directly been asked. The existence alone of that relationship can encourage administrators to question whether they should modify their behavior to avoid potential offenses against its partner. After all, who wants to alienate or offend a business associate? And as I will discuss in the next chapter, that is how many university administrations operate: not as values-driven institutions, but as global corporations that must protect the bottom line.

But that instinct to protect financial relationships becomes especially troubling when the partner is an authoritarian government. The actual frequency with which administrative self-censorship occurs is very difficult to measure, as university officials are not exactly likely to shout from the rooftops that they have made decisions to appease an authoritarian government in contrast with their expressive values, or that they feel some pressure to do so.

But we do have some examples of how this decision-making can work behind the scenes. Hollywood is an industry where this acquiescence is well-documented and instructive to those seeking to understand the bind higher education finds itself in. A 2020 report released by PEN America, *Made in Hollywood, Censored by Beijing: The U.S. Film Industry and Chinese Government Influence*, investigated how American film studios' desire to participate in the lucrative Chinese market has resulted in an industry where "there is widespread compliance with Beijing's censorship strictures," which often "goes further, with studios actively cooperating with Beijing's propagandistic goals."[61] Unsurprisingly, films released in China are edited to appease censors and gain approval for distribution. Blockbusters like *Mission: Impossible III*, *Skyfall*, and *Casino Royale* were released with some scenes removed and lines redubbed. Other films like *Cloud Atlas* and *Bohemian Rhapsody* had discussions or depictions of homosexuality removed.

Countries like Russia and Saudi Arabia also require censorship of certain films and topics for release in their country, but few have the power to make widespread changes in Hollywood the way China does. Studios are often part of massive multinational corporations that fear the domino effect of releasing a film—even one not intended for release in China—that features just seconds of content that would offend the Chinese government. When institutions are global, whether they are movie studios or universities, they must consider what international consequences will result from politically charged speech.

The fear of blacklisting is a real concern for companies who worry that by releasing a politically divisive project for American audiences, they could jeopardize other lucrative ventures in China, whether they are hotels, theme parks, or video games. That fear can shape what projects studios will pursue, what actors or directors they will work with (as some have been blacklisted for working on projects depicting China in an unfavorable light), and what stories they are willing to tell—all without Chinese officials ever needing to issue any threats or edicts.

The 2014 hack of Sony executives' emails divulged that Sony cut scenes, like the depiction of aliens destroying the Great Wall, from sci-fi comedy *Pixels* out of fear that they would harm the film's ability to run in China. Even more troublingly, Sony cut the scenes from *all* versions for release (rather than just the Chinese version) because, as one executive explained, "if we only change the China version, we set ourselves up for the press to call us out for this when bloggers invariably compare the versions and realize we changed the China setting just to pacify that market." Sony applied China's censorship policies *globally* to avoid accusations of submitting to them at all. That certainly backfired.

"In a sense, the Party's influence on Hollywood has enabled it to practice its technique of friend recruitment on a global scale," Isaac Stone Fish wrote in his book *America Second*. "It will never be able to invite every American voter into a closed-door meeting for tea and blandishments; so it propagandizes its view of China via the most powerful mass media the world has ever seen."[62]

Director and producer Judd Apatow, known for comedies like *The 40-Year-Old Virgin* and *Knocked Up*, argued that "a lot of these giant corporate entities have business with countries around the world, Saudi Arabia or China, and they're just not going to criticize them."[63] In 2018, Netflix locally cut an episode of Hasan Minhaj's news-comedy show *Patriot Act* to "comply with local law" and a "valid legal request," because it criticized Saudi Arabia's government.[64] And in India, Netflix willingly committed to not offer content that "deliberately and maliciously" offends religion or national symbols.[65] But Apatow noted that while comedians and writers individually wonder which jokes they can pen, "on a much bigger level, they have just completely shut down critical content about human rights abuses in China, and I think that's much scarier." The content you see in the United States may be pared down to appease the unstated expectations of the strict censors in Beijing without a request ever being handed down. Does that sound familiar?

It could be the case with the books you read too. In 2014, Reader's Digest Australia dropped an author's novel from a volume intended for distribution *outside* China after printers in China demanded references to Falun Gong be cut from the work, and the author refused.[66] Eight years later, two British book publishers were caught removing material including mentions of Taiwan and Hong Kong so their books intended for Western audiences could be printed cheaply in China in accordance with local censorship laws.[67] A string of similar incidents have taken place since. More than we may realize, it could be the reality in higher education too.

What is taking place in the movie industry echoes the events at Harvard Law. Bureaucrats in American institutions are aware of, and may even be following, the unstated preferences of bureaucrats in the Chinese government. No commands or threats are issued. No official interference is to blame.

These subtle decisions made behind the scenes within institutions can negatively impact the people within them who find themselves unable to speak freely. But it also affects the public, who may be deprived access to ideas and information that is financially or politically inconvenient to the bureaucracy of censorship. The implications of this censorship rarely end at one individual or one institution, and will have downstream effects in the coming years and decades that we cannot yet fully predict.

CHAPTER 3

How Did We Get Here?

Tensions accelerated in the United States after the leak of the *Dobbs v. Jackson* draft opinion, which foreshadowed the overturning of *Roe v. Wade* and *Planned Parenthood v. Casey*. The nationwide upending of abortion policy and precedent, unsurprisingly, provoked passionate responses on and off campuses across the United States.

But when a group of American University law students took to a class group chat to discuss the ramifications of the *Dobbs* leak, they learned that sharing their strong reactions to the opinion would result not just in a disagreement with a classmate, but a fight against their school's Office of Equity & Title IX as well. Eight students were placed under investigation for harassment after their classmate, who claimed the exchange was "deeply offensive" to his Greek Orthodox faith, reported their private conversation.[1]

While spirited—"we are allowed to call each other out on our fucked up opinions if it challenges our very right to exist in this world without regulations, restrictions, or fear," one student wrote[2]—no student critical of the leaked opinion engaged in any speech remotely close to unprotected. That fact, though, was irrelevant to administrators because at American University, students are subject to a harassment policy banning speech that subjectively "offends." Law students, who must grapple with the challenging complexities and contentious questions about the legal system, were expected to do so without offending one another. That is an impossible task for anyone with any opinion at all on abortion, regardless of where they stand on the issue.

How did American campuses reach the point where criticism of another country's government could prompt the investigation or sanctions discussed in the previous chapters, like at George Washington University or Emerson College? Or where a Harvard Law administrator believed it proper to tell a Chinese dissident his expression could harm the university's business opportunities abroad?

To understand how universities are failing to grapple with international censorship concerns, we first need to look at how institutions like American University are mishandling free speech fights that arise at home. Cultural, economic, and political developments related to China occurring outside campus and in broader society no doubt played a major role. But here we will look at a few trends that have been blooming on American campuses that are largely unrelated to events involving China—like the punishment of students arguing about abortion—but nevertheless help tell the story of how campuses are open to the "sensitivity exploitation" and academic censorship discussed in previous chapters.

First is the already existing administrative interest in appearing proactive or responsive to speech that could be perceived as controversial, insensitive, or offensive. This interest is coupled with administrators' willingness to use the authoritative tools at their disposal to punish that speech. Second is administrations' tendency to prioritize, to a fault, the protection of their universities' brand or business interests. The line between university and corporation has grown thin, sometimes nonexistent. And the last trend is legislative efforts in the United States to constrain other forms of political speech taking place in the classroom and on the quad. Taken together, these trends are helping create a campus environment where critical conversations about China and other authoritarian governments are becoming less feasible.

Many of the challenges discussed already in this book exist because campus bureaucrats and legislators have lost sight of why universities exist. Their failures at protecting academic freedom in the United States have made universities easier targets for foreign censorship as well.

The Sensitivity Crackdown

Imagine you are a professor hired to teach a class on global art history. So, you do exactly that, offering a section on Islamic art throughout history and showing a famous—and respectful—medieval Islamic painting of the Prophet Muhammad with the Angel Gabriel, one intended and commissioned to honor Islam.

Knowing that depictions of the Prophet are today considered inappropriate or blasphemous by many followers of Islam, you take care to sufficiently and repeatedly warn students that the image will be shown, so that students can choose to avoid seeing it if they wish. You teach material necessary to the subject, but in a way that would still respect individual students' sensibilities.

For Erika López Prater, it seemed that doing her job is how she lost it. López Prater, an adjunct professor at Minnesota's Hamline University, was nonrenewed from her position by the administration in 2022 after a Muslim student complained about her decision to show the painting in class.[3] In a letter to the campus, then–President Fayneese Miller wrote that "respect for the observant Muslim students in that classroom should have superseded academic freedom" and decried the "harm" caused to them.[4]

Soon after, she doubled down, asking "does the claim that academic freedom is sacrosanct, and owes no debt to the traditions, beliefs, and views of students, comprise a privileged reaction?" and complaining of the "purported stand-off between academic freedom and equity."[5] Miller failed to mention that it was she, herself, who needlessly put the two values at odds.

It did not matter that López Prater thoughtfully taught material that was undoubtedly germane to her course, that Hamline University committed itself to academic freedom, that there is disagreement within Muslim communities about the viewing of such images, and that even the national Council on American-Islamic Relations chapter denounced the treatment of López Prater and the unfair allegations of Islamophobia against her.[6] Hamline's administration heard student complaints about alleged offense and bias on campus, and decided to use an adjunct professor with few job protections as a sacrificial lamb.

These calls to censor critics of China under the guise of sensitivity or inclusion did not appear out of nowhere. Indeed, these efforts have sometimes found success precisely because, on subjects *other* than China, administrators have grown accustomed to reaching for censorship as the first tool when challenged with controversies surrounding speech, offense, and sensitivity. Readers are no doubt familiar with some of these stories—like administrators canceling students' invitations to controversial speakers, or professors punished for unpopular class material—as questions about free speech on campus have dominated headlines in recent years. But they likely do not know the scope of speech that has been censored for causing or risking offense.

For readers unfamiliar with the legal background here, public universities are bound by the First Amendment to the United States Constitution, meaning they cannot punish or retaliate against students and professors for engaging in protected expression simply because they do not like what they have to say. The First Amendment does not require the same of *private* universities, but those institutions often make extensive promises to protect speech and academic freedom in their handbooks and policies. After all, expressive freedom is the backbone of American higher education, so promising it is a strong selling point to prospective faculty and students. Such universities are obligated to stand by those promises—as policy commitments they have made, terms of their accreditation, or in some cases, contractual requirements. But these obligations—moral, contractual, or legal—are frequently cast aside in the face of controversial speech, as the court of public opinion often rewards suppression of unpopular speech (the very dynamic expressive rights are intended to ward against) and the potential legal consequences are unlikely to materialize anytime soon, if ever.

So, what does it look like when an institution adopts offense avoidance as a guiding force? Truman State University offers a stunning example of how institutionalized sensitivity can reign supreme. In 2017, a student revealed that staff members had been rejecting recognition for well-meaning (and sympathetic) student organizations because of the theoretical possibility that the groups' members might encounter disagreement or upsetting things in the course of their activities.

It started when undergraduate student Naomi Mathew approached staff members, trying to start a campus group associated with People for the Ethical Treatment of Animals. Concerned about the possibility of "emotional risk" engendered by "hostile" confrontations over the group's message, Truman State denied the request. Consider that: Truman State chose to violate a student's rights rather than risk the mere *possibility* that her speech could result in hurt feelings. Not done yet, administrators also fretted over the "reputational risk" for the university to have its students associate with PETA. Mathew responded by using public record laws to find out who else's rights had been violated. In cases like these, lightning rarely strikes just once.

She discovered that the university had implemented a standardized system of assessing the "emotional risk" and "reputational risk" for proposed student organizations—then deployed that system to deny recognition to a club for transgender students (emotionally risky to provide support for other students), a group calling on fraternities to prevent sexual assault (due to "risk management" concerns), and a club that creates hats for children with cancer (an issue with "high" emotional risk). That system came to a grinding halt, and Truman State revised its policies, because Mathew raised questions.[7]

Truman State's censorship was stunning in the sheer breadth of speech it targeted and its efforts to formally evaluate risk to emotions and the institution's reputation. Plenty of universities, however, have long cracked down on speech about race, politics, and gender to temper controversies, placate critics, or mitigate risks that such expression might be upsetting to donors, alumni, or lawmakers. Sometimes the crackdown is initiated before anyone complains, even when nobody complains, or when the aggrieved group raises dubious concerns.

This systematic aversion to offense did not appear overnight and is an extensive problem today in part because of all the years in which it has been allowed to grow deep roots in higher education. Look, for example, at Indiana University—Purdue University Indianapolis, where janitor and student Keith Sampson was charged with racial harassment back in 2007. The charges came after he was found reading *Notre Dame vs. the Klan: How the Fighting Irish Defeated the Ku Klux Klan* during one of his breaks. The book is, of course, *not* an endorsement of the KKK—as anyone who bothered to read to the end of the book's title might grasp. Instead, the book tells the story of a group of Notre Dame students who got into an altercation with members of the white supremacist group in South Bend, Indiana. But that did not matter. In response to a handful of complaints, IUPUI's Affirmative Action Office launched an investigation and quickly found Sampson guilty of racial harassment, writing that he "used extremely poor judgment by insisting on openly reading the book related to a historically and racially abhorrent subject in the presence of your Black coworkers." Sampson was given no opportunity to defend himself and was ordered not to read the book again near his colleagues.[8]

Ten years later, little had changed except that such cases were becoming more common. Tenured Rutgers professor James Livingston was found guilty of violating Rutgers' Policy Prohibiting Discrimination and Harassment for sarcastically mocking gentrification in Harlem, writing "I am a white people, for God's sake, but can we keep them–us–us out of my neighborhood?" on Facebook.[9] Nobody at the university—much less any students—had complained about Livingston's comment, but he was initially found responsible anyway, with an administrator citing the "reputational damage" to the institution, evidenced by public complaints about his remarks.

That same year, another New Jersey institution acted on even *less*—and got caught red-handed. Essex County College fired Professor Lisa Durden after she debated then–Fox News host Tucker Carlson on his show, with Durden coming to an animated and, true to the form of talking heads commentary, rhetorically pugilistic defense of a controversial Black Lives Matter event. Durden did not mention that she worked as an adjunct lecturer at Essex, and none of the media coverage of her exchange with Carlson mentioned it.

But administrators there noticed—first suspending, then firing, Durden. Essex County College president Anthony Munroe published a video message of his own, lamenting that his hand had been forced, as the "College was immediately inundated with feedback from students, faculty and prospective students and their families expressing frustration, concern and even fear" about "the views expressed by" Durden. Munroe went on to suggest that the college received an "outpouring of concern regarding [the] student body" and had a "responsibility to investigate those concerns."[10]

Here's the kicker: The sudden "outpouring of concern" from students did not exist. Using New Jersey's Open Public Records Act, I requested records of the complaints Munroe cited as justifying his decision. The college stonewalled for month after month, resulting in a lawsuit from FIRE for the records. When we finally obtained them, the records showed that the college had received only one complaint within the first thirteen days after Durden's appearance. And by the time that *one* complaint was received—from someone with no relationship to the college whatsoever—the college had already decided to suspend Durden. Ultimately, the college received less than three dozen emails, Facebook messages, and voicemails in total—all of which were sent *after* Durden's suspension had been announced by the college, and mostly by out-of-state strangers to Essex.[11] In this case, the college appeared to be using invented claims of sensitivity to students to rid itself of a professor that the college's *administration* found too controversial.

For decades, campus speech codes have been litigated in the courts—and the codes have been losing. But while individual policies have been struck down as unconstitutional over the years, attacks on faculty members' right to speak have nevertheless increased. Between 2015 and 2022, there were over 550 attempts, many successful, to sanction, punish, investigate, or fire faculty members for their academic or extramural speech, with

117 resulting in terminations.[12] Unconstitutional and illiberal policies can be rescinded, but that does not mean the practice of censorship will depart with them. These attempts have also disproportionately occurred at top US universities, ones that tend to produce America's next generation of political and business leaders. We are currently arming future leaders with the wrong tools to understand living in a free society. This is not a trend that portends well.

If you are wondering why these attacks are ramping up over time, the answer is simple: Because they are working. Behavior that is rewarded will be repeated. When our universities signal that they are willing to conduct investigations or initiate suspensions because someone—or anyone—complains, they are not too many steps removed from posting a billboard that reads, "Did a professor's tweet make you mad? Please call our complaint line."

Among students, speech-related disciplinary cases have also become more common. A sample of recent punished or censored students include a Students for Justice in Palestine chapter denied recognition by the administration against the wishes of the student government because it was considered polarizing,[13] a nursing student expelled for an "insensitive" writing assignment about chronic disease,[14] a conservative student group whose "divisive" pro-life cross display was rejected,[15] fraternity members whose private skit "threatened the mental health, physical health and safety" of the campus,[16] and a libertarian student group whose event was canceled after the invited speaker showed "inten[t] to violate the safety of our community" after tweeting a joke about safe spaces at the college.[17] Efforts to censor by and among students have taken place alongside dozens of well-known incidents of speaker shutdowns, demands for firings and expulsions, and public disputes over how universities respond to offensive speech. The list goes on.

Students and student governments have contributed to this overcautious, censorship-prone environment. In recent years, student governments at colleges across the country have denied recognition or funding to groups for holding controversial or unpopular viewpoints on campus, including a "Churchill Club,"[18] a pro-Israel student group,[19] a libertarian group,[20] a free speech forum that could cause "harm,"[21] and a conservative group that could have a "negative impact on campus climate."[22]

Student press has a target on its back too. At Texas State University, the student body president threatened the funding of a student paper after it published a poorly received op-ed about destroying "whiteness." Students also organized a petition to demand revocation of the paper's funds.[23] And at Wesleyan University, a lengthy censorship debate unfolded after the campus paper published a student opinion piece critical of the Black Lives Matter movement. Students "recycled"—threw in the trash—copies of the paper en masse and circulated demands for its defunding, which some members of the Wesleyan Student Assembly were eager to take up.[24]

Opinion polling shows students are feeling the effects of, and in some part fueling, this environment. A 2021 survey of 37,000 students at over 150 of America's top campuses found that two-thirds of students reported that shouting down speakers was sometimes acceptable. Equally troubling is students' lack of confidence in administrators' support for their rights—only one third of students say administrations make it very or extremely clear that students' right to speak is protected.[25] Students are not only confused about their own rights and the rights of their peers, but also doubtful that they can look to their universities for clarity.

Perhaps it should be no surprise that students looking down the barrel of thousands and thousands of dollars in debt might expect that administrators will accommodate their specific expectations of the campus experience. After all, people tend to believe that the more we pay for something, the more we should expect it to cater to our preferences. The customer is always right—especially when they are paying for a luxury good. This is a valid complaint for students to have and, as someone who has spent over a decade working through my own student debt, one to which I am sympathetic. But finding ways to make college more affordable and accessible is the better alternative than making college an environment where the price tag determines how deep the commitment to free speech goes, or does not, and who gets to dictate the rights of their peers.

It can be tempting to downplay these incidents as isolated horror stories from a few of America's thousands of educational institutions. But surveys, polling, and other data suggest that these schools are institutionalizing methods of policing and suppressing speech, contributing to a chill on campus and likely violating students' rights. A 2016 survey of nearly 250 Bias Response Teams (BRTs) at public and private institutions offered some troubling findings of how universities deal with offensive speech.[26] Colleges, of course, must investigate student claims of discriminatory conduct or hostile environments. But these teams often go well beyond that, casting a wide net for reports of broadly defined "bias" and, in the process, providing administrative channels for reporting offensive speech or conduct that is nevertheless protected under the First Amendment or free expression policies. Only half of these universities mentioned their First Amendment or free speech obligations in their BRT materials.

Among the BRTs whose membership was publicly available or discernable, even more concerning details emerged: Over 60 percent included student conduct administrators, and over 40 percent included law enforcement. In short, hundreds of universities have been asking students, faculty, and members of the public to report speech they dislike to official university bodies—often including student conduct boards or law enforcement—for investigation and perhaps punishment. It is possible for universities to carefully craft such teams so that they offer *support* to students who feel unwelcome because of controversial speech, while still protecting basic speech norms, but that is not what generally happens in practice.

A survey of nearly 450 universities' speech policies from that same year found over half maintained codes that could be interpreted to censor constitutionally protected speech, and nearly 40 percent had severely restrictive speech codes that clearly and substantially prohibit constitutionally protected speech.[27] These numbers have improved somewhat in the past few years, but the underlying issue remains: On the whole, universities are keeping policies on the books that violate their First Amendment obligations or their other written commitments to free speech. This is bad for both students whose speech is chilled or censored and students who are given the wrong idea about how expression operates in a free society.

The thing is, if you tell students that administrative action should be taken against offensive speech, they might start to believe you.

Stories of administrative overreach could fill an entire book on their own. While the purpose of this book is to address the growing difficulties China and other authoritarian countries pose to higher education in the United States, these preexisting pressures on free speech should be understood as one of the aggravating factors worsening the "sensitivity exploitation" we are seeing regarding China on campus.

Put simply, once universities set a standard of punishing speech because it offends *some* listeners, that standard is available for all to demand, including those who are offended by criticism of the CCP or other oppressive governments, and even those claiming offense in bad faith. This leaves administrators in an uncomfortable position, one some of them have helped craft: How do they decide *which* complaints of insensitivity are more valid than others? Which political views are extended the protection of university policies and which are the subject of investigation? These are difficult questions already when viewed through the lens of American politics with which administrators are familiar. They are even more complicated when applied to political questions in different parts of the world—for example, the Chinese government's relationship toward its Uyghur community—that administrators are likely less familiar with and which carry the potential for embarrassing missteps.

The solution is for universities to steadfastly abide by their existing legal or moral obligations to respect speech rights in a viewpoint-neutral manner. Some of the speech at the center of these controversies has, in my view, been offensive, insensitive, obnoxious, or hurtful. But that is exactly why we need neutral principles on speech: so that our personal feelings about speech do not set the standard for others' rights.

In the short run, this may look like the harder path, and will no doubt leave universities in the sometimes-uncomfortable position of defending the right to engage in speech that leaves many different people angry from time to time. I can admit from experience that this is not always pleasant. But in the long term, it is truly the easier path, the right path, and the one that does not result in an environment where students, angry internet mobs, or foreign government officials can cite standards against insensitivity or offense to demand censorship of an authoritarian regime's critics. Hemming closely to a speech-protective approach when the going gets tough is how institutions remain steadfast when the calls for censorship come from new, and perhaps unexpected, quarters.

Branding and the Corporate University

In my years of working with censored students and faculty members, I often encountered critics who wanted to break down campus censorship into a simple story where the left or the right—or whichever political faction they least liked—bore responsibility. What commentators so often cannot see, though, is that fired professors and censored students do not always tell tales of a political battle or follow clear partisan lines. Sometimes the story is as simple as a university acting more like a business seeking to protect its interests and its brand. But these cases—which often fail to receive as much attention because they do not easily fit into political narratives that commentators prefer—tell an important part of the story of how universities fail to protect free speech.

As I discussed in this book's introduction, the COVID-19 pandemic helped bring to light free speech issues that had long been simmering under the surface. On campuses, that often manifested in the form of restrictions on community members whose criticism of their university's handling of the pandemic could cause embarrassment or bad press. Few institutions, including universities, like bad press. Even fewer like bad press suggesting they bungled their response to a deadly pandemic.

At Juniata College, a tenured professor was formally reprimanded by his college's administration after he wrote a Facebook comment pointedly arguing that Juniata's decision to hold in-person classes, rather than continue to host classes online, could possibly lead to death. "That is what is at stake," he wrote. In February 2021, notorious bad actor Collin College decided that professors Audra Heaslip and Suzanne Jones would be dismissed after their contracts expired, citing their criticism of the college's handling of COVID-19—a pandemic that the college's president said was "blown utterly out of proportion."[28] FIRE would go on to represent Jones and history professor Michael Phillips, who was fired due to his public advocacy for Confederate statue removals in Dallas (advocacy which "made the college look bad"), as well as his comments about Collin's COVID policies and the necessity of masking during the pandemic. After one of his Facebook posts about Collin's pandemic response, an administrator asked him: "Do you still want to work here?"[29]

Students were intimidated too. Schools, including the University of Missouri, Louisiana State University, University of Virginia, University of North Carolina at Chapel Hill, and Frostburg State University, enacted policies limiting student employees' or residential assistants' ability to speak to the media, including student press. That meant that RAs who worried about the spread of COVID or lack of pandemic protections in shared dorms were under pressure to keep those fears to themselves. To their credit, some of these universities dropped their policies after being called to do so by advocates, student press, and the affected students themselves. Others ignored these efforts, confident that the court of public opinion would not punish them for censoring student employees.

Such policies governing community relations with members of the media existed long before COVID hit. In 2014, California's Skyline College instituted—and later revoked, after criticism—a policy directing staff not to speak to the media, and to instead direct reporters' requests to the college's marketing director. "The Skyline College Media policy is designed to protect the Brand and image of the College," the policy stated. "Therefore, we request that you do not directly answer any questions, but follow the procedure as outlined below."[30] Central Washington University, Chicago State University, Pima Community College, Loyola University Chicago, and others have attempted similar policies for staff, faculty, or both.[31]

Universities have also sought to abuse claims of trademark infringement to target critics or distance themselves from controversial expression. FIRE fought a four-year legal battle with Iowa State University after administrators approved—and then rescinded after complaints from state officials—a T-shirt design for the campus National Organization for the Reform of Marijuana Laws (NORML ISU) chapter featuring the school mascot's head in place of the "O" in NORML. The censorship in service of protecting ISU's brand proved costly for the university, which was ultimately responsible for nearly $1 million in damages and attorney's fees.[32] UCLA has tried its hand at trademark infringement too, *twice* targeting a former student who started a website criticizing the university over a period of ten years,[33] as well as the National Students for Justice in Palestine, whose conference at UCLA faced cancellation demands from Los Angeles-area congressman Rep. Brad Sherman, among others.[34]

How have universities reached the point where brand supersedes all else, and protecting image matters more than protecting values? Some of the fault no doubt lies in the corporatization of higher education and the changing idea of what a university should entail. Readers' minds might immediately go to some of the more glamorous additions to university life at some campuses, like state-of-the-art gyms or lazy rivers, and the luxury price tag I discussed earlier, but one of the biggest shifts in what comprises a university has not been *what* it offers, but *who* it employs. Over "the last forty years the number of full-time faculty at colleges and universities has grown by 50 percent—in line with increases in student enrollment—but in this same period the number of administrators has risen by 85 percent and the number of staffers required to help the administrators has jumped by a whopping 240 percent," journalist and professor Nicolaus Mills wrote in 2012.[35] The fastest growing wing of the university is not the faculty or the student body, but the administration.

Occurring alongside this rise in corporatization has been "adjunctification," an arrangement where universities rely on professors working short-term contracts with no guarantees of renewal. Universities are more easily able to rid themselves of adjunct professors—who do not benefit from the protections of tenure—that prove controversial, outspoken, critical, or bad for the brand. The *Los Angeles Times* editorial board, among others, decried this "diminishment" of academic freedom, writing that "most adjuncts know that they can be let go for any reason and may avoid saying anything remotely controversial to students."[36] Take, for example, the case of Babson College adjunct professor Asheen Phansey, who was fired after making a joke on Facebook about President Trump's threat to bomb Iranian cultural sites and Phansey's negative view of American cultural landmarks.[37]

By 2013, tenured and tenure-track professors constituted only 24 percent of teaching positions, meaning that adjunct professors and other part-time or non-tenure-track teachers comprised over three-fourths of the workforce.[38] "Most adjuncts teach at multiple universities while still not making enough to stay above the poverty line. Some are on welfare or homeless. Others depend on charity drives held by their peers," writer Sarah Kendzior explained in *Al Jazeera* that year. "Adjuncts are generally not allowed to have offices or participate in faculty meetings. When they ask for a living wage or benefits, they can be fired. Their contingent status allows them no recourse."[39]

What this means for the modern campus environment is that the number of administrators, who prioritize universities' often tightly controlled public image and who safeguard the "brand," keeps growing, while the presence of tenured faculty, who are most free to speak their mind and more likely to be concerned about the state of academic freedom, fades away. There are, of course, faculty members across the country who courageously advocate for these values. But for decades, the numbers have been decidedly moving in favor of administrators, and academics are simply outmatched.

Universities' obsession with marketing appeal has materialized in more than just media policies and administrative staff. In 2014, Northwestern University's Feinberg School of Medicine successfully pressured faculty-run bioethics journal *Atrium* to take down an online version of the journal featuring a "Bad Girls" theme to protect the "brand" of both the school of medicine and its corporate parent. Officials especially objected to the inclusion of an article by a professor who wrote about how his consensual sexual encounter with a nurse aided his psychological recovery when he was paralyzed at the age of 18.[40] And with no warning or due process, Linfield University fired tenured professor Daniel Pollack-Pelzner in 2021 after he embarrassed the university's leadership by criticizing its handling of sexual assault allegations and accused several employees, including the university's president, of anti-Semitism.[41] The president, Miles Davis, rejected the allegations of anti-Semitism, but later admitted he had discussed "Jewish noses" with Pollack-Pelzner.

One of the most stunning examples of reputation enforcement and donor service in recent years took place at Washington's Bellevue College in 2020. Early that year, Gayle Barge, vice president of Institutional Advancement, admitted that she was responsible for the use of correction fluid to cover up parts of an art installation about Japanese-American internment camps. Barge specifically sought to censor this sentence from the display: "After decades of anti-Japanese agitation, led by Eastside businessman Miller Freeman and others, the mass incarceration of Japanese Americans included the 60 families (300 individuals) who farmed Bellevue."

Why would a college vice president feel the need to protect the reputation of Freeman, who died decades before? Material obtained via a public records request suggested a reason: The college wished to avoid embarrassing Freeman's grandson, billionaire Kemper Freeman, Jr., a donor to the college who administrators viewed as a prospective heavy hitter.[42]

And public records revealed in 2019 that Polk State College looked to its liability insurance provider for "crisis communication service . . . to assist with public relations/ media concerns" after it became public that the college rejected Professor Serhat Tanyolacar's anti-Trump artwork for being too "controversial" for an art show. Polk State's first thought was not to protect its faculty members' speech or consider its obligations toward free expression, but how to defend its decisions in the media. Even worse, campus officials reached out to *law enforcement* to ask them to determine whether the artwork constituted obscenity because it depicted President Trump and other political figures in sexual situations. They got the stamp of approval they sought; the Polk County Sheriff said police would "enforce Florida's obscenity statute" against the work should it be displayed. (To be clear, the image does not meet the narrow definition of obscenity laid out in Supreme Court jurisprudence.)

Brand protection efforts extend to social media too. A 2020 survey of over 200 universities found that three in ten schools employ a private, curated blacklist to block comments on their Facebook pages. It is no surprise that these tools were often used to hide commentary that could be harmful to their reputation. Around the time it joined a massive fifteen-year, $250 million dining contract with Aramark, the University of Kentucky began blocking the terms "birds," "chicken," "chickens," and "filthy" in response to animal rights activists protesting the deal. Mississippi State University also blocks mentions of "Aramark," its food services provider, almost certainly for the same reason. Texas A&M University and Santa Monica College blocked mentions related to animal abuse after receiving unfavorable attention from PETA. And the University of North Carolina at Chapel Hill blocked a series of words relating to its controversial campus Confederate monument, a professor whose commentary about 9/11 drew national criticism, and sexual assault.[43]

Bad for the brand? There is a secret blocklist for that. And when comments are "hidden" because they include words from these blacklists, the person posting them will never know: Their comment remains visible to them—it just seems like nobody is listening.

After reading all of this, you may think: Well, of course, it is no surprise that a large institution acts in its best financial and reputational interests. Offensive artwork about the president, criticism of a donor's grandfather, public knowledge of COVID health concerns, accusations of mishandled sexual assault claims—all of these could embarrass a university in front of donors, social media, prospective students, parents, the general public, lawmakers, and corporate partners. But universities have, or should have, higher interests than corporations. Protecting free expression should matter more than protecting reputations—especially for public institutions that are legally obligated to do so. Time and again though, universities get it backward, betraying values and obligations for the sake of the brand.

And when it comes to China, as many corporations have shown, offending the government is bad for business. Audi, Mercedes-Benz, Versace, Givenchy, McDonald's, and many more have apologized in recent years for accidentally causing offense by "incorrect" mentions of Hong Kong, Tibet, or Taiwan.[44] At one point, Marriott even promised an "eight-point rectification plan" after a string of offensive incidents, including a survey appearing to suggest Hong Kong and Tibet were separate countries from China.[45] More recently, actor and wrestler John Cena posted a video in Mandarin in which he said, "I'm very sorry for my mistakes. Sorry. Sorry. I'm really sorry," after stating Taiwan would be the first "country" to see his upcoming film, *Fast & Furious 9*.[46]

Not long after Cena's expression of regret, American photography company Kodak sought forgiveness after posting on its Instagram an image of Xinjiang from photographer Patrick Wack, who had called it an "Orwellian dystopia." Kodak's English statement on Instagram explained that its account is not a "platform for political commentary" and cautioned that the "views expressed by Mr. Wack do not represent those of Kodak and are not endorsed by Kodak. We apologize for any misunderstanding or offense the post may have caused." But, unsurprisingly, its other statement on Chinese social media site WeChat took a significantly more groveling tone. "For a long time, Kodak has maintained a good relationship with the Chinese government and has been in close cooperation with various government departments. We will continue to respect the Chinese government and the Chinese law," Kodak wrote. "We will keep ourselves in check and correct ourselves, taking this as an example of the need for caution."[47] To protect their interests, businesses are very willing to throw other values out the window and do what they believe is necessary for the brand.

This is, of course, behavior from corporations, not universities. But as universities act more and more like corporations, the potential that they will choose financial ties with China over commitments to expressive values increases. And it has already happened. As I discussed earlier, at North Carolina State University, for example, the university prioritized its relationship with the college's Confucius Institute, as well as the state's business ties with China, over a speaking invitation to the Dalai Lama. Savannah State University censored a mention of Taiwan to protect its Confucius Institute relationship. A Harvard Law vice dean interfered with a Chinese dissident's event so that it would not harm the university's efforts at the time in China.

And in 2022, Syracuse and Duke mirrored their corporate counterparts when they issued apologies for missteps related to statements mentioning the Lunar New Year. Dean of Syracuse's Newhouse School of Public Communications, Mark Lodato, wrote: "By including Hong Kong and Tibet alongside China in a list of countries, I implied that they are not part of China; however, I know that is incorrect. It was a mistake to present the list that way, and I apologize."[48] Similarly, Duke's engineering school apologized for its own "incorrect and insensitive statement to the Chinese community and the government of China" and reaffirmed that "Tibet is a part of China and not a separate country."[49] These statements of regret appear indistinguishable from corporate apologies to China.

Governmental Interference in Campus Speech

As I discussed earlier in this chapter, the standards universities set forth for speech are important. If you enforce a rule against offense or insensitivity, that rule may be cited to demand censorship of government criticism that some listeners find uncomfortable. On this test, American universities are performing poorly.

Unfortunately, our elected officials are also active participants in the game of weighing offense against campus speech rights. In recent years, both state and federal policymakers have pursued, sometimes aggressively, legislative or regulatory means to influence how some controversial social and political issues are discussed in the classroom and the quad, opening universities up to more demands that complex political discussion be silenced. Today it may be critical race theory. What will it be tomorrow?

While I have been writing this book, a flurry of legislative activity has been taking place across the United States to produce what are generally known as anti-critical race theory (CRT) bills. While many of these bills target K–12 education, which is governed by different legal precedents and principles than its counterpart in higher education, a number have sought to police what takes place in *college* classrooms—where adults, not children, are supposed to grapple with difficult subjects. While they proclaim to target discrimination or advance freedom of expression, what many of these initiatives do instead is seek to limit how "divisive concepts" can be taught or discussed. States, including Alabama, Indiana, Oklahoma, Missouri, New York, Kentucky, and more, put forth bills containing unconstitutional provisions in the form of curricular bans.

Florida's HB7, which was passed by the state's legislature in March 2022 and stands out at the time of writing as one of the worst of such bills, bans in public universities the "instruction" of material "that espouses, promotes, advances, inculcates, or compels" students to "believe" a number of concepts related to race and sex. Those concepts include "that a person should feel guilt, anguish," or other discomfort because of their "race, color, national origin, or sex," or a person "by virtue of his or her race, color, national origin, or sex is inherently racist, sexist, or oppressive." This bill is, of course, outright unconstitutional (not that this fact has historically stopped many public officials intent on legislating against speech). Supreme Court precedent makes clear that, in the university context, academic freedom is not a right that legislators can revoke because they dislike what takes place in classrooms. Around the same time, Texas Lieutenant Governor Dan Patrick also promised to "ban" CRT "in publicly funded higher ed,"[50] and followed up with a threat to end tenure.[51]

FIRE has since challenged HB7, also known as the "Stop WOKE Act," arguing in federal court that the law violates the First Amendment rights of Florida's students and faculty. Judge Mark E. Walker of the US District Court for the Northern District of Florida agreed. In November 2022, he ordered a halt on the enforcement of several provisions of the law that violated campus rights.[52]

Measures to give government officials the power to determine what is said in the college classroom about controversial political or social issues are wrong on their own merits and should be opposed on that basis alone. But they also run the risk of lending legitimacy to other campaigns to limit what dicey political issues are raised in a college classroom. How broadly should "divisive concepts" be defined?

Aside from the clear constitutional issues presented by the Florida bill, consider what it means to ban material that could cause students "discomfort or guilt because of their race, color, national origin, or sex" in the context of the issues discussed in this book. Criticism of Russia's invasion of Ukraine, China's abuse of Uyghurs, the United States' war in Iraq, Ethiopia's ethnic cleansing of Tigrayans, or Qatar's treatment of migrant workers could no doubt make students from those countries feel "discomfort or guilt" related to their nationality. Should we limit those discussions too? Discomfort is oftentimes a natural result of education. By interfering with these discussions, legislators not only harm academic freedom, but also limit adult college students' ability to learn how to cope with unpleasant, but nevertheless true, facts.

Who has a right not to feel discomfort in the classroom? And whose discomforting stories therefore cannot be told? Supporters of laws like these may believe that the inherent vagueness of them is a boon and will allow them to be wielded successfully against so-called CRT in the classroom. But vague laws are a Pandora's box; when opened the consequences are not always easy to predict or control.

There is already evidence that universities may take these bills, even when they do not directly target classroom speech, as directives to censor. After Iowa's legislature passed House File 802—another "divisive concepts" bill, but limited to mandatory staff or student *training*—Iowa State University advised its faculty they could not approach even germane material related to one of the banned topics if the class could be considered mandatory to a student.[53] If Iowa State's administration found the bill vague, which is not unreasonable, they could have appealed for further guidance from the state on enforcement. Instead, they applied an unnecessarily expansive reading to their faculty body. When pressed, the university claimed that faculty members do not have First Amendment rights while teaching—an approach that would, if upheld, give legislators free rein to dictate what college professors can or cannot say in the classroom.

These bills are troubling for what they do on their face, which is to unconstitutionally introduce government controls on what can be said in the classroom. But I also worry that, while they are not responsible for the uptick on campus of appeals to limit criticism of foreign governments, they will provide another tool in the arsenal of those who seek to limit such speech. When we pass vague restrictions on "divisive" material about race and gender in class, we should not be surprised if appeals to limit "divisive" conversations about international political issues are next. As a preview of what that might look like, the New York State Senate, for example, has repeatedly considered bills that would disallow funding of student groups that "permit" either "hate speech" or encourage boycotts of *some* allies of the United States, with a special eye toward those that support the Boycott, Divestment and Sanctions movement against Israel.

Bills governing the teaching of "divisive" content in classrooms were not the only campus issue lawmakers turned their attention to in recent years. Legislators and federal officials also pursued efforts to combat incidents of anti-Semitism, the rates of which have been rising both on and off campus over the past decade. While the safety and protection of Jewish students is a vital concern, these efforts have often relied on language that presents serious First Amendment concerns.

One of the most notable developments was President Trump's 2019 signing of the Executive Order on Combating Anti-Semitism, which commanded federal agencies to "consider" the International Holocaust Remembrance Alliance's definition of anti-Semitism, as well as the accompanying "Contemporary Examples of Anti-Semitism," in its enforcement of Title VI of the Civil Rights Act, which prohibits discrimination based on race or national origin. This definition, while potentially useful in tracking or understanding incidents of anti-Semitism, contains language posing a clear risk to protected political speech when it is used for other purposes. It states: "Antisemitism is a certain perception of Jews, which may be expressed as hatred toward Jews. Rhetorical and physical manifestations of antisemitism are directed toward Jewish or non-Jewish individuals and/or their property, toward Jewish community institutions and religious facilities."

Listed among the "Contemporary Examples of Anti-Semitism" are "drawing comparisons of contemporary Israeli policy to that of the Nazis" or "applying double standards by requiring of [Israel] a behavior not expected or demanded of any other democratic nation." Because most campuses, regardless of their status as public or private, receive federal funding, they are subject to the requirements of Title VI, and thus, pursuant to the executive order, could have complaints against them evaluated using the IHRA definition and examples.

Readers will likely disagree about whether the IHRA examples constitute anti-Semitism in every hypothetical case. But when it comes to the legal question, such speech would clearly be protected by the First Amendment, regardless of how listeners perceive it. Criticizing a country's policies, comparing it to Nazi Germany, holding one nation to different standards than other countries—all of this is, even if not subjectively right or fair, core political speech. Effectively, under this standard, any country's policies *except* Israel's could be compared to Nazi Germany. Universities, which are already trigger-happy when it comes to censoring controversial expression, would feel even more pressure to censor political speech to avoid falling afoul of the order.

If the concerns of free speech advocates are not enough, just listen to the protests of one of *the IHRA definition's authors*. "The definition was intended for data collectors writing reports about anti-Semitism in Europe. It was never supposed to curtail speech on campus," Kenneth Stern, then–executive director of the Justus & Karin Rosenberg Foundation, wrote in *The New York Times* in 2016 about the federal Anti-Semitism Awareness Act proposed at the time.[54] "What's next? Should Congress define what speech is Islamophobic? Anti-Palestinian? Racist? Anti-white? How about defining 'anti-United States' speech? We could dust off the files of the House Un-American Activities Committee."

Stern gets exactly to the point that I and other free speech advocates worry about. Where does this end? Interestingly, his concerns about officials trying to establish what speech is "racist," "anti-white," or anti-American now look prophetic in light of the spate of unconstitutional "divisive concepts" bills. And regarding "Islamophobic" speech, Reps. Ilhan Omar and Jan Schakowsky introduced the 2021 Combating International Islamophobia Act that would compel the State Department to increase its efforts to combat and monitor Islamophobia, though it was not entirely clear what acts and speech would fall within its scope. At a House floor debate, Omar stated that "this legislation is modeled on the Special Envoy to Combat Anti-Semitism, and I was proud to co-sponsor and vote last Congress on legislation to elevate that envoy to a Cabinet-level position."[55]

In the late months of 2023, concerns about campus anti-Semitism reached a peak after Hamas' October 7 terrorist attack, Israel's subsequent military action in Gaza, and the widely panned congressional testimony from the presidents of MIT, Harvard, and Penn. Advocates are right to worry about anti-Semitism on campus, and unprotected speech like true threats—for example, those from the Cornell student who threatened to "shoot up" a kosher dining room on campus[56]—must be taken seriously by administrators and law enforcement.

But as with every crisis, the rush to respond resulted in missteps, some small and some great, that risked encompassing broad swaths of political expression, not just threats or harassment. Claire Finkelstein, a faculty member from Penn's Open Expression Committee and its law school's committee on academic freedom, wrote in *The Washington Post* that the university "must restrict speech" to fight anti-Semitism.[57] State Senator Art Haywood announced that he intended to pursue bans on "hate speech" in Pennsylvania's public and private universities.[58] State University System of Florida Chancellor Ray Rodrigues, "in consultation with Governor DeSantis," temporarily attempted to ban Students for Justice in Palestine chapters within the university system.[59] Institutions like Brandeis[60] and Hunter College[61] cracked down on pro-Palestinian expression and Columbia University announced it would "not allow or condone language that promotes or supports violence in any manner."[62] And at the University of Texas at San Antonio, the site of an alarming police response to campus encampments, administrators reportedly banned students from chanting "from the river to the sea" or even speaking in Arabic at protests.[63]

Charged expression about the conflict no doubt deeply upset many listeners, on campus and off. But limits on speech that is hateful or justifies violence would effectively make the political and historical discussions that must take place in classrooms impossible. Supporting any policing, revolution, or military action—including Israel's war against Hamas—is, at its core, an endorsement of violence. How can we approach conversations about the Irish Republican Army's tactics, John Brown's raid on Harpers Ferry, or even America's Revolutionary War under such standards? In efforts to respond appropriately to hate and threats, we cannot create standards that ignore the complexity of political debate and the ever-changing analysis of current and historical events.

Legislative or executive efforts to moderate speech in the campus or quad, however well-intended, will only fuel arguments that we must widen the restrictions to encompass even more political speech and limit the breadth or views that can be expressed. Which political speech could be next?

Administrators and legislators may think they are solving a problem by regulating away controversial and offensive speech. Instead, they are creating a system of turnkey censorship for factions hoping to eliminate political commentary, including about authoritarian governments. It is evident that the desire to censor such criticism on campus already exists—and we run the risk of continuing to hand censors the tools that we have created. When we create standards for punishing political speech, we should not be surprised to see them put to use, perhaps by authoritarian government officials seeking to limit, on a global scale, criticism against them.

CHAPTER 4

The Global Threat of Authoritarian Censorship in Academia

As protests swept Hong Kong in 2019, they did not just mobilize one-fourth of the city's population to participate in demonstrations.¹ The protests also inspired showings of solidarity at campuses around the world, as international students and their peers in Canada, Europe, Australia, and elsewhere expressed support for pro-democracy activists in Hong Kong. While the spread of these protests indicated how rapidly activism can transcend borders, it also revealed how efforts to silence these protests can go global as well.

The developments covered in previous chapters—from student protests against the CCP to questionable arrangements with Confucius Institutes to consulates' demands for censorship of government critics—are not unique to universities in the United States. Far from it. Like American universities, academic institutions around the world, as they seek global status, encounter many of the same challenges as their counterparts in the United States.

In this chapter, I will discuss how the trends I have witnessed in the United States fit into a larger effort to influence how authoritarian countries are discussed on campuses anywhere and *everywhere*, from Canada to Ireland to Australia. The events documented at American universities are disturbing on their own, but when put into a larger context, it is evident that authoritarian pressure is reshaping higher education on a global scale. The question is not whether this influence exists, but how deep it goes and how dangerous its downstream effects will be.

Authoritarian interference in higher education is not an American problem. It is a global problem. In the short term, self-censorship and fear pervade institutions. In the long term, this interference could reshape how the entire world understands and discusses authoritarian regimes today and tomorrow. History is written by the victors, the saying goes. But how are authoritarians rewriting the present and the future?

Canada

"We hope MSU can monitor lecture room bookings and ensure they are not being used for talks and activities regarding sensitive political issues and misleading information," Bonnie Chen, vice president of McMaster University's Chinese Students and Scholars Association, wrote in 2019 to the Equity and Inclusion Office and the McMaster Students Union. "The Chinese students community is deeply hurt by this incident, response and explanation from MSU and McMaster University are highly needed."[2]

The email, sent on behalf of the CSSA and a handful of other McMaster student groups, was prompted by a speech from Rukiye Turdush, a Uyghur activist who gave a talk at the campus in February that year about the Chinese government's mistreatment of Uyghurs. It is a perfect archetype of sensitivity exploitation—unserious accusations of hurt and offense lobbed to silence a victim of genuine harm.

In addition to demanding surveillance of political speech and appealing to administrative concern for "hurt" caused to students, the CSSA made a number of other statements. The club explicitly asserted that it was "associated" with Toronto's Chinese

The Global Threat of Authoritarian Censorship in Academia

consulate, which was paying attention to the events unfolding at McMaster, and that it expected the university to punish the student groups who had invited Turdush to speak, citing campus policies against hate speech and defamation. The message? Through its consulates abroad, the Chinese government is watching, and expects action.

Their efforts backfired. Rather than securing sanctions against the students hosting Turdush, the CSSA would instead be decertified later that year by McMaster's Student Representative Assembly.[3] SRA members cited multiple reasons, including the CSSA's open coordination with the Chinese consulate, as well as members' involvement in filming and vocally disrupting Turdush's speech. Sympathetic attendees at the speech had good reason to fear their presence may have been recorded and sent to government officials at the consulate, potentially endangering students from China who could be outed as dissidents.[4] They certainly would not be the first students in Canada to catch the attention of government officials abroad.

"Now I am living in Canada, but I am living with fear from the Chinese government," a recently graduated international student told journalist Joanna Chiu in 2019.[5] The student, "Dan," explained to Chiu that while studying in Canada, he shared only three retweets, one a satirical video about Xi Jinping and two others commenting on developments in China, on his anonymous Twitter account that had just two followers. But those three posts were enough to catch the attention of Chinese authorities.

Months after he posted the tweets, Dan was warned by his father that his family in China received multiple calls from the public security bureau because of Dan's social media use. Some students in the United States have shared the same experience. Then a police officer contacted Dan personally on WeChat with a threat: He would "face trouble" if he did not take responsibility for the posts. The officer promised that authorities had evidence proving he owned the account. Dan, unsure what else to do and spurned by the Canadian police officers he contacted for help, deleted the posts, becoming another victim of the censors without borders.

Chiu wrote that Dan, an international student studying law in Canada, was "an ideal target" for China's United Front Work Department, which coordinates international influence and opposition campaigns "to coerce into someone who would support the motherland rather than become a detractor." The United Front Work Department has gained vast importance under Xi Jinping as a strategic tool to interfere with both foreign public opinion and diaspora communities abroad, increasing the range of the censors without borders.

"The fact that the United Front is a political model and a way for the party to control political representation—the voices of groups targeted by united front work—means its overseas expansion is an exportation of the CCP's political system," the Australian Strategic Policy Institute wrote in 2020. "Overseas united front work taken to its conclusion would give the CCP undue influence over political representation and expression in foreign political systems."[6] Those political systems include Canada's, as well as the Chinese international students—around 140,000 as of 2020[7]—attending universities there.

Even in Canada, China's repression is not far away. Such has been the case for some common targets of the Chinese government—like Hong Kong democracy activists, Uyghurs, Tibetans, and Falun Gong practitioners—who are located in Canada.[8] These individuals have faced tactics including threats, harassment, intimidation, vandalism, surveillance, and violence, often from groups and individuals loudly supportive of Beijing and likely including government agents. The intended outcome?

The Global Threat of Authoritarian Censorship in Academia

The export of China's censorship regime to freer communities overseas.

I spoke to one of those individuals, Chemi Lhamo, about the abuse she suffered after daring to run for—and win—a student leadership position at the University of Toronto Scarborough as a Tibetan-Canadian. "My campaign wasn't even about raising awareness for Tibet, it was about protecting student interests," Lhamo told me. She had been personally involved in activism regarding Tibet as a student and was open with her identity, often wearing a chuba, a traditional Tibetan garment, on campus. But Lhamo said her 2019 campaign was intended to reach all students, including Chinese students. She focused on issues like housing and wages, rather than her activism for Tibet. For the most part, ahead of the election for student union president, nothing much happened, at least nothing to hint at the wave of harassment she would soon receive.

The night of the election, Lhamo slept in her office, awaiting the results. It became clear she would win the next day, but Lhamo's opportunity for celebration was quickly cut short. Ahead of the announcement of her victory, fellow students began circulating her photo on WeChat, thousands of signatories added their name to a petition demanding her removal, and trolls filled Lhamo's social media accounts with abuse. Lhamo sent me some of the ugly, politically and sexually charged messages she received on Instagram. A sampling included: "Tibet always belongs to China . . . fuck you bitch," "fuck u bitch your mother is dead," "China is your daddy," and "Your mom is a whore, you are a whore."

The comments veered into even darker territory: "Ur not going to be the president of UTSC. Even if u do, we will make sure things get done so u won't survive a day. Peace RIP," "U can say whatever u want but ur mom die," and "Degenerates like you belong on a cross." Lhamo said there were rape threats, and a comment about Chinese-made bullets waiting for her. It is difficult to imagine that all of this punishment could be meted out over an election to a campus leadership position.

Initially, she gave the university time to look into the threats levied against her. But that did not lead to any results; she thinks campus officials just wanted to "wipe their hands" of her situation and played down the threats because they had taken place online rather than in person. For a time, Lhamo actually had to close her campus office for her own safety. Aside from giving her a walkie-talkie to contact campus security and a meeting with a safety officer, university officials did little for her.[9] Lhamo ultimately went to Toronto police to investigate the situation, but as of the time of this writing, she still does not know who was threatening and coordinating harassment against her.

The Chinese Consulate General in Toronto rejected questions about their potential involvement in coordination of the harassment against Lhamo, but certainly did not sound troubled by her experience. If anything, the office appeared to be openly pleased. "It is believed that this is an entirely spontaneous action of those Chinese students based on objective facts and patriotic enthusiasm," the Consulate General wrote in a statement shortly after Lhamo's election. "The Chinese government firmly opposes anti-China separatist activities by 'Tibet independence' activists who are plotting to split Tibet from China [and] the move of any country or organization to provide support or convenience of any kind to 'Tibet independence' activities."[10]

Lhamo, though, has "no doubt" that the consulate was involved with the "patriotic enthusiasm" she experienced. "The people that are at the forefront of it, the students sending threats, some of them do not have a choice and are being used by the Chinese government in their long arm tactics," Lhamo told me. She also learned that an individual who was with the campus CSSA chapter, which Lhamo was unaware of at the time, attempted to join her campaign early on, but the position she wanted was unavailable. She later messaged Lhamo, pretending they had never been introduced before, and asked her to explain her "stance on a Free Tibet." To Lhamo, this looked like a questionnaire the student had been told to send.

The CSSA would often set its table outside the student center near her office after Lhamo's election, leading Lhamo and other students to feel that they were being surveilled. Some students from Hong Kong were hesitant to discuss their concerns and activism with her out of fear they would be photographed and reported to authorities. One student from Hong Kong even wore a Guy Fawkes mask when he would go to her office to protect his anonymity. This troubled Lhamo for obvious reasons—feeling that she was being surveilled for political reasons after facing death and rape threats—but also because it made her "inaccessible" to the students she hoped to represent in office.

Aside from the immediate challenges Lhamo faced in the aftermath of the election, she told me that, in general, it is getting harder to openly talk about China in higher education, where "the Chinese government is definitely using academic institutions and their influence to garner support and infiltrate conversations." On campus and elsewhere, pro-government activists are "co-opting spaces" and "progressive language" to equate criticism of the Chinese government with support for imperialism and anti-Asian racism. Sensitivity exploitation is not just an American problem.

"I'm an Asian woman too, and I'm subject to anti-Asian racism," Lhamo told me, "but I have to deal with left progressive spaces where they're telling me you can't criticize the [Chinese] government. So where do I go? I'm advocating for fair wage and housing and I'm not accepted into these spaces."

A 2020 report from Canadian human rights groups found that other students had experiences like Lhamo and Dan. At a testy confrontation between protesters supporting Hong Kong and their pro-Beijing counterparts at the University of British Columbia, one of the pro-Hong Kong activists was hit with a microphone. Like the student who wore the Guy Fawkes mask to Lhamo's office, many UBC participants took pains to conceal their identities "as they expressed fear of Chinese governmental surveillance and retaliation, both personally and against their families." At the University of Guelph, students engaged in a back-and-forth, painting over each other's artwork about Hong Kong and China on a cannon located on campus and open to student art. At one point, students stationed themselves around the area to prevent the pro-China messages from being replaced. Similar incidents occurred at some Canadian high schools as well.

While these controversies became more common as Hong Kong-related activism spread globally in recent years, questions about China's role in Canadian higher education have existed for much longer. Around three decades ago, immigration officials, in denying permanent resident status to a man from China, alleged that he used his position in Concordia University's CSSA chapter to spy on pro-democracy student activists for the Chinese government. The refusal letter noted that the man admitted he "identified and reported on these [pro-democracy] individuals to the Embassy" and "sought to change the direction of the CSSA using funds provided by the Embassy in support of certain activities, to make it 'sensitive to the Chinese Government and Chinese officials.'"[11]

More recently, at McMaster University, where the CSSA chapter coordinated with the consulate in response to a Uyghur activist's speech, administrators were compelled to eliminate their Confucius Institute. In 2013, the university announced the closure in light of concerns over "the hiring decisions that were being made in China," referencing a previous employee's claim that she had to sign an agreement in order to work at the institute, declaring that she would not engage in Falun Gong spiritual practice.[12]

And in 2010, the academic careers of Chinese students at the University of Calgary were thrown into disarray when the Chinese government moved to derecognize it as an accredited university in the country, in retaliation for the Canadian university's decision to grant an honorary degree to the Dalai Lama.[13] While the university's status appeared to be restored in China the following year,[14] the temporary punishment was perhaps a precursor to what the University of California, San Diego would experience just a few years later after its own invitation to the Dalai Lama, as I discussed earlier in this book. These somewhat random punishments, which are issued with no clear end date or resolution, serve as a warning to other universities to stay in line. Maybe there will be consequences, maybe not. Is it worth the risk to find out?

Europe

Between a ban on gender studies,[15] the expulsion of Central European University from the country,[16] expanded state control over research institutes,[17] restrictions on LGBTQ books,[18] and other encroachments into civil society, Hungary's prime minister Viktor Orbán's incursions into the country's higher education system have been numerous. During his leadership, Orbán has overseen the decline of academic freedom and free expression in Hungary, attracting concern from academics around the world.

While Orbán has orchestrated this internal attack on expressive rights in Hungary, he has also been courting another external threat: Beijing. Orbán has made it no secret that he is untroubled by Xi Jinping's authoritarian tendencies, perhaps because he happens to share some of them himself. While developing greater economic connection between the two countries, Orbán has also advanced academic ties in the form of a massive deal with China's Fudan University, seeking to give the university its first campus in the European Union, despite strong public dissent among Hungarians.

Ties already existed, like Fudan University's joint degree program with Corvinus University of Budapest. But this new deal would be much more expansive. Initial government proposals for what would be Fudan Hungary University estimated over 500,000 square meters of buildings spaced out over dozens of acres, with a $1.687 billion cost for taxpayers. That amount is "more than Hungary spends on the annual operation of its over two dozen state-run public universities combined." Documents obtained by investigative journalist Szabolcz Panyi revealed that Orbán's government hid the project from the public for years and "already agreed that the construction can only be carried out as a 'Chinese only project'—meaning that only Chinese companies and banks could be involved."[19] The project was in consideration by the time Fudan cut the phrase "freedom of thought" from its charter in 2019, and instead added a commitment to the CCP.[20]

Public opposition proved fierce, with around two-thirds of Hungarians reportedly against the deal.[21] Protests ranged from thousands of demonstrators marching in Budapest to Mayor Gergely Karacsony's decision to rename streets near the proposed campus to highlight China's human rights violations: Uyghur Martyrs' Road, Bishop Xie Shiguang Road, Free Hong Kong Road and Dalai Lama Street.[22] "We have our problem with dictators. . . . And we are not in the least protesting against Chinese people who live together with us peacefully in this marvellous city," Karacsony said. "What is unacceptable is when the Hungarian government serves the broadening of Chinese political-economic influence instead of Hungarian interests."[23]

Efforts to hold a public referendum on the deal were thrown out as unconstitutional by Hungary's top court in May 2022.[24]

Orbán's courting of Fudan is notable due to the scope of the deal, its groundbreaking significance in the EU, and the severity of the public backlash against it. But Hungary is not alone in the maintenance and pursuit of troubling academic ties to Beijing. Throughout the rest of Europe, concerns about China's role in higher education have continued to bubble up to the surface in recent years.

Conference materials at the European Association for Chinese Studies in Portugal were seized in 2014 after the chief executive of Confucius Institute Headquarters—whose Confucius China Studies Program provided a grant for the conference—complained about the contents.[25] Three years later, in Spain, the University of Salamanca canceled the public events for a Taiwan cultural celebration after China's embassy in Madrid intervened. "We demand your university adhere to the 'one China principle' and take measures to avoid and eliminate the adverse effect," the embassy wrote in an email.[26]

In 2021, the publisher of *Xi Jinping—The Most Powerful Man in the World* alleged that a book event at University of Duisburg-Essen's Confucius Institute was canceled "due to Chinese pressure," referring to the Chinese consul in Düsseldorf. Leibniz University's Confucius Institute, another German institution, canceled an event for the book that same week after its partner in Shanghai, Tongji University, reached out to file a complaint.[27]

In Sweden, newspaper *Dagens Nyheter* found proof that at least thirty doctoral students studying through the Chinese Scholarship Council were required to essentially sign loyalty pledges to the Chinese government. The letters required them to agree to "serve the interests of the regime" and "never participate in 'activities' that go against the will of the authorities."[28] Even worse, the agreement required that a "guarantor" for the student, likely a relative, not leave China for long periods of time while the student is abroad. To students, the meaning was likely clear: If they err overseas, it could be a relative at home who suffers.

And in 2020, a PhD student watched his academic career, and years of work, implode at Switzerland's University of St. Gallen over a Twitter account with only a handful of followers.[29] Oliver Gerber—a fake name, as his partner's family is in China and risks retaliation—received an email from his doctoral supervisor warning, "Very urgent: Complaint from China about your Twitter." She told Gerber she had received "angry emails from China" because of the "neo-Nazi-like content" he posted about the country on Twitter.

"Ultimately, it may even turn out that I won't be able to get a visa to China because of you," she went on. "This is definitely going too far, and I would have to end our advisory relationship." Gerber was baffled, considering that he had mostly just posted criticism of China's handling of COVID. *Neue Zürcher Zeitung* obtained a copy of the so-called "complaint from China"—a Chinese doctoral student contacted Gerber's adviser to complain that a comic he posted criticizing China's Hong Kong and Taiwan policies contained racist depictions of Chinese people. Gerber admitted he did not pay enough attention to the depiction and was sharing it for its political commentary.

Within days, Gerber's adviser had dropped him and the university, which boasts fifteen cooperation agreements with Chinese universities, deleted his email account. St. Gallen alleged that Gerber had technically deregistered from the university in 2019, but Gerber's emails show that the university's doctoral program manager specifically advised him to do so while he temporarily studied in China, and affirmed that the university would facilitate his return. Gerber initially contested the situation, but eventually gave up and left the field. He told reporters, "I don't

The Global Threat of Authoritarian Censorship in Academia

want to have to censor myself, certainly not in Switzerland." That is one of the short-term consequences I discussed at the start of this chapter: A student feels pressure to self-censor when it comes to China. What are the long-term consequences for the university department he studied in, and that university as a whole?

Fears about interference from China are especially fraught in the United Kingdom, a destination for a significant number of Chinese students—assuming they are allowed to leave China to get there. Sophia Huang Xueqin was set to begin gender studies at the United Kingdom's University of Sussex on the Chevening scholarship, a British government-funded program meant to foster future global leaders. But she never made it to Sussex, and her supporters fear that the university downplayed her fraught situation.

Huang, a journalist, led the spread of the #MeToo movement in China, where she talked about her personal experiences with harassment. She was punished for it with a state-led disinformation campaign meant to discredit her and her story. In September 2021, when Huang headed to the airport for her flight to the United Kingdom with a fellow activist, they disappeared—until a 2022 BBC investigation revealed they were detained and put in solitary confinement in one of China's secret "black jails" on subversion charges. In 2023, Huang and Wang Jianbing went on trial. Wang's time studying in the United Kingdom, as well as an online course he allegedly took there, were cited in the indictment against him.[30] Huang has since been sentenced to five years in prison, and Wang to three and a half.[31]

While China's covert arrest of an inconvenient activist, who received no access to attorneys or due process, is disturbing, it is not exactly out of the ordinary. The University of Sussex's response, however, raised eyebrows. Immediately after her disappearance, the university issued a short statement expressing concern, but public silence followed. An email later obtained by the BBC revealed that the university warned students that a reporter had been reaching out to community members about the case, and asked students and staff not to comment on Huang's disappearance and instead direct media to the university's publicity team.[32]

Sussex defended its actions, asserting that the sensitive nature of Huang's case would be best handled by the university and confirmed that the administration remained in contact with UK officials regarding the case. Huang's supporters, though, did not see a university looking out for her best interests, but one seeking to avoid overstepping against China. Did Sussex do everything it could in Huang's case? Likely only the university's leadership knows in full. But a university's vague claims that silence is in an imperiled student's best interest should be met with skepticism, when silence serves the universities' financial interests as well.

And the financial interests are staggering in some cases. Over a five-year period beginning in 2016, Cambridge University, for example, accepted £25.7 million in grants and donations from Chinese tech conglomerate Huawei. Around that time, Oxford was awarded between £500,000 to £2.49 million from Huawei and an amount ranging £2 million to £4 million from the Chinese Ministry of Education's China Scholarship Council.[33] Among some of the top UK universities, Huawei and other Chinese corporations dealt out £40 million.

While the amounts given in donations and grants at Jesus College were less eye-popping, the details of the college's relationship with China nevertheless caused a stir. In 2020, the UK-China Global Issues Dialogue Centre at Jesus College, a constituent college of the University of Cambridge, released a white paper that "referred to Huawei favourably."[34] A freedom of information request made by *The Times* found that Huawei had given the college £155,000 for a two-year research partnership, and that the 2018 founding of the Centre was supported by a £200,000 grant from an agency with China's government-run State Council.

Leaked transcripts also revealed that Professor Peter Nolan, director of Jesus College's China Centre, warned students against holding a campus discussion about the plight of Uyghurs, which he suggested would not be "helpful," because if "both views" were not represented, "the college will be perceived as being a campaigning college for" Uyghurs.[35] When the head of the college's student union used the term "cultural genocide" to describe the events in Xinjiang, Nolan reportedly asked if the student "could give us maybe an hour's lecture on Xinjiang" and suggested that the student should be "trained to think in a different way."[36] The insinuation was that the student only criticized the situation in Xinjiang because he was uninformed.

In 2022, Jesus College announced the Centre would be renamed the "China Forum" and that it would commit to greater funding transparency after reports revealed that a trust Nolan led, the Cambridge China Development Trust, offered classes annually to senior officials from "major state-owned enterprises and government departments in China."[37]

Like grants and donations, Chinese students' tuition contributions are sizable too. Annually, thousands of students from China seek out the United Kingdom for their studies, with an estimated 144,000 in the country in 2022, a number that has rapidly risen in recent years.[38] Unlike Sophia Huang Xueqin, most of these students are not public figures with a history of angering officials, and do not expect to disappear on the way to the airport. But just because they are allowed to leave China does not mean that the pressures of the Chinese government stay behind.

"Many universities rely on the income that international students from China generate," Andreas Fulda, associate professor at the University of Nottingham's School of Politics and

International Relations, told me, "because of the dwindling public finance of higher education they basically use that funding to subsidize research in universities." It is a trend that readers may recognize in the United States too. Chinese students contribute roughly £2.5 of the £7 billion paid annually in tuition fees in the United Kingdom.[39] But this reliance can "create real dependencies" that result in "all kinds of issues of self-censorship," Fulda says.

Fulda told me that he, personally, does not feel pressure to self-censor, and that if he did think his university wanted him to toe a political line around China, he would leave. But he also does not have to operate under the knowledge that his commentary could limit his ability to get a visa, a frequent source of worry for academics who study China. "That boat has sailed," Fulda said. "I decided after what happened in Xinjiang that I could not justify engagement anymore."

Other professors, though, acknowledged self-censoring. A 2022 survey completed by 1,500 humanities and social science professors in the United Kingdom offered a stunning finding: 41 percent of scholars specializing in China self-censored "when teaching students from autocratic states." The number for scholars concentrating on Africa was nearly as high.[40] When asked if they have ever self-censored when reporting fieldwork findings, 22 percent of China-focused scholars confirmed they had, along with 26 percent of scholars specializing in Africa.

A smaller 2019 survey of twenty-five scholars and administrators who deal with China found that "a majority expressed concern about the prospect of—and some described facing—professional reprisals for speaking out on sensitive China-related issues," and fear retaliation from the Chinese government *and* from their universities.[41]

"If many people choose to engage in self-censorship then, of course, you could say the Communist Party succeeds with their rule by fear," Fulda told me. "If it just works with half of colleagues then that's 50% too much." He knows well the consequences of speaking openly. After Fulda took part in an Oxford Union panel about China with journalist and broadcaster Mehdi Hasan in 2019, and spoke to a reporter for *The Times* in 2020, his colleagues received emails attempting to smear Fulda's reputation. Fulda specifically remembered one email telling him "university politics will eat you from the inside out, watch and learn." The opposite happened, fortunately. Fulda's managers defended him and he was asked to help implement institutional guidelines on risk management and authoritarian regimes at his university.

Dr. Jo Smith Finley, a reader in Chinese studies at Newcastle University, knows about these consequences too. In 2021, the United States, European Union, United Kingdom, and Canada issued sanctions against China related to the country's treatment of Uyghurs. In retaliation, Beijing issued its own set of sanctions against those who "maliciously spread lies and disinformation"—including lawmakers, government bodies, and Smith Finley, one of multiple academics named in the sanctions tennis match. Targets of the sanctions would be banned from entering China, along with their families, and Chinese citizens would be disallowed from engaging in business with them.[42]

After the sanctions became public, Smith Finley wrote that she was sanctioned not just for research and "speaking the truth about human rights violations against Uyghurs," but for "having a conscience and standing up for social justice."[43] She added, regarding the developments in Xinjiang, that she "would lack academic and moral integrity" if she failed to share what she had observed. "I have no regrets for speaking out, and I will not be silenced."

This is a sentiment shared by many of the students and professors I spoke to while writing this book: They recognized the potential consequences of speaking out on what is occurring in

China, especially in Xinjiang, but felt both a professional and a moral responsibility to speak openly and honestly about the situation. This clarity is less present among university administrations by far. There are resolute academics who have stood strong against these intimidation tactics, but their courage alone cannot reverse widespread institutional shifts that influence how global populations, within and outside higher education, understand the perils of authoritarianism today.

While the consequences—documented and potential—as well as the urge to self-censor have escalated among academics, the students they teach experienced pressures of their own. Like those in Canada and the United States, the ebb and flow of student protests and controversies about China in the United Kingdom often mirrored political developments occurring in Hong Kong.

As democracy protests swept Hong Kong in 2014, over 150 Durham University students met to debate the movement. Chinese officials, though, were not pleased to learn the intended topic of discussion. Prior to the conference, representatives from the Chinese Embassy Education Office contacted Jake Zhou, one of the organizers and then-president of the Durham Chinese Students and Scholars Association, to recommend that speakers avoid negative comments about China.

"It is not compulsory for the CSSA to listen to the Chinese Embassy," Zhou said, but he reportedly also "spoke of concerns that the embassy could withdraw support for Chinese students who are studying at Durham if the relationship was undermined."[44] Other participants were more troubled by the intrusion. University of Bristol professor and panelist Jeffrey Henderson called it "a clear attempt to interfere in activities that are normal in Britain." The attempt "might have been OK had the conference been in China, but it is unacceptable to try to restrict freedom of speech here."

Three years after this incident, a Chinese embassy official again attempted to interfere at Durham. When Durham Union Society invited former Miss World Canada and Chinese government critic Anastasia Lin for an event, an official at the London embassy phoned the group and told them to "take a second and think between this debating and the more grand background of UK–China relations."[45] The official asserted that "Chinese students are not comfortable about Lin because she's not friendly to the Chinese government."

Durham's CSSA, along with some students at the school, issued complaints of their own to the group and university officials. "Hereby we sincerely ask you to cancel this debate on behalf of the majority of Chinese students in Durham university," the CSSA's representative wrote. "Our members find both the topic and the guest they invited a violation of the belief and feelings of Chinese students. Anastasia Lin has been banned by the Chinese government and she is obviously not an appropriate person to be invited to debate in a topic like this, which put China in a position to be discriminated." Sensitivity exploitation, once again.

As protests in Hong Kong spiked again in 2019 in response to a proposed extradition bill that would ship people accused of some crimes to the mainland, students in the United Kingdom clashed once more. Protesters viewed the bill as another crack in the facade of the "one country, two systems" agreement made by China. For over a century and a half until midnight on July 1, 1997, Hong Kong had been under British rule as a concession from China during the First Opium War. The policy of "one country, two systems"—which promised to allow a higher degree of autonomy to the Special Administrative Region for fifty years after the handover returned Hong Kong back to China's rule—was meant to be honored until at least 2047. To many activists in Hong Kong, and their supporters around the world, it seemed clear that China was not abiding by its promise.

Students took up the cause on campus, with counterprotesters supporting the Chinese government joining the fray, leading to some fiery back and forth among the camps. At the University of Sheffield, though, the heated protest resulted in more than just jeering. Around thirty students gathered to protest for Hong Kong, but before long they were escorted indoors by police after counterprotesters arrived. Those students, who had organized their demonstration on WeChat, reportedly called the pro-democracy activists "insects," sang the Chinese anthem over their chants, and some threw broken bottles at them.[46] Ultimately, one of these counterprotesters, a Sheffield student, was suspended and arrested "under suspicion of committing a public order offence."[47]

Though the violence may have been limited, students nevertheless feared consequences worse than thrown bottles. The family of a student at a Scottish university was contacted after the student took part in a campus protest for Hong Kong. Other activists alleged that that pro-CCP students from mainland China had harassed and intimidated them. Students who anonymously spoke to *The Times* shared that the presence of CSSAs and Confucius Institutes on campus made them uneasy. "I worry about any kind of Chinese Communist Party influence on campuses, not only potential government employees but also the Chinese Students and Scholars Association in each university," one student explained. "Confucius Institutes have brought so much money to universities but they are taking away priceless freedom, fairness, privacy and integrity," another student said. "Our universities don't seem to care about this with all the construction and redecoration work they are doing with Chinese money."[48]

Across the Irish Sea, one university reckoned with a series of controversies and scandals surrounding its relationship with

China. University College Dublin (UCD) attracted international criticism in 2020 when it shared proposed changes to its academic freedom policy that would have overtly prioritized international engagement over student and faculty rights. A working group created by UCD proposed drafts suggesting that "a university with a large international footprint" should "consider and appraise the risk of tension arising between the obligations regarding academic freedom and the strategic imperative to internationalize higher education." It further suggested that UCD determine "whether divergent approaches to academic freedom can be reconciled or accommodated" in international partnerships. "Divergent approaches" is a rather generous way of explaining that some countries have encoded academic freedom protections into law and practice, while others regularly sentence academics to long prison sentences.

"It was really worrying. I don't know where it came from or why it was proposed in the first place. It just came to us out of the blue," UCD associate professor in the School of Politics and International Relations Alex Dukalskis told me in an interview. While Dukalskis, who has spoken frequently about UCD's questionable foreign ties, told me he did not know the origin of the proposed change, he did hypothesize that because universities are under strain to internationalize and most EU students pay lower fees, there is pressure to accommodate less free countries. Again, this is a truth across higher education in the United States as well: The desire to seek higher paying tuition constituents can lead universities out of their own borders, and into less free ones.

UCD, which is home to the first Confucius Institute in Ireland, has certainly set its focus abroad in recent years. In 2012, UCD founded the Beijing-Dublin International College, a joint college with Beijing University of Technology. UCD operates two more joint colleges in China, as well as colleges and partnerships in

Hong Kong, Singapore, and elsewhere. The community at UCD is global as well, with international students comprising about a third of its population.[49]

Hundreds of academics reacted quickly to the proposed academic freedom changes, signing a petition stating that "either UCD has principles or it has not, and they can't be limited by geography" and "if it has principles, then these will not be available for negotiation whatever the circumstances." As a result of the backlash, the proposal was dropped. But while the abandonment of this language was a victory, it hinted at an unresolved underlying issue, which I will discuss more in the next chapter: Do these proposed revisions to the academic freedom policy simply reflect the blunt reality of international engagement with countries like China, and is it naive to pretend otherwise?

Tim Crowley, an assistant professor in UCD's School of Philosophy, suggested that it would even be appropriate for the university to conduct an inquiry into how the statement originated. Crowley identified it as one of a series of concerns surrounding free expression and free speech at UCD, concerns which led him to seek a review of the university's speech policies. "You don't go for these reports if you think your university will do well," Crowley told me. To the school's credit, Crowley said UCD has begun to address some internationalization concerns since the failed update to the academic freedom policy, creating department-specific academic freedom officer positions, for example.

UCD's near-miss with gutting its academic freedom protections would have been concerning on its own, but similar incidents have plagued the campus in recent years too. "Enough other stuff has happened at the university that this was a big alarm bell," Dukalskis told me. One of those other incidents involved the UCD Irish Institute for Chinese Studies, which taught (and, as of this writing, still teaches) a course on Chinese politics that students could credit for some minor degrees. Dukalskis and colleagues in the School of Politics and International Relations objected, citing concerns about the role of the Chinese government in the class. Unlike the Irish Institute for Chinese Studies, UCD's Confucius Institute does not teach credit-bearing courses.

But, as Dukalskis explained during the controversy, "the reality is that the two entities were established at the same time, have the same director, the same email address, the same phone number, the same building, overlapping senior staff, and share the same mission to promote teaching Chinese studies."[50] To what extent was UCD's Confucius Institute teaching credit-bearing courses at the university? UCD academics raised these legitimate concerns internally to their university's leadership and were offered a laughable concession: UCD simply removed the word "politics" from the title of the course.

UCD's leadership again raised eyebrows when its outgoing president Andrew Deeks sent an email to staff saying he was "disappointed by some of the misguided commentary" about the university's Confucius Institute. Deeks went on to write that he was "particularly disturbed by implicit suggestions that the political loyalties of some colleagues can be inferred from their ethnicity, given our ongoing campaign against racism."[51] He was "basically calling criticism of the Confucius Institutes racist, that was the strong subtext," Dukalskis told me. "This infuriated people because it was so disingenuous." Crowley was similarly troubled, calling it "his nadir as president."

There are likely some people who criticize the presence of Confucius Institutes for bigoted purposes. But to imply that critiques of academic partnerships and financial ties to a global superpower—one with a documented disdain for human rights, especially those of minorities in its country—are presumably racist is simply not credible. Regardless of one's opinions about the benefits and risks of Confucius Institutes, it remains entirely appropriate, and even necessary, to question how university ties with authoritarian governments can strain academic freedom.

Shortly after Deeks' accusation against "misguided" commentators, UCD found itself at the center of controversy *yet again* over a statement posted in response to Russia's invasion of Ukraine. The university wrote that it "joins the Irish Government and wider society in its concern with the situation in Ukraine, and in particular with the violation of international law and the unnecessary and tragic human suffering and loss of life."[52] The university later released an updated statement after weathering strong pushback.[53]

Critics were especially troubled by the university's use of the word "situation" and their inference that UCD did not want to take sides. Professor Ben Tonra announced that he was resigning from his role as vice principal for internationalization and global engagement, as the handling of the Confucius Institute controversy and Russia's invasion made it "clear to me that I do not share the values underpinning UCD's global engagement strategy."[54] Tonra, who was "deeply, profoundly ashamed" by UCD's behavior, posited that university management was hesitant to make a statement condemning Russia's invasion of Ukraine because it might then be expected to condemn the Chinese government too.[55] And that is what may be at risk with universities' partnership in authoritarian countries: Administrators may feel an implicit pressure to adjust their behavior to suit that government's preferences.

Academic ties to China can of course have immediate effects on academic freedom. But it is clear they have these long-term reverberations on other aspects of university operations, like how a university might respond to Russia's invasion of Ukraine. "The shadow of that relationship hangs over things that you might not expect it to hang over," Dukalskis said.

Australia and New Zealand

The COVID-19 pandemic sent international higher education into a tailspin, as public health measures complicated student travel and basic university functions, and threatened to permanently alter the state of the education market. While Australian institutions no doubt felt the hit, the pandemic did not succeed in devastating the country's international education industry, which was still Australia's fourth highest export in 2021.[56] The successes of this export are in large part due to the steady inflow of students from China, who made up 13 percent of enrollments in Australia before the pandemic hit, and about a third of international students in the country, with around 133,000 in 2019. But the windfall brought by students from China and the deepening ties between Australian and Chinese academic institutions has accompanied serious strains on campus dissent.

"China is part of our national identity. We have a permanent, postcolonial identity crisis," "Edward," an Australian academic who preferred to remain anonymous, told me. "The past is Britain, the future is Asia. And it makes talking about China very difficult and it makes it easy for China to play Australian universities." When the 2019 protests in Hong Kong made their way to his campus, he said his university "saw the protests as a public relations challenge, not a free speech challenge." The goal was to avoid controversy, not to set a standard for protecting students' free speech. As with American universities, brand protection can supersede institutional values.

I asked Edward about the sensitivity exploitation I have seen taking place at US campuses and he suggested that similar issues plague Australian campuses, whose leaders fail to understand the situation they are in. "They lack the vocabulary to make sense of the party system. The university has committed to government anti-interference efforts but only in a box checking way,"

Edward told me. "There's an incredible amount of anxiety about being seen as anti-Chinese. That's part of the problem with influence. There's a complete mismatch for what Chinese universities mean on campus. For Australian universities they represent corporate money making and diversity and for China they represent state development and ideological control."

And that is where Edward sees the future of China's interference on campus: not angry calls from consulates or demands from CSSA chapters—an "inefficient and expensive" method—but cooperative educational models that split students' academic careers between a Chinese university and a foreign university, in this case Australian. "The Chinese government has moved on and is moving into a joint educational management model which gives them much more control" over students, Edward says. This way, the Chinese government can hold onto students and "blast them with party ideology for two years before they leave" for a foreign partner university.

"With this model of engagement, the question of influence is one of institutional autonomy and it's clear the university has given up on it. It has no control over its partner. Would the university have the power to protect me if [the Chinese partner] decided it didn't want an academic saying things about Taiwan? And I think it wouldn't be able to if it has no institutional autonomy. And I think that's more serious than the CSSAs," Edward told me. At his university, the discussions about the Chinese government on campus "end up being very acrimonious," Edward says. "You tell them they shouldn't do this and they ask, 'why are you anti-China?'"

It is possible CSSAs and embassies may not be the future of interference on Australian campuses, as Edward predicts, but they have undoubtedly been a force. In 2005, a Chinese embassy "provided flags, transport, food, a lawyer and certificates for students that would help them find jobs back in China" to CSSA attendees of a rally welcoming a government official to Australia. This may sound familiar—in the United States, a Chinese embassy coordinated similar schemes with George Washington University's CSSA. Years later, 10,000 students from China were shuttled in chartered buses to Canberra "to protect the torch" at a 2008 Beijing Olympics torch rally.[57]

Members of these groups have also been active in demanding censorship of their peers' speech. "It's an environment of real fear and intimidation," according to Kevin Carrico, a senior lecturer in Chinese studies at Monash University. Carrico told me that tensions were high on his university's campus during the 2019 protests. Students at Monash held their own demonstration in support. At the beginning, it was running smoothly when Carrico checked in early in the day. But things quickly went downhill, and Carrico was contacted by students who said counterprotesters had joined and were physically intimidating them and screaming in their faces. "I rushed down there and witnessed this and then I realized I have no idea what to do; it looked like there's about to be physical clashes and I don't know what to do." Security officers came to separate the groups, but students were left discouraged, Carrico said, feeling that the university "tried to pretend nothing really happened."

"You can imagine for students who've been intimated like that, to not have their university standing behind them is deeply disappointing," Carrico told me. "I've also encountered Uyghur students who speak to me about things in private but naturally feel deeply uncomfortable about speaking honestly about any of these issues with students from China around."

Similar clashes to the one Carrico witnessed took place on campuses across Australia around that time, resulting in tense confrontations and, in isolated examples, physical violence. One of the victims of such violence, Drew Pavlou, became embroiled in a dispute with the University of Queensland (UQ)—which maintains extensive ties within China and a campus population where one in seven students came from China—that continued for years.[58]

On July 24, 2019, Pavlou and Jack Yiu, a student from Hong Kong and leader of the campus Hong Kong Student Association, coordinated joint protests addressing both the events in Hong Kong and the University of Queensland's extensive ties to the Chinese government. It was the first protest Pavlou had ever planned. At that time, UQ was in negotiations over its contract with the Confucius Institute, which in previous years gave Hanban the authority to assess teaching quality at the institute.[59] UQ's then–vice chancellor and president, Peter Høj, also maintained a cozy relationship with Hanban, winning a 2015 Outstanding Individual of the Year Award for "his active approach to integrating the UQ Confucius Institute into the University and the local community, and for his contribution, guidance and support to the UQ Confucius Institute and the Confucius Institute global network."[60]

Initially, the protest proved peaceful, even though Pavlou received threatening messages ahead of the event. But as the day wore on, the energy changed. "We were surrounded by Chinese government supporters," Pavlou told me, with crowds reaching close to 400 people. Students blasted the national anthem and ripped up signs lamenting the treatment of Uyghurs and advocating for freedom in Hong Kong. Someone attempted to take Pavlou's megaphone, and he was soon assaulted with a hit to the back of the head and punches to the face. One student, a business major from Hong Kong, was "grabbed by the throat and thrown to the ground." Another student from Hong Kong "said a sign was torn from her hands and her clothing ripped," but she was brushed off by police when she tried to report it.[61]

The Global Threat of Authoritarian Censorship in Academia

Pavlou attempted to hold a follow-up rally the next week, but was stymied by UQ, who said the protest could only be held in a designated free speech area—what Pavlou described as a "patch of grass" by a car park far from the university center. Even worse, administrators wanted every student involved to be identified with their ID badge, a serious concern for students from Hong Kong who already felt at risk in the aftermath of the previous protest. On this occasion, administrators backed down. But this marked the beginning of a long and ugly saga pitting Pavlou against his university.

Just one day after the initial protest, Chinese state media weighed in, with *The Global Times* accusing Pavlou and other protesters of "spreading rumors about Xinjiang and Hong Kong." In a statement, Brisbane consul general Xu Jie specifically thanked counterprotesting students for their "spontaneous patriotic behavior" at a rally that saw multiple acts of violence. Because of this attention, Pavlou and his family would go on to receive death and rape threats. It took eleven months for UQ's leadership to condemn Xu's comments.[62] But Xu Jie was not *just* a Chinese diplomat. Less than two weeks before Pavlou's protest, Xu was quietly appointed to an unpaid position as visiting professor of language and culture—at, where else, the University of Queensland.[63] Pavlou attempted to sue Xu, alleging that his comments incited violence against him, but a Queensland magistrate dismissed the case, citing Xu's diplomatic immunity.[64]

For Pavlou, disturbed by the worsening human rights situation in China, it became a personal vendetta to take on his university's ties to the country, sometimes in provocative ways. His advocacy ranged from sparring with critics and lambasting university leadership on social media to controversial on-campus stunts, like wearing a hazmat suit outside UQ's Confucius Institute during the pandemic. He also conducted a successful candidacy for a student position on the university senate. "I wish some of the things I had done, tactically I had changed, but I wouldn't have changed my overall strategy, and I wouldn't have changed it even with the assault, the death threats, the effect on my education," Pavlou told me.

But Pavlou's joy at winning the university senate election was short-lived. On April 9, 2020, the University of Queensland slammed Pavlou with a 186-page dossier detailing a set of eleven accusations of misconduct against him. Pavlou says documents obtained by freedom of information requests show that UQ first initiated its investigation hours after it became aware of his stunt suggesting the Confucius Institute was a "biohazard risk."

"UQ's disciplinary processes seek to address alleged contraventions of university policy—they do not seek to prevent students from expressing their views or to limit their right to freedom of speech," the university said in a statement about the charges.[65] Nevertheless, many of the allegations directly related to his speech, like his social media use and his alleged damage to the university's reputation. "They basically started an investigation in search of a crime," Pavlou alleged. "They searched through three years' worth of social media to find any example of me potentially breaching [university rules] because there was a political vendetta against me." *The Guardian Australia* reviewed the allegations when they were first aired and confirmed that none identified unlawful acts. Chinese state media outlet *The Global Times*, though, was pleased by the news, writing that "Chinese and Australian students at UQ" had "expressed their support for the university's possible punishment against Pavlou and felt that expulsion would be reasonable."[66]

"The really extraordinary thing was that the university launched a perfunctory investigation into these guys [who assaulted me] and never found anything, and then launched an investigation into me," an incredulous Pavlou told me, "and even brought in external legal help and PR firms." One of the accusations that troubled Pavlou most was the university's use of some intemperate comments he had made on social media to paint him as a bully. But he says UQ ignored the context—some of the "swear words" he had used online were in response to trolls who were mocking his friend's recent suicide.

As with most political provocateurs, Pavlou's style of protest could at times be polarizing or off-putting to observers. But even for those opposed to his brand of activism, it is hard to look at the situation and conclude that UQ acted appropriately. *The Australian Financial Review* reported that a spokeswoman for UQ had even bizarrely "mocked the student for allegedly being a 'virgin.'"[67] Hundreds of thousands of dollars, multiple PR and law firms, public criticism and mockery, and a nearly 200-page dossier painstakingly documenting years of social media posts and behavior, all laser focused on punishing a rabble-rouser student who focused his attention on China, his university, and the relationship between the two. Was it necessary to use this much administrative firepower to hobble a student's academic career and future?

Pavlou and his attorney countered with a lawsuit and appeals. UQ's initial effort to expel him was whittled down to a two-year suspension, then six months, and a majority of the charges against him were dropped, though he could not keep his position on the university senate. "I ended up losing about a year of my studies," Pavlou, who also took some time off to run for office, told me. "I found it hard to transition back to my studies after that."

At the time we spoke, Pavlou intended to return to finish the last few months of his degree, but he also said that his whole experience with UQ made him question his status in academia and his future career. He is not sorry it happened though. "I'm overall happy that it's raised awareness on a national level, even internationally," Pavlou said. "It's clearly become a national political issue. Given all my mistakes and everything I went through I'm glad with what I did and I'm proud of the contributions I've made."

Pavlou's story made national and international headlines, putting a highly public name and face to the murky stories about China's influence on college campuses in Australia. But a number of other students and academics have quietly suffered aggressive pressure and fear in recent years—students who cannot share their name or show their face because of the potential repercussions, but whose stories illustrate the strain present in higher education today.

In a 2021 report, Human Rights Watch conducted interviews with twenty-four international students studying at Australian universities—eleven from mainland China and thirteen from Hong Kong—to investigate self-censorship about China taking place on Australian campuses. Over half of the twenty-two academics interviewed, chosen because they study China or teach large numbers of students from the country, said they "practiced regular self-censorship" while talking about the subject. Among individual students, the stories were grim. More than half of the pro-democracy students interviewed reported that they were intimidated, harassed, doxxed, or threatened with violence by their peers from China. One student from Hong Kong, then in the process of applying for asylum in Australia, shared that police interrogated him at the airport in Hong Kong, demanding to know, "Did you do anything about supporting the movement in Australia?," and when the student relented and admitted he had, they asked if he had been paid by the American or Australian governments.

Much like the imprisoned University of Minnesota student I discussed in chapter 1, a Chinese student in Australia reported that he began speaking out on Twitter because he "thought it was safe here." It was not. In March 2020, police in China contacted his parents and brought them to a station to inform them that the student should "shut the fuck up." The student was never contacted himself, but his parents were sent threats to relay to him. "They said I must shut down my Twitter, stop spreading antigovernment messages and if I don't cooperate, they may charge me with a crime if I ever come back home," the student alleged. "They said I would face a minimum three years." Out of concern for his family, the student deleted his account. Other students reported threats to dox them, alert police of their behavior, or physically harm them.

It is not just about what individual students can say though. It is also about what they can hear. Human Rights Watch suggests that the climate began to change in 2013, as Chinese consulates started to robustly insert themselves into campus politics. In the following years, incidents readers may now be unsurprised by began occurring with greater frequency at Australian campuses.

The University of Western Australia student guild passed a resolution acknowledging the "negative impact" a visit by the Dalai Lama may have had on Chinese students a year after his visit, and asked that the university consider the "cultural sensitivities of all groups" and that speakers not "unnecessarily offend or upset groups within the student community."[68] Victoria University canceled a screening of *In the Name of Confucius*, a documentary directed by a Falun Gong practitioner, just one day after the director of the university's Confucius Institute passed along complaints from the Chinese consulate about the event.[69] In 2021, an art gallery at Australian National University—on the campus, but not run by the university—took down two works critical of human rights violations and surveillance in China without the artist's permission, because of "unintended hurt caused to the Chinese community who felt the work was feeding into negative racial narratives."[70]

Another professor I spoke to who preferred to tell his story anonymously, "Liam," shared that he is troubled by the general worsening environment on campus, and specifically by the behavior of his colleagues. When we talked over the phone, Liam was in the process of reviewing his university's Chinese studies program and redesigning the capstone curriculum to offer more relevant and interesting classes. What started out as a promising update to the curriculum turned into a dispute between Liam and his colleagues over the direction of the department and the role of political controversy in the classroom.

Liam thought the capstone classes at his university were too often essentially language classes with superficial research elements, so he proposed capstones addressing Tibet, Xinjiang, and Chinese politics, topics he thought could be more intellectually engaging and rigorous for students. His discussions with administrators went well, so he pitched the proposal to his colleagues. That is when it started to go downhill.

At first, Liam says some colleagues in his department suggested they opposed his plan because "students just want to learn language, they don't want to take classes about politics." They put forth a new language-focused capstone, but were rejected by the university, Liam says, and their next complaint was that it would be too challenging to introduce political science and anthropology perspectives in their students' last year of school, when capstones took place. He countered, arguing that it is better to introduce these ideas later in students' learning than never at all.

Then the conversation changed. "One of my colleagues said, 'these classes seem interesting, but I really hope you won't discuss controversial issues.' That's literally what my colleague said." Liam, incensed, said he told his colleagues that "the university is not a kindergarten," and he would of course broach controversial topics. Then he says colleagues asked that he not do so in a "provocative" manner.

"When we're talking about China-related issues, anything that deviates even slightly from official orthodoxy is viewed as a provocation," Liam told me. "'Yeah, I'm going to talk about controversial things and in ways that don't meet the demands of the CCP.' And that's when things got really rowdy. I was very calm, but this was the most ridiculous conversation I've ever had in my life."

And then, Liam said, they finally got to the real heart of the matter: Colleagues complained that if he taught in a provocative manner, he could imperil students or the university's programs in China. Liam said some of his colleagues argued it was unfair for him, as an academic with no intention of returning to China, to teach sensitive material while associated with colleagues who *do* want to travel to China again. One of his colleagues even openly admitted he did not want to be on the wrong side of the local consul general, Liam alleged. Ultimately, what disturbed him most was the feeling that his colleagues transferred their frustration with China's retaliation against scholars onto him, an easier target.

"Rather than standing up and saying we need better protections for Australian researchers, we're offering classes on buzzwords and the Chinese internet," Liam said. "I think that speaks to a lot of the issues in China-focused research today. First of all, you don't know where the 'red lines' are. From my perspective, it's highly implausible that one of my colleagues would be detained when visiting China simply because I taught a class on Chinese politics," he added. "The problem is that people tend to displace blame for the Chinese government's bad behavior onto academics who are just trying to do honest work in discussing some of the challenges China presents today. I was really quite disappointed in my colleagues in their seeming eagerness to just give me a hard time."

Despite the arguments with his colleagues, Liam still expected his proposals to go forward. But the damage was done with respect to his opinion of his colleagues. "If I had to write a script satirizing obsequiousness toward China I couldn't come up with a more ridiculous example," he told me.

The exchanges Liam described painted a worrying picture of the private fears and concerns that could shape how topics like Tibet or Xinjiang are taught (or maybe *not* taught) at universities. But equally interesting to internal disputes over what goes on in classrooms is what universities express outwardly about China, and to whom they express it. In earlier chapters, I discussed institutions expressing different public sentiments in their English- and Chinese-language statements. The University of New South Wales (UNSW) certainly knows this tactic well. In 2020, UNSW's media team asked Elaine Pearson, a director at Human Rights Watch and an academic at the institution, to comment on the developments in Hong Kong and the surrounding international political climate. In the article UNSW posted, Pearson suggested that the United Nations needed to survey the developments taking place there more aggressively.

The university shared Pearson's thoughts on social media, tweeting that she "says 'now is the time' for the international community to put pressure on China to wind back infringements on human rights." The campus response was not entirely supportive, with WeChat posts "indicat[ing] multiple students made complaints to the university and requested a response from the Chinese consulate."[71]

By the next morning, the tweet was gone. UNSW justified the removal by stating that the tweet was "being misconstrued as representing the university." And by that evening, *The Global*

The Global Threat of Authoritarian Censorship in Academia

Times had published an article claiming UNSW was "under attack from its Chinese student cohort" who were "outraged" that "the university's behavior brings 'shame to Chinese students.'"[72] But what happened next was even more interesting. Within a two-day period, the university issued separate statements, one in Chinese and the other in English. Their content, and tone, varied greatly.

In English, UNSW's vice chancellor, while restating that the issue was that the post appeared to imply the university's views, called the deletion "a mistake," stated the tweet "should not have been removed," and affirmed an "unequivocal commitment to freedom of expression and academic freedom."[73] The Chinese-language statement did not show the same support for free expression.

That statement, from a UNSW Global executive officer, did not mention free expression or academic freedom, or express regret for the tweet's deletion. "UNSW does not take any political stance, so any political views expressed by its staff or relevant personnel of the school cannot represent the position of the school. Because its content was misleading, the tweet has been deleted by the school," the statement read. "We are deeply disturbed by the trouble this incident has caused to you. Thank you for your understanding."[74]

Why would a university feel compelled to write that it is "deeply disturbed" by the "trouble" caused by an anodyne tweet sharing a measured statement—which was sought out by the university's own media team—from one of its own academics about human rights?

Across the Tasman Sea, campuses in New Zealand have experienced many of the same pressures and controversies as their peers in Australia—posters torn down, events canceled, and scholars targeted. The Auckland University of Technology

(AUT), for example, was embarrassed when emails released under New Zealand's Official Information Act (comparable to the United States' Freedom of Information Act) revealed not only that the Chinese Consulate General in Auckland attempted to interfere with a 2019 Tiananmen anniversary event, but that the university sought to appease the consulate.[75]

The Chinese Consulate General first reached out days before the event to request a meeting to discuss the memorial, leading the director of International Relations & Development, Lester Khoo, to ask that colleagues contact him "as soon as possible" with details about the event. Director of Hospitality David Green confirmed he would notify Khoo "before confirming any bookings related to the Chinese government or Chinese national groups."

Head of the vice chancellor's office, Andrew Codling, wrote Vice Consul General Xiao Yewen on May 31 to thank him for "alerting" the university to the event and wrote that he "was pleased to inform [Xiao] that this event has been cancelled by the university" and that "it was an unsanctioned event about which the university had no prior knowledge."

"I highly appreciate the right and wise decision made by AUT, which will definitely help promote further growth of exchanges and cooperation between AUT and the General Consulate and China in general," Xiao replied. "I understand that with the kind support of AUT, such uninvited scenario will not take place anymore."

Vice Chancellor Derek McCormack quickly met with Xiao to further assuage the situation, and in the emails between them, McCormack explained that "the rooms had not been booked correctly or paid for by the group" and that the building would be closed for a holiday. "Happily," McCormack wrote, "on this instance your concerns and ours coincided, and the event did not proceed at the University." Though he cited AUT's commitment to free expression, he added that "the University has no wish to deliberately offend the government and people of China."

"Happily"? Why would a university's administration so adamantly seek to appease consular officials offended by an event highlighting human rights abuses in their country? If anything, universities should err on the side of fostering more, rather than less, discussion about government officials of all stripes. These emails were, fortunately, uncovered. But how many other universities have conducted similar campaigns to appease and satisfy Chinese government officials and remained undiscovered? And what has this done to their communities' understanding of the Chinese government of today and the past?

One professor who, in 2020, dug into the relationship between New Zealand universities and the Chinese government, quickly learned that this topic was not open for discussion. Anne-Marie Brady, a professor at the University of Canterbury, coauthored an investigation of the ties connecting universities in the country to China's military. A handful of academics and students objected to the research, alleging "manifest errors of fact and misleading inferences."[76] One of the complainants was the deputy vice chancellor of the University of Auckland, Jennifer Dixon, who also oversaw the university's Confucius Institute in Auckland.[77] Academics sparring over the content of each other's writing is nothing new or unusual. That is how academia works, after all. But what was outside the norm was the University of Canterbury's response. The university did not encourage disagreeing parties to publish competing research and criticism. Instead, it opened an investigation into Brady. Even worse, Brady's lawyer reported that the university "ordered her not to communicate about their 'review' and the complaint."[78]

Other academics were understandably outraged, inspiring nearly 200 of them to sign onto a letter of support for Brady. "We would have expected you to stand up for your university, the right of any of its members to publish their research freely, however contentious, and for Professor Brady as a brave colleague. She has been the target of a harassment campaign and threatening menace because of the serious implications of her important research," they wrote. "We know of no valid basis for any 'review' of Professor Brady's work other than by her peers and other researchers and commentators, as is normal for academic research and publication. That will and should include informed criticism as and if grounds emerge."[79]

Brady and her protesting colleagues were vindicated, and the university dropped the investigation a few months after initiating it. "The University of Canterbury affirms its support for 'the freedom of academic staff and students, within the law, to question and test received wisdom, to put forward new ideas, and to state controversial or unpopular opinions,'" the administration stated.[80] But even when they end in favor of academic freedom, these investigations nevertheless take their toll both on the professors targeted by them, and on the general sense of trust that can be placed in higher education. It certainly does not inspire confidence in the industry when an academic is targeted by her university for investigating institutional ties to the Chinese military.

While writing this chapter, the parallels between Chemi Lhamo and Drew Pavlou stood out to me. Though on opposite sides of the world, within months of each other, both faced serious threats of violence, threats which were seemingly endorsed by their local Chinese consulates. Even the language of the consulates' statements was starkly similar: Brisbane's consulate lauded the "spontaneous patriotic behavior" at the protest at which Pavlou was assaulted, and Toronto's consulate called the harassment against Lhamo an "entirely spontaneous action . . . based on objective facts and patriotic enthusiasm."

The takeaway is clear: No matter where you are, how young you are, or how relatively powerless you are, you might be a target of the censors without borders. Some activists, like Pavlou and Lhamo, may decide that this is a price they are willing to pay for their beliefs. How many other students and academics have suffered through similar abuse, but whose stories have gone untold? And how many have understandably decided that the cost of speaking in the first place is simply too high to pay?

Their enforced silence robs their peers of learning more about the Chinese government and about its role in the world today. But, in the aggregate and the long term, it also shapes how populations around the world do or *do not* understand the CCP and other authoritarian regimes, especially given that global higher education is now more interconnected than ever. The protests, debates, discussions, and research that are silenced today leave their mark on our shared future—not with their presence, but with their absence.

CHAPTER 5

Compromised Campuses

Every day, we make compromises in life. In relationships, at work, with our families. We compromise because we get something of value for doing so, even if it comes with conditions we would normally reject. We believe what we get in return justifies what we have to give up. Does this apply to higher education too? Universities that have expanded into unfree countries—through satellite or joint campuses or global centers—have done so under the assumption that they will create or obtain something valuable, even if they may have to make certain compromises to get it. These losses and gains cannot always be easily quantified, especially when the compromise involves something intangible that is not necessarily measurable in dollar signs or square footage. In the case of universities, that unquantifiable compromise often includes commitments to expression and protections for academic freedom.

This prompts a question that is nearly impossible to answer: What price tag do you affix to your values?

Whether university leaders are willing to admit it, opening a campus in China, the United Arab Emirates, or other countries with aggressive restrictions on speech will fundamentally create tensions with institutional commitments to expression. A university handbook is not going to supersede a country's legal code. The tensions will vary in scope and severity, but they will always exist. These campuses do tend to operate with greater freedom than most citizens enjoy in the countries where universities put down roots. But the restrictions still linger, even if they apply to a different degree.

How do you weigh what universities have achieved in unfree countries against how much of their commitments to expression they must compromise, both overseas and at home? It is a question without easy answers. But it is becoming increasingly difficult to argue that the risks universities have taken on are worth what they have gained. As I will discuss in this chapter, universities have doggedly pursued expansion with the justification that it would build bridges and open doors. But is what they have built worth the free expression and academic freedom protections they have given up? In the age of the censors without borders, this reality is one universities can no longer ignore.

"The Vision That Took Us There"

"It's true that affairs in China have developed," Duke president Vincent Price told concerned faculty amid growing human rights issues in 2021, "that are not positive since we entered into this relationship with DKU." Price nevertheless defended Duke Kunshan University (DKU), the university's partnership with Wuhan University in China, arguing that engagement in China "stood to provide benefit to the students who attend DKU and ultimately longer term to China and the world." Duke possessed certain "bright lines" on academic freedom at the campus that could not be crossed, Price assured.[1]

"I don't think at this point that we collectively at Duke want to step back from the vision that took us there," Price said. According to DKU's mission statement, that vision included "an effective blend of Chinese, American, and global techniques and values and a culture of academic excellence and freedom."[2]

Since its inception, that vision has had its critics, including the editorial board of student newspaper, *The Duke Chronicle*. "Although the administration has promised to ensure that DKU operates under guiding principles that include academic freedom and open access to information, given China's legacy of censorship, we have serious doubts that Duke can live up to that commitment," the board wrote in 2013. "Given the overwhelming evidence of censorship in Chinese academic culture, however, there is little reason to think that DKU will remain immune to constraints on academic freedom."[3] The board asked Duke to "abandon empty rhetoric and wishful thinking and confront the issue of academic freedom squarely."

Though the outlook for academic freedom and free expression in China has undoubtedly worsened in recent years, there were already serious concerns at the time Duke launched DKU. That year, the Central Committee General Office issued a directive to Chinese officials warning of threats in the "ideological sphere." According to a (later deleted or censored) post about the directive from a local party committee's website, officials should "fully understand the dangers posed by views and theories advocated by the West" and "cut off at the source channels for disseminating erroneous currents of thought."[4]

Some Chinese professors—whose posts about the directive were censored on social media—alleged that they too were warned about this series of troubling topics by leadership at their universities as part of the directive against Western influence. They reported that these topics, including freedom of the press and negative history of the CCP, were not to be discussed in the classroom. "We are worried we will go back to the Mao era," Zhang Ming, then a professor at Renmin University, said. "After the document was issued, the government has not come out and acknowledged it. . . . It seems the top leadership hopes to shake up the party and the government but does not want the outside world to know."[5]

Officials at American branch campuses in China at the time were less concerned. "We have received assurances from our partners and authorities that Duke-Kunshan University will be accorded the highest level of academic freedom," DKU executive vice chancellor Mary Brown Bullock said. Bullock also stated that the university had "not received any written or verbal decree from the Chinese government."

DKU may have been spared much of the aggressive authoritarianism its academic peers have faced in China, but Bullock's claim that the campus maintains the "highest level" of freedom is rosy. Students are provided VPNs and access to Duke's libraries, a freedom not shared by many others in China, but that freedom has come with occasional disruptions to VPN access—and can be revoked.[6]

The US Government Accountability Office identified internet access as a central concern to the functioning of these campuses and their relative level of freedom in a 2016 report.[7] Of the twelve American institutions in China surveyed by the GAO, only five offered uncensored internet obtained through virtual private network access. The remaining seven acknowledged they "do not have complete access to uncensored Internet content in China." An administrator at one of the institutions with uncensored internet access admitted "that the university is required by the Chinese government to track and maintain records for several months of faculty, student, and staff Internet usage, including the Internet sites visited by faculty and staff," though at that time, no officials had yet requested access to those records. Students and faculty at some of the universities with limited internet access reported difficulty accessing scholarly material and educational resources.

Unlike their counterparts in the United States, DKU students are not freely allowed to start student groups to organize around religious, political, or other values. One student who attempted to form a Christian student group "was told anything religious is frowned upon."[8] In 2019, Vice Chancellor Denis Simon admitted that DKU would be unlikely to hold an event commemorating the Tiananmen massacre, and the following year stated that DKU would in subtle ways discuss sensitive issues in China, but would follow this rule: "Never unnecessarily stick your finger in the eye of your Chinese counterpart."[9] Indeed, it was Duke's US-based engineering school that issued an apology for its "incorrect and insensitive statement to the Chinese community and the government of China" and clarification that "Tibet is a part of China and not a separate country," an incident I discussed earlier in this book.

Similarly, an administrator at the Johns Hopkins University–Nanjing University Center for Chinese and American Studies admitted that "we are not trying to be instigators in sensitive areas. The mission of the center is to build better relations with the Chinese, so we're not going to stir that up." Leadership would not "be deliberately insensitive to our partners by trying to be provocative in whatever we do at the center."[10]

Professors have not disappeared. Tanks have not been deployed to silence unrest on campus. But leaders also clearly shy away from institutional decisions that would provoke or challenge government officials, and students and professors must internalize the laws and expectations of the Chinese government. And therein lies one of the fundamental problems with this form of engagement: American universities have not made China any freer—in fact, China has grown demonstrably less free since American campuses have expanded into the country—but universities have risked making *themselves* less free institutions.

That may be a price worth paying for some students, academics, and administrators, but it is one that should be openly acknowledged, not covered up with flowery language about openness and exchange.

Peter Hessler, who I spoke to in the summer of 2022, is a believer in the benefits of engagement and exchange despite its risks. First sent to China to teach for the Peace Corps in the mid-90s, Hessler has written eloquently about his time there and the students whose lives have changed and grown in the decades since he taught them English literature. "We were pushing boundaries—not by design, it's just bound to happen. I think that kind of disruption is good, and the risk to America is negligent," Hessler told me about his time in the Peace Corps and in defense of the now-shuttered program in China. But while Hessler is a supporter of engagement, he thinks it should be done with intention and care. That is where Sichuan University-Pittsburgh Institute (SCUPI) comes into the story.

In May 2022, in a *New Yorker* piece two and a half years after his ordeal started, Hessler first opened up about the events that led to the nonrenewal of his position at SCUPI.[11] When I spoke to Hessler, he did not broadly describe a poor environment at the campus. "Generally speaking, I did not feel this political weight in the classroom, and I found students to be much less afraid than I did in the 90s," Hessler said. While "no one ever told me I couldn't talk about X, Y, Z," he did acknowledge that "the system depends on that, they prefer not to set boundaries" because "once you set up a boundary people will try to go up against it."

Though Hessler found his students to be less afraid than their parents' generation, that did not mean *he* had no reason to fear. He would soon become personally acquainted with *jubao*, a verb describing "when a student reports a professor for political wrongdoing," which Hessler says "happens rarely, but the possibility is always there, because potential infractions are both undefined and extremely varied."

In late 2019, his firsthand experience with jubao began. Hessler's wife called to warn him about a Weibo post alleging that Hessler had "possibly been reported for his behavior/speech." Posts on Weibo claimed Hessler was "finished." Expecting an investigation from party officials, Hessler hunted down what had likely prompted complaints—comments he had left while grading a student's argumentative essay defending, coincidentally, state restrictions on expression—and sent it to the head of his department. "It's not accurate to say that in a civilized country with rule of law, people are not allowed to make statements that challenge national sovereignty and social stability," Hessler had written in one of his comments on "John's" essay. "In the United States, Canada, Europe, etc., anybody can make a statement claiming that some part of the country deserves independence." The anonymous Weibo commenter fibbed and exaggerated details, implying Hessler had argued with students in class and made inflammatory claims about the CCP.

The investigation went forward, Hessler reported, but party officials' interviews of students yielded no evidence of the Weibo posts' claims. These officials then shared their report with Minking Chyu, SCUPI's dean and the University of Pittsburgh's representative in the joint campus arrangement, who met with Hessler and confirmed there were no discoveries against him. Later, though, Hessler says Chyu disowned any knowledge of the investigation.

At a departmental meeting after Hessler's meeting with Chyu, professors sought clarity about the investigation and what it meant for their academic freedom rights. Instead, they found vagueness. A campus party official, when prompted to explain what issues were banned, read from a statement saying impermissible topics "include sex in a graphic or degrading manner, political opinion that may not be generally agreed upon, religious material promoting or degrading the tenets within, and topics deemed politically sensitive."

Later on, after the pandemic began and in-person classes shut down, Hessler reached out to John, who shared that he "was mortified to learn that the attack had been connected to his essay" and denied that he had shared the story on Weibo. The most likely source of the leak was fellow students, possibly roommates with whom John had discussed the essay comments, or tutors present at SCUPI's writing institute. "I totally agree with you about the comments, if we don't consider the politics," John told Hessler. "But I had to consider the politics, because I am under a certain circumstance in China. Your comments were against the traditional politics."

Chyu, in April of 2021, notified Hessler his contract would not be renewed. Hessler wrote that Chyu cycled through a series of different excuses, first alleging there were other candidates and then claiming short-term contracts could not be extended. Those excuses did nothing to convince Hessler, who experienced other attacks on social media after the incident with John's essay, and was certain politics were in play.

When I interviewed Hessler about the situation and his eventual nonrenewal, he told me it was "definitely" Chyu's decision to end his employment at SCUPI. "Basically, I know pretty much for sure that there were messages or ideas conveyed to him that I was making people nervous by my writing," he said. "It reflects the general political uncertainty and nervousness. People are trying to read signals." Uncertainty is the point—it is better to err on the side of self-censoring or expelling potentially problematic individuals than risk crossing a line you cannot see or define.

I asked Hessler if, after everything he experienced, he would be willing to return to China to teach again. He was adamant that he would. "I was definitely not banned and there was no top-down order to get rid of me," Hessler told me. As a believer in academic engagement, it seemed that Hessler's biggest frustration was not the complexities of the political situation on the ground, but the University of Pittsburgh's "refusal to engage with it and talk about it at all." He told me the university failed to show any curiosity about his treatment. When he reached out to Pittsburgh while writing about his experience, he said he was brushed off. "All these things reflect that this program is not being properly monitored by Pittsburgh. I think they're out to lunch on it and just cashing the check. They're being willfully blind. They need to conduct proper investigations but there's no curiosity about it."

In one of Hessler's earlier reflections on his time in the Peace Corps, he wrote that China's "programs involved university expansion and improvement, and they reflected a strategy that was hard for Americans to grasp: the idea that education and restriction could proceed in tandem." That observation struck me, and I asked Hessler if he believed one or the other would, or could, ultimately win out. Restriction "obviously limits education all the time. It's the same in the US where there's different restrictions or sensitivities," Hessler said. "The question is whether you're cutting off everything useful. In China we don't know the outcome yet and it remains unclear whether this can continue indefinitely." Like Hessler, I do not know how long this can go on, but for the most part, American universities have shown little interest in asking such questions themselves.

The same could be said for UK institutions like the University of Nottingham.[12] In 2018, University of Nottingham Ningbo China (UNNC) removed academic Stephen Morgan from his management board role, though not his faculty position, after party officials reportedly said he "embarrassed the university." The move occurred after Morgan published an essay critical of a meeting held by top CCP members.¹³ Three years later, an academic anonymously spoke out against the changing environment at UNNC. Initially, he felt "mostly free and able to express myself," but over time, found that "the political and social climate in China" was "seeping" into the campus. "I am not naive to the challenges of operating a foreign university in China, but I do feel that, whereas there was some wiggle room previously, now this has been shut down," he said. "The longer I worked, the more I came to realise that UNNC is actually a Chinese university masquerading as a British one."

"Accept, Tolerate, and Ignore the Repression"

Over the years universities have expanded into China, their advocates have suggested that they create small oases for academic freedom in an authoritarian desert. That is true, to some extent. But they have also arguably lent their credibility, as well as their flowery commitments to justice and intellectual freedom, to a government traveling down an increasingly authoritarian path, helping to soften the ugly edges of widespread human rights violations. After all, one might argue, how oppressive could China really be if some of the most respected and revered universities are willing to put down roots in its soil? But the reality is that expansion into unfree countries says more about the compromises that universities are willing to make than the situation on the ground in the countries into which they expand.

For decades, political, cultural, and economic policy was conducted under the assumption—or claim—that by engaging with the United States, the Chinese government would improve the outlook for human rights and democracy in the country. Education exchange is one of those forms of engagement believed to have the potential to liberalize China. As I discussed in chapter 1, this was part of a broader push in the twentieth century to use American higher education as a democratizing force and cultural export. Readers will likely hold differing opinions about whether the pursuit of such goals in China was naive, inappropriate, or even hypocritical. I will not make sweeping statements within the scope of this book about the intent or outcomes of this effort. It is impossible to know what would have happened differently, in both the United States and China, had engagement been conducted without "liberalization" as one of the intended goals. But it is evident that, regardless of the intent, recent engagement has taken place alongside a steady nosedive into repression in China, and that certain American industries, like Hollywood and higher education, have found themselves changed by their participation in the Chinese market.

Cornell University was one of the institutions to feel those changes over the years. "Most people in central administration are former professors," Richard Bensel, a professor of government at Cornell, told me in a July 2022 interview. "There's something that happens to them when they cross that line and become administrators. This notion of having a higher morality that you ascribe to, you leave that by the door."

In recent years, Cornell has been a campus of note for those interested in how universities grapple with global expansion. In 2019, I praised Cornell because the university had done something few, if any, other campuses were willing to do: craft guidelines for international engagement that acknowledge the strain on student and faculty rights.[14] The guidelines advised those "working in a place where certain speech or expression is prohibited" to consider "how your academic freedom and that of your colleagues, students, and collaborators, may be limited or threatened." The guidelines also encouraged those working with international partners to offer a context-based response to academic freedom violations, "from dialogue-based responses to amendment of the terms of the program or termination of the program and relationship." Willingness to abandon or end a partnership is important.

This was not just a hypothetical question for Cornell. The year before, Eli Friedman, an associate professor of international and comparative labor and a member of the council that created the engagement guidelines, successfully pressed Cornell's School of Industrial and Labor Relations to suspend its student exchange partnership with Renmin University of China. Friedman was instrumental in initially coordinating the partnership, but grew troubled upon collecting "enough evidence of students being subjected to forms of punishment that . . . represented in sum pretty gross violations of academic freedom."[15] Renmin was one of a number of universities that took part in a government-ordered effort to crack down on student labor activists at the time.[16]

In the case of Renmin, Cornell recognized that its exchange program was putting its students' rights at risk and did something about it. And that willingness to do the right thing at Renmin is what made Cornell's later conduct so much more disappointing. Less than two years after issuing its guidelines on academic freedom in international programs, the university announced its intentions to create a dual-degree program between its School of Hotel Administration and China's Guanghua School of Management at Peking University.

Bensel was a leading critic of the proposal, one of several professors in the university's Faculty Senate opposed to it. At a February 2021 Faculty Senate meeting, Alex Susskind, associate dean for academic affairs at Cornell's hotel school, shared plans for the program, but refused to address "the larger political cultural issues" that were "above [his] paygrade."[17] That excuse did not fly among faculty. Professor Neil Saccamano suggested Cornell could not protect its community when "the people teaching next door can get hauled away by the Chinese government."

The Cornell Daily Sun, the student paper, called the faculty response an "intense rebuff." Weeks later, the Faculty Senate voted against the proposal, but while it represented a significant rebuke of the administration, it did not have the authority to bind its actions.[18]

Bensel suggested that two main issues concerned the faculty. "The first is that, when it was presented by the central administration, the major justification for the dual degree program was money. In the first year there would be a $400,000 profit and in subsequent years there would be a million-dollar profit. There didn't seem to be any academic justification beyond this monetary one," Bensel told me. The money, he said, was important for a university that had suffered financially since the financial crisis of 2008. Beyond that, Cornell likely sees the wind blowing in this direction in certain scientific and political fields, and views its connections and partnership in China as "an investment in the future."

The second concern is obvious: academic freedom. "It's seriously constrained, and that's a natural result of having pedagogical and research institutions in authoritarian regimes," Bensel said. Further, he suggested that Cornell's expanding involvement in the country has been "almost in lockstep with increasing repression of the Chinese government." According to Bensel, he and other professors have "asked many times whether the Cornell statement on academic freedom applies to the programs in the PRC," only to be meant with silence. "We have taken that refusal to mean that they accept, tolerate, and ignore the repression that goes on in the PRC."

Cornell's Student Assembly seemed to agree. The body issued a resolution asserting that "it would be unethical for Cornell to champion the safeties and liberties of its own students while their academic counterparts are systematically oppressed in adjacent classrooms."[19] Much of the resolution addressed the plight of China's Uyghurs and the ongoing mistreatment the community faced at the hands of the government. While the violations committed against Uyghurs is a concern worthy of consideration for Cornell's expansion, it is not just a question of morality. Discrimination against Uyghurs is an unfortunate reality in China's hotel industry—but is it one that could be freely discussed in the School of Hotel Administration's new program? It is hard to imagine so. Questions like these directly implicate the university's academic freedom commitments.

Aside from the campus CSSA chapter, which called on the university to "avoid ideological conflicts, political disagreements and other factors affecting pure academic exchanges,"[20] there were few supporters of the program to be found outside of the university's administration. That, however, did not deter Cornell from plowing ahead with the program. Its decision to make the announcement of its approval just as the semester ended, though, suggests that the university was well aware the community would not be pleased, and was hoping to avoid further controversy.

In the announcement, Wendy Wolford, vice provost for international affairs, wrote that "the university's role is to create bridges across what might be considerable cultural or political difference."[21] What these bridges actually produce, and what compromises must be made to build them, proved irrelevant once again. Wolford went on to argue that "the vetting process" for the university's new program, in a country that successive secretaries of state Mike Pompeo and Antony Blinken both accused of committing genocide,[22] "has been very extensive."

The supposedly well-vetted Peking dual-degree program is not Cornell's only venture in China. At a 2022 teach-in organized by Bensel, Friedman spoke about his experiences with the university's internationalization and what he called a "legitimacy crisis" in academic freedom. Specifically, Friedman recounted his invitation to chair a small ethics committee for engagement with China "after agitating about academic freedom issues in China for a number of years."[23] He pursued a policy on free speech, academic freedom, and engagement in China for the committee, which was housed with the university's China Center, a part of Global Cornell. The Center's board is "a normal list of billionaires and CEOs," Friedman pointed out, that also includes Ma Huateng (also called Pony Ma), a former delegate to the National People's Congress and the founder and CEO of Tencent, which operates the messaging app WeChat. "This company oversees the largest and probably the most technologically advanced censorship regime in the world. Its technology is also deployed in the mass surveillance and persecution of Muslims in northwest China." If Cornell is concerned about its associations with censorship and surveillance in China, it is certainly not showing it.

"I did not pursue an absolutist perspective on academic freedom and eventually proposed what I thought to be sort of a compromise position," Friedman said. "My proposal was that the center would state publicly number one that Cornell does not engage in censorship and number two that Cornell's overseas operations are bound by local law. So in cases where officials or someone else asked us to not host an event or to modify an event the committee would then review that request and make a decision about how to proceed that would be transparent and would be available to Cornell's community." His proposal did not get far. "The director refused this proposal and subsequently she removed me as chair of the committee. As far as I know that committee does not exist at all."

I asked Bensel if anything—a potential invasion of Taiwan, perhaps—could convince Cornell to revoke the program. "Those people who can tolerate the atrocities in Xinjiang, they're going to tolerate anything," he told me. Bensel also described an administration that "has gotten more repressive itself" and specifically sought to "constrain" and exclude faculty members who have challenged the university's expansion plans. "This is really a litmus test now for the central administration," Bensel explained. "You oppose them on this and you would be denied influence."

"One of the reasons I am so active is that they can't do anything to me. I'm near the end of my career," Bensel said. For the most part, Bensel feels protected by his status and is willing to accept his unpopularity among administrators, but when junior faculty members encounter this issue, "I tell them to duck." This was a constant theme I have encountered both in the context of global expansions *and* domestic university management: Most of the time, the only professors who feel comfortable criticizing administrators are the ones with tenure, near retirement, or both. Otherwise, the personal risks are too high to bear.

Who Is in Charge Here?

A major appeal of universities' expansion into China is that it offers what is meant to be a largely American-style education, with the associated infrastructure and institutional values, but abroad. Unique opportunities and experiences around the world with a respected American university's degree. Best of both worlds, right?

These international institutions have not been around that long, but cracks are already starting to show in their foundations. It turns out, when you open a joint campus in a country with a different, and more repressive, legal system, it is unclear who exactly is running the show—the American university, the Chinese partner university, or the Chinese government? In this, New York University Shanghai is a poster child—or cautionary tale.

In 2015, Vice Chancellor Jeffrey S. Lehman testified before the US House of Representatives that NYU Shanghai "would have absolute control over the school's curriculum, faculty, teaching style, and operations." Even further, he said NYU "would receive an ironclad guarantee that it could operate the school according to the fundamental principles of academic freedom." Academic freedom does not just protect the freedom of individual scholars to teach, research, and study without undue interference from legal or administrative authorities. The concept of academic freedom also entails the freedom of educational *institutions* to conduct their business without interference from the state.

Four years later, NYU Shanghai's "ironclad guarantee" appeared to have sprouted a few holes, when reporting revealed that the university added a course "at the behest of the Chinese government" and "included a visit to a monument commemorating a close advisor of Mao Zedong and screenings of video lessons like 'Promoting the Prosperity and Development of Socialist Culture with Chinese Characteristics.'"[24]

Curiously, the course was not made public on NYU Shanghai's online registration site and was instead privately shared with students by administrators through WeChat messages. The course is not required to receive a degree at NYU Shanghai, but it is required for all Chinese citizens in attendance. An NYU spokesperson defended the confidential manner the students were notified, arguing that it is "a Chinese government requirement of Chinese citizens attending college" and "not taught by NYU Shanghai faculty, nor is it given during the regular semester." The syllabus, though, listed NYU Shanghai chancellor Yu Lizhong as a class speaker.

While NYU is bound by Chinese law and must offer courses the government requires to those obliged to take them, it does not have to do so in such a hush-hush manner. Privately telling students over a messaging app about a required course, rather than listing it with clear explanations about who must take it and why, gives the appearance that NYU has something to hide. And it is not hard to imagine that NYU might not want to draw attention to this, given that it casts doubt over Lehman's testimony that NYU "would have absolute control over the school's curriculum."

"I hesitate to speculate what's in their minds at this point but the testimony that Lehman gave to Congress is incredibly emphatic in asserting that NYU has absolute control over the operations of NYU Shanghai and that's certainly been my experience," Matthew Belanger told me in July 2022. Beginning in 2015, Belanger was hired to teach at NYU Shanghai, part of a cross-appointment role between NYU and its Shanghai campus. Belanger said NYU has attempted to downplay the cross-appointment, calling it an honorific role, and cast him entirely as an employee of NYU Shanghai, *not* NYU. It turns out that it is a very important distinction.

Belanger, now no longer employed at either university, sued in 2021. One of Belanger's claims was that NYU and NYU Shanghai discriminated against him, in violation of New York and federal law, after he suffered a debilitating disc herniation on his way to work years prior and required the use of a cane afterward. The injury "immediately left me very profoundly disabled," Belanger told me. "It's been years of recovery."

While I am not equipped to weigh in on Belanger's allegations regarding disability or discrimination claims, I think his battle with NYU is worth noting, even though it does not directly implicate academic freedom. Because in a response filed to the US Equal Employment Opportunity Commission disputing his claims, NYU said something interesting: Legally speaking, NYU is not in charge at NYU Shanghai, and American legal protections for employees do not apply. Chinese law does.

"To be clear, NYU Shanghai is a registered Chinese university established with East China Normal University, and a separate entity from NYU," the university's associate general counsel wrote in the school's filing. That is a far cry from Lehman's promise of "absolute control" of "operations."

Calling its status "analogous to that of a minority shareholder," NYU asserted that Chinese rules

> state that foreign investment in the higher education sector is limited to Sino-foreign jointly run schools and programs (i.e., programs jointly established by a Chinese party and a foreign party), over which the Chinese party *must* have control. This includes the requirement that the Chancellor must be a Chinese citizen, and that the board members appointed by the Chinese party must be no less than half of the total board.

"NYU Shanghai contracts with NYU and pays NYU service fees for a range of professional and administrative support services," the filing states, "but the ultimate authority and decision-making for hiring, execution of contracts, licensing and the like for NYU Shanghai rests with that institution, not NYU."[25]

Despite how his career at NYU ended, Belanger was initially optimistic about his job at NYU Shanghai and the broader meaning of the campus. "I went and participated in this with great enthusiasm. I really thought engagement was a hopeful mechanism for US and China relations and I saw this as a positive thing," he told me. But he quickly noticed self-censorship in the community. One of his students, for example, wanted to focus a project on China's online censorship behemoth the Great Firewall, but "abruptly shifted gears" and admitted that he feared producing "problematic" work.

But the censorship was not just on the student side. Belanger recounted multiple incidents where books were delivered to campus "with big black marks across censored portions," leading to concern from faculty. Reporting from a student publication at NYU Shanghai confirmed that in the 2015–2016 academic year, censored copies of Wang Gungwu's *The Chinese Overseas* and another textbook were distributed to students. Officials cited "a mistake conducted by Chinese customs and delivery services" and redistributed the books.[26] Belanger told me that what most concerned him were the "mechanisms" in place at NYU Shanghai. Freedoms could easily be revoked. Yes, the university utilizes VPN access, "but that's a single point of failure that can be cut off."

Belanger also described the unnerving feeling of seeing the campus modified to support online blended learning during the pandemic. When he saw the cameras in classrooms—cameras from Hikvision, he says, a company facing US sanctions for its role in government surveillance in Xinjiang—"it immediately hit me, 'This is a big brother eye.'" Indeed, when I asked Belanger if he had ever consider returning to China to teach, he told me that his experience with the pandemic in general was a major factor guiding his decision-making. "Nobody in the US has the perspective of what it's like to be padlocked into your home," he told me. "The only way to get to the hospital might be to walk or beg to be let out. For months I was left without medical care or treatment. That's an awful place to find yourself."

NYU Shanghai is not alone in disowning responsibility for its China-based institution. Kean University is a mid-size public university in New Jersey that set its sights on China in the early 2000s, years ahead of some of its peers. Kean boasts that

Wenzhou-Kean University, a joint venture between Kean and Wenzhou University, is "the only public university in the United States to have a campus in China."[27] (Just a few sentences later, Kean University's "About" page highlights its Human Rights Institute, which "offers a broad range of programs to raise awareness of human rights violations worldwide.")

Wenzhou-Kean did not receive approval from the Chinese government until 2011, but the eventual project was lucrative: China's Ministry of Education promised nearly $250 million in funding. "It doesn't cost us a penny," then–President Dawood Farahi boasted, adding that the campus "helps us with our reputation, and it has financial advantages in internationalizing our curriculum and bringing in some revenue."[28]

It may not have cost Kean's administration a penny, but it certainly cost their faculty. In 2018, the Kean Federation of Teachers made a troubling announcement: Within months, teachers at the campus in China would no longer be employees of Kean University in New Jersey and would instead be employees of Wenzhou-Kean. Kean defended the move, asserting that it was a more efficient management setup, and that Kean would "retain academic control over the institution after the change in the employment structure."[29] President Farahi, too, wrote that it is "worth noting that our sister institutions in China, [New York University] Shanghai and Duke Kunshan, are already using the local employment model, and have been successfully for a few years."

As I have written before in this book, public institutions in the United States are bound by strong legal precedent protecting professors' right to speak and teach. This is a defining strength of American higher education. So to see a public university create a campus in China and willingly hand over management of professors to a system with so few rights protections is jarring, to say the least. The transfer of faculty to Wenzhou-

Kean was not even the joint university's first employment scandal. In 2015, job postings for residence life and student conduct positions asserted that "membership in Chinese Communist Party is preferred." And Wenzhou-Kean's standard staff employment application also asked prospective employees to disclose their "politics status."[30]

Kean Federation of Teachers president and professor James A. Castiglione, who likened the decision to "saying we're moving your address to the moon," strongly protested the change. "To say that you're an employee of Wenzhou-Kean versus an employee of the government—there's no distinction," Castiglione argued. "The government bought the land; it paid for the construction of the building; it provides the money that runs the university. . . . If you go to the Wenzhou-Kean website and you print out an organizational chart of Wenzhou-Kean, what you'll see is that the very top of the organizational chart is the CCP secretary—that is, the Chinese Communist Party secretary."

John Kean Jr., a member of both the Kean Board of Trustees and the Wenzhou-Kean Board of Directors, defended the university's conduct in an op-ed that made some far-fetched claims about rights in China. WKU "students enjoy the same academic freedom their peers in the United States enjoy and come to appreciate American culture and values through their education," he wrote.[31]

That claim would soon be challenged by anonymous faculty members who alleged that the campus was not truly under the control of Kean—or the promises it had made. "We have no academic freedom, basically, and there's a lot of self-censorship that goes on," one former lecturer said.[32] And the limitations were not subtle either. The lecturer claimed that Wenzhou-Kean professors received a set of topics they were warned not to touch. The list included Tiananmen Square, protests in Hong Kong, and oppression of Uyghurs.

"In the Context of Qatari Laws"

Earlier in this chapter, I raised a question: Who makes the decisions at American institutions in China? The same could be asked of universities, like Northwestern University, in Qatar. Is NU-Q in charge? Its partner, the Qatar Foundation? Offended social media users angry about what takes place on the campus?

In Education City, an academic initiative spearheaded and infused with billions of dollars by the state-linked Qatar Foundation, a group of universities started setting up shop around the early 2000s. In the years since American institutions expanded into Qatar, critics have challenged the wisdom of deepening educational ties in a country with immense wealth, but deeply impoverished political and civil rights. Do the financial benefits of expansion into the Gulf states outweigh the associated limits on free expression?

These concerns have been justified numerous times. A 2020 incident, where a campus event clashed with legal and social attitudes about homosexuality in the country, offers useful insight into these tensions. That February, NU-Q was set to host an event on media revolutions in the Middle East, with Lebanese indie rock band Mashrou' Leila, whose lead singer is gay, taking part. In Qatar, sexual activity among same-sex individuals was then, and still is, punishable with prison time. News of the event had provoked cancellation demands on social media, with complaints that NU-Q was denigrating local law and culture.

The demands were met. Northwestern's director of media relations asserted that both the campus and the band mutually agreed to cancel the event "out of abundance of caution due to several factors, including safety concerns for the band and our community."[33] Instead, the event was scheduled to take place at Northwestern's home base in Illinois. It was troubling that, as Northwestern alleged, safety concerns necessitated the event's cancellation, but at least the university sought an alternate venue for the event to continue. A change of venue is better than a total cancellation. End of story, right?

Not according to the Qatar Foundation, a campus partner and Education City leader, which released a statement completely undercutting Northwestern's claims about its decision-making. "We place the utmost importance on the safety of our community and currently do not have any safety or security concerns," a spokesperson told media. "We also place the very highest value on academic freedom and the open exchange of knowledge, ideas and points of view in the context of Qatari laws as well as the country's cultural and social customs. This particular event was canceled due to the fact that it patently did not correlate with this context."[34]

So, rather than undefined security threats, the Qatar Foundation made clear why Mashrou' Leila was unwelcome at NU-Q: Qatar's laws and social customs. In 2022, Northwestern's claims were challenged yet again—this time by Craig LaMay, who was dean of the Qatar campus at the time of the Mashrou' Leila cancellation. LaMay asserted that the Qatar Foundation directly ordered him to shut down the event because of the lead singer's sexuality.[35]

It is now difficult to avoid the conclusion that Northwestern not only canceled an event because of a participant's identity, but then openly lied about why the event was canceled, and that its state-affiliated partner in Qatar ordered the cancellation.

At the time, I wrote that this incident flew in the face of NU-Q's promise to protect the "freedom to communicate, assemble and peaceably demonstrate" and the "freedom to join organizations, to speak freely, and to exercise one's civil rights as long as the student does not claim to represent the institution."[36] It was quite clear that there were unwritten limits to that freedom.

Those limits did not escape the notice of Northwestern's faculty. In 2021, the faculty senate passed a resolution to its handbook's academic freedom policy, one that had been in the making even before the dustup the year prior. The new policy, applicable to all Northwestern campuses, abandoned the phrase "to the extent that applicable laws allow," replacing it with: "While academic freedom essentially coexists with established legal frameworks, on rare occasion the two may be in conflict."[37]

While researching for this book in 2022, I found that in the two years since the incident, NU-Q's previous student rights commitment, now only accessible via internet archive tools, had changed. New policies were posted and appeared, to my eyes, weaker. Now the policies stated that "students will be free from censorship in the publication and dissemination of their views as long as these are not represented as the views of Northwestern University and do not violate any University policies" and have "freedom of research, of legitimate classroom discussion, and of the advocacy of alternative opinions to those presented in the classroom."[38] The new promises on student rights emphasize the freedom for "legitimate" *classroom* discussion over the freedom to assemble and demonstrate. These may look like subtle changes, but they suggest where American and branch campuses diverge on important speech protections: What a student could write in an exam paper or suggest in a class discussion might not be as freely stated in the public quad. Negotiated protections on paper only go so far.

The dustup over Mashrou' Leila was far from NU-Q's first bout with censorship. When Everette E. Dennis, a professor of journalism and dean of NU-Q, conducted a survey of citizens of six countries, funded by the Qatar National Research Fund, one of the questions was whether respondents thought their country was "headed in the right direction." The views of citizens from the United Arab Emirates, Egypt, Tunisia, Lebanon, and Saudi

Arabia were included, but "someone in the government refused to let Northwestern ask that question" of Qataris.[39] And like their peers at branch campuses in China, some professors at NU-Q have been forced to cut books from their syllabi "because they were held by ministries or Qatari customs for review," and book shipments—especially those addressing topics like sex, religion, or Gulf politics—have been held up weeks at a time.[40] Similarly, the director of the Virginia Commonwealth University libraries in Qatar reported that, on occasion, "boxes are opened before they arrive with some books missing from the original shipment order."

These incidents and controversies are not limited to NU-Q. A recent anonymized survey of seventeen academics and administrators at five branch campuses in Education City found that nearly all of them praised the material conditions of their working environment, with better salaries, perks, travel budgets, and living accommodations than what faculty members at American campuses would likely receive. But Christopher M. Davidson, the survey's author, also found that those benefits came with certain costs.

Nearly all surveyed "agreed that there does exist a culture of self-censorship" and confirmed "sporadic episodes of direct censorship." Sensitive topics that tended to face censorship pressure, either internal or external, included criticism of Islam and Qatari leaders, laborers' rights, terrorist groups, and Israeli relations. And "almost all reported that they felt restricted in their ability to teach in a fully objective manner."[41] That is the reality of university expansion into a state like Qatar: An improvement in benefits and material conditions (though these conditions may not extend to many laborers in the country) may come with the tradeoff of impoverished rights and limited recourse for faculty rights violations. Is what is gained worth what is given up?

Georgetown's "Free Exchange of Ideas"

A short walk down the road from Northwestern sits Georgetown University's Qatar campus (GU-Q), first instituted in 2005. In Qatar, Georgetown offers "a vibrant, multinational community" that "focuses on educating the whole person through exposure to different faiths, cultures, and beliefs, and through critical engagement with a range of points of view."[42] That sounds promising, assuming you can get there with no issues. Kristina Bogos could not.

In 2016, Bogos, then a master's student at Georgetown's School of Foreign Service in Washington, DC, was working on a thesis about migrant workers' rights in Qatar. What better opportunity for a master's student focusing on Qatar's labor issues than a semester spent studying and researching at her university's campus in Qatar? Bogos told me in a 2022 interview that it just made sense for her to study abroad at GU-Q's campus, even though she was the first master's student to make the request, a guinea pig of sorts.

Weeks before she left, Bogos received a troubling email from an unknown sender, "Wahedk87," about her "planned visit to Qatar." The sender warned that authorities in the United Arab Emirates—where Bogos had previously spent a semester—"have informed their counterparts in Qatar regarding your planned visit" and knew of her "dirty mission" to "gather some confidential information." (The "dirty mission" presumably referred to Bogos's research on migrant workers' rights.) Working with a cybersecurity expert, Bogos learned that her email had been hacked the previous month, with all of her sent and received emails available to the hacker.[43]

Wahedk87's threat proved true. When Bogos arrived in Qatar in June—on a tourist visa because she did not have time to obtain a student visa before traveling—she was stopped and warned that she was on a national security blacklist. Officials would not say why, only that she should not try to enter any Gulf country because she would likely be stopped in others too. With assistance from the US embassy in Doha, Bogos was allowed in after her temporary detainment.

"The first month in June I really kept a low profile," Bogos told me. "I started to do my research but because I was on a tourist visa I knew I'd have to leave the country and come again." But something strange was happening, Bogos said. "I started to notice I was being followed by state security. Cars with tinted windows would follow me on the campus and were parked outside the library while I was inside. I thought it was interesting that Georgetown would be okay with state security following a student."

Through June, July, and August, Bogos had to enter Qatar three separate times because of the limits of her tourist visa. Each time, she was subject to questioning, and with each visit the length of time she was held at the airport increased. And then during August, she finally got the news: A liaison at GU-Q informed her that her student visa was denied. With no other options, no explanation for the denial, and no opportunity to appeal, Bogos returned to Washington, DC. I asked Bogos if her research into labor rights in Qatar cemented her denial. She had "every reason to believe" that was the case, she told me, referencing the emailed threat that UAE authorities knew of her "dirty mission" and informed Qatar. The research, she said, was also why she was initially denied entry for national security reasons.

Bogos stressed that she was grateful for Georgetown's initial efforts to get her into Qatar in the first place, and to the people who wanted her to be able to continue her research in Qatar. But she offered less praise for officials at Georgetown's home campus, with whom she raised the issue of her visa denial and found to be "very much taking the side of the government," Bogos told me. "To be honest it was a very uncomfortable experience. I was basically told that the university does not control immigration policy and that there was nothing they could do. They somehow made me feel as though I should feel stupid for having even thought the university could facilitate it."

A defining question of these institutions, and one that increasingly looks to be answered in the negative, is whether universities' international expansion has the ability to pressure countries in favor of openness, at the very least in academic matters—a visa approval for a student undertaking critical research, for example. In China, while American universities may be pockets of relative freedom, the world outside them has not grown any less strict or surveilled (in fact, the opposite has happened). Bogos suggested a similar situation in Qatar. "Yes, you can talk about things all you want in a space like GU-Q but the minute you leave those walls," that openness stops.

"If you were to ask any teacher that teaches at GU-Q, 'how do you feel about being able to talk about homosexuality in the classroom?' I'm sure they could talk about it," she said. "But if someone tried to go out in the field and do research they wouldn't get very far. In terms of actually producing scholarly research, I think that's where it stops." Essentially, do not look for what happens in class to have a significant effect outside of it.

That is the experience she had speaking to migrant workers at GU-Q's campus. Some people might argue that Georgetown's presence in Qatar offered better labor conditions, Bogos said, but that did not mirror what she found. "If you talk to them like I did, they'll tell you they don't have passports, their boss is making them stand outside in the sun, and there's deep seated racism within the workforce at the university. And then you hear the university say they're treating them well." Bogos called it "a lot of self-serving introspection" where "it's hard to get an answer from them whether they think they have actually created any change."

They have, though, created useful branding opportunities for a country eager to signal its openness to foreign investment. In a televised commercial run during its controversial hosting of the 2022 World Cup, Qatar proclaimed that the country was "committed to that idea and growing its potential as a partner, investor, and innovator, with possibilities that are unlimited and rewards that are priceless." The ad showed the country's museums and stadiums, and then panned to American satellite campuses in the country. During a sporting event marred by controversy over migrant workers' rights and censorship of players' pro-LGBT advocacy, you could not ask for a better illustration of how the presence of American universities serves as a tool for a government seeking to deflect attention from its human rights record. It is reasonable to argue that universities should not be in the business of spreading freedom abroad in the first place, but they cannot have it both ways, promising the same rights as those on their home campuses and claiming they promote the common good, while then passively citing the limits of local law when it suits them.

It is doubtful that what happens within GU-Q's walls can change what happens outside of them. But that does not mean events in Qatar do not affect what happens in GU-Q.

In 2018, GU-Q, which boasts "a commitment to open discourse and the free exchange of ideas,"[44] found itself in a spot of trouble. That October, the university's debating union scheduled a discussion on the topic: "This house believes that major religions should portray God as a woman." (Yes, this was planned not long after the release of the Ariana Grande song on the same subject.) The debate topic did not go over well online. Social media users accused the university of "disrespect" and called the event "offensive" and "unacceptable."⁴⁵ And then the hashtag "Georgetown Insults God" went viral in Qatar. That is not exactly great PR.

The day before the event was scheduled to take place, GU-Q announced its cancellation and took down event flyers from campus,⁴⁶ tweeting that it was "not sanctioned" and did not follow appropriate university policy.⁴⁷ But just one day later, the university administration sang a different tune. "Georgetown is a global research university guided by a commitment to engage all over the world to promote the common good," but the debate was "cancelled after it failed to follow the appropriate approval processes and created a risk to safety and security of our community," the Office of Communications said in a statement. "GU-Q is committed to the free and open exchange of ideas, while encouraging civil dialogue that respects the laws of Qatar."⁴⁸

Was the reason a "risk to safety and security of our community"? Or creating "civil dialogue that respects the laws of Qatar"? Those are very different justifications than blaming organizers for failing to follow proper event guidelines. And most interestingly, the statement's reference to "the laws of Qatar" makes clear that university officials believed a campus debate about God and gender—basic academic discussion that takes place at campuses every day—could run afoul of Qatari laws—presumably its blasphemy law, which punishes offenders with fines and/or prison time.

It is not easy to square GU-Q's "commitment to open discourse and the free exchange of ideas" with a blasphemy law, which is why FIRE put the campus on its 2019 list of the 10 Worst Colleges for Free Speech⁴⁹ (the first branch campus to make the list) and asked the university to explain itself. In a statement to *The Hoya*, the student paper, GU-Q again doubled down on its earlier comments: "Faculty members and student groups with access to university benefits may host events on campus that are in accordance with Qatari law."⁵⁰ Obviously, given that Georgetown's campus is in Qatar, there is the reality of Qatari law. But Georgetown cannot explain how its campus both celebrates and protects free expression, but also abides by Qatari law. It simply does not add up.

In the aftermath of the debate's cancellation, The Hoya reported that the university's administration and student government sped up plans to open the Red Square, "a replica of the main campus's forum for tabling, flyering and other forms of public discourse" to "ensure students had a platform for free expression."⁵¹ It is promising that GU-Q looked for ways to encourage student expression. But as GU-Q's online rules for the Red Square remind, "as with any other form of expression, content on posters may not violate the laws of Qatar."⁵² At the end of the day, what matters is likely not the number of spaces for expression, but what can actually be said in them. And, under Qatari law, there are many words that must go unspoken.

"There's No Protection for You"

Over thirty foreign universities have expanded into the United Arab Emirates in the past few decades, the most branch campuses hosted by any country.⁵³ Like Qatar, the lucrative opportunities offered in the UAE have attracted storied institutions like Paris-Sorbonne University, New York University, and London Business School. For these universities, expansion into the UAE can offer high rewards. For students, it can prove high-risk. Few know that better than Matthew Hedges.

When Hedges traveled to the UAE in 2018, it was far from his first visit. Hedges had spent time there throughout his life for family, work, and research. But this visit turned out differently when, on May 5, Hedges was arrested at the Dubai International

Airport at the end of a two-week fieldwork trip. A PhD student at the United Kingdom's Durham University, Hedges had traveled to the UAE to conduct research on Emirati state security. A sensitive subject, sure, but one well within the traditional bounds of academic study and Hedges's documented area of work and pedagogical expertise. Emirati officials, however, did not see it that way.[54]

So began a harrowing seven months for Hedges. From the airport, Hedges was detained, blindfolded, and driven to Abu Dhabi, where security officials threatened him with torture and subjected him to weeks of "intense and grueling daily interrogations, sometimes for 15 hours at a time."[55] Eventually, under worsening physical and mental conditions, Hedges signed a confession—written in Arabic, a language he does not speak or read—admitting to what authorities falsely accused him of: working as a spy for British agency MI6. Only once he signed the confession asserting that he was a British spy was he granted a six-minute meeting with a UK consulate official.

Over the following months, Hedges was kept in solitary confinement, "arbitrarily given high doses of medication, including antidepressants, anti-anxiety pills, antihistamines, and sleeping pills," and denied visits from his wife or others, worsening his depression. While incarcerated, Hedges said he attempted self-harm and experienced suicidal thoughts. And then, in a five-minute hearing with no lawyer present for Hedges, an Emirati court sentenced him to life in prison in November 2018.[56] Days later, thanks to public advocacy from Hedges's wife, fellow academics, and British Foreign Secretary Jeremy Hunt, President Khalifa bin Zayed Al Nahyan pardoned Hedges, in part because of "the historical relationship between the UAE and the UK," but UAE officials continued to assert Hedges's guilt.[57]

Academics were understandably troubled by Hedges's experience—after all, some of them working on sensitive subjects risk suffering the same fate—and began asking questions not just about conditions in the UAE, but of the institutions proud to partner with the country. At the University of Exeter, where Hedges studied previously, lecturers at a general meeting issued a unanimous call for an academic boycott of the UAE, including suspension of Exeter's Dubai programs, until Hedges's release.[58] Similar campaigns succeeded at Heriot-Watt University and the University of Birmingham. And at Durham, Hedges's university, officials advocated a moratorium on staff and student travel during their academic's imprisonment.

When I interviewed Hedges about his experiences, he told me that these ethically dicey partnerships between universities and the UAE are "part of the neoliberal environment that's taken over the higher education sector." Money is, clearly, the driving force. "You get the bureaucrats, academics who have climbed a corporate ladder within the university and they get massive bonuses for doing this. It kind of requires this type of engagement if there's a lack of national funding," Hedges said. "One of the clearest examples, and the most dangerous, to highlight is NYU. When you have members of the Abu Dhabi executive council on the board of a US university, and that affects the ability to discuss issues in New York, that's the clearest illustration of that influence and money changing critical thinking in the US." He said this same incentive was driving expansion into both China and the Gulf states, but at least in the United Kingdom, China was perceived as more of a security threat than Saudi Arabia or the UAE.

Hedges is not alone in his criticisms of NYU Abu Dhabi. Members of the community, both at the New York and Abu Dhabi campuses, expressed outrage at Hedges's treatment and questioned whether the administration understood the gravity of what it meant for NYU. Over 200 NYU professors signed onto a statement calling for better academic freedom protections and on President Andrew Hamilton to "make it clear" that Hedges's situation has "grave implications for NYU's ongoing operation in Abu Dhabi."[59] In his reply, Hamilton wrote that he spoke to senior Abu Dhabi officials about Hedges's case.[60]

The editorial board of *The Washington Square News*, the campus paper, weighed in too. "The administration must recognize the extra responsibility it takes on by exposing its students to a government that has been consistently proven to inhibit academic freedom in various ways," the WSN board wrote. "The safety of students is paramount, and in the wake of Hedges's sentencing, it is frightening to consider how student life could be affected by the limits of free speech in Abu Dhabi. It is the responsibility of NYU and NYUAD leadership to recognize the patterns that leave students and citizens at risk."[61] In a faculty forum to discuss Hedges's case, NYU Abu Dhabi assistant history professor Lauren Minsky shared that she had personally suffered some intimidation while teaching at the campus, and was followed by government officials for hours while driving her car. She reported the harassment to NYU, "but it was almost like nothing ever happened."[62]

In a months-later interview with Hamilton, WSN wrote that Hamilton refused to release the memorandum of understanding between NYU and the UAE government.[63] When WSN questioned Hamilton about academic freedom in the UAE, he asserted that he was "not aware of any constraint on discussions that take place on the Abu Dhabi campus or discussions that take place in the classroom at Abu Dhabi," but "dodged the question of whether NYU has policies in place to protect students should they be detained in the UAE."

I asked Hedges what protections, if any, universities could provide in these situations. You cannot force countries to change their laws, Hedges said, "but what you can do, if you're going to have a partnership in another country, you have to ask, 'Can you have a free space to discuss ideas?' If this isn't the case you have to communicate this to students and faculty then so they can be informed. Then you can say 'you might not like partnerships but we're not hiding anything.' The problem comes when they try to pretend they do have the ability to genuinely engage in academic practice."

I prompted Hedges to share any advice he had for students who may someday find themselves in his shoes, pursuing research in countries with heightened risks. "In my experience, you have to be not just realistic, it's a very serious thing for you to do, to step outside of the US or UK, the rules, regulations and norms of wherever you're going may not be the same as you'd expect in your country." Even UK students, he said, should understand that the United States will have its differences. "From the top, this needs to be institutionalized: You're there by yourself. There's no protection for you, you have to be aware of those limitations. I don't want to close the door but you have to be aware of what restrictions and limitations there are to your own safety and livelihood." Hedges also criticized the lack of preparation offered to academics undertaking high-risk opportunities, and warned that, with the lack of social awareness about the risks of academic field work, "these abuses can get normalized."

It is hard to imagine a faster way to normalize these abuses than for universities to continue pursuit of expansion into the UAE, business as usual. But that is exactly what the University of Cambridge intended to do. A 2021 report revealed that Cambridge, despite what happened to a student from one of its peer institutions, was pursuing a historically massive deal with the UAE, one that would help "weather the challenges faced by universities as a result of Covid, Brexit and a constrained funding environment."[64] Under this deal, the UAE would commit £312 million to the collaboration and Cambridge would contribute £90 million through staff time to form the UAE-Cambridge

Innovation Institute, which would eventually host a physical home in the UAE.

Cambridge knew very well the risks that this kind of partnership could pose, both to its community and to its reputation. Internal documents on the proposal, according to the *Guardian*, "acknowledge the risk of reputational damage posed by the collaboration. They also raise concerns about a 'values gap', 'academic freedom and institutional autonomy', and 'the potential burden such a large partnership could place on parts of the university and attendant mission drift.'"[65]

"We are fully aware of the UAE's recent treatment of UK researchers and other visitors, which reflect a dramatically different cultural and legal context than that which may be familiar to our staff and students," university documents stated. "We will put in place sufficient support to ensure that our staff are prepared before their work in the UAE begins."

As with Cornell's dual-degree plans in China, I was shocked when I saw what Cambridge intended to do. Pursuit of these deals even ten years ago was an ethical quagmire, but the appeal, and the belief that their potential gains outweigh their harms, were understandable then. But now, after a doctoral student had been arrested and tortured? Cambridge, of course, was "fully aware" of that violation—but was either foolhardy enough to believe its community would never pay the price for its lucrative deals, or eager enough for the deal not to care.

Just weeks after this news broke, a majority of the directors at the Cambridge Centre for Chinese Management were accused of sharing close ties with state-linked Chinese tech company Huawei.[66] In the aftermath of both of these controversies, Cambridge vice-chancellor Stephen Toope announced the release of principles to steer international engagement. The guidelines promised to "seek to advocate" core values, including academic freedom and free expression in cross-border deals, and would "review, pause or withdraw from international engagements that threaten them."[67]

Cambridge soon after announced it put the UAE deal "on hold" over reports that UAE leadership utilized spyware to hack targets' phones.[68] A spokesperson said the university would reflect and evaluate its long-term options. Will the trickle of damaging reports be enough to sway Cambridge against ultimately approving the deal? Or is the university just waiting until time passes and people lose interest, so a very lucrative deal can pass through under the radar? We will have to wait and see.

Time will also tell as to what future awaits the Emirati students who bear a higher risk of meeting a fate like Hedges, but without citizenship in another country to protect them. I spoke to one of those students, "Jane"—her name and identifying information concealed for her and her family's protection—in August of 2022.

In the early 2010s, Jane taught as an instructor at a university in the UAE, but quickly found the environment devolving around her. "There was creeping authoritarianism in the aftermath of the Arab Spring. We lost a lot of professors who were vocal on social media supporting the revolution," Jane told me. "The red lines that we were familiar with shifted and it became very constricted after that. That prompted me to pursue a PhD as an escape."

So, with the walls closing in, Jane left to seek a PhD. But, years later, when she published an article critically assessing challenges to higher education in the UAE, she was now the one being pursued. An employee of the UAE's foreign minister reached out to her with a request: He wanted her to meet him in a nearby hotel for a chat. This took place just a few years after Jamal Khashoggi's murder, Jane emphasized, giving her an increased sense of fear and awareness of the potential consequences that could await her.

When they met, the hotel restaurant they sat in was completely empty—no waiters or waitresses, and Jane struggled to get phone reception at the table. Two bottles of water, already opened by the Emirati official, sat on the table. Jane told me he had also placed a set of books—including one by Judith Butler, another about the Muslim Brotherhood—on the table, and brought them up for discussion. It seemed to Jane like an effort to figure out how she would react, if she would reveal any political leanings.

Through a two-hour conversation, he asked her questions and offered her prompts, and told her that he may have had the wrong impression of her. "We thought you were undermining the government and its efforts," he said. He asked her about her plans—she told him she had no specific ones—and repeatedly asked her when she planned to return home. He appeared just a little too curious about when Jane would be back within Emirati borders.

"At that moment I made the decision not to return," she told me.

He left the meeting reassured, Jane said, but that was not the end of officials' contact with her. The consul general kept calling. "It was very patronizing. They come from this fatherly place where they kept asking if I needed anything," Jane explained. "Every time they called me I felt more uncomfortable." Then officials contacted her university, requesting a copy of her dissertation. To her knowledge, it was not handed over. And then they organized a meeting between her and a fellow, more compliant Emirati scholar, whose first question to her was about her dissertation. The meeting took place at an expensive hotel he had been staying at, suggesting to Jane that he was "very well rewarded for acquiescing." He asked her why she was writing daring articles and warned her she was crossing red lines. She asked him where the red lines were, Jane reports, and he pointed up to the sky and said, "the higher ups were unhappy." He then mentioned an imprisoned Emirati rights activist and asked Jane if she wanted to end up like her. "I'm an academic, not an activist," Jane told him.

"What kind of government is shaken by an article? How fragile are you as a system?," Jane asked me as she recounted the conversation.

The news of Hedges's arrest and sentencing troubled Jane, both because of what it meant for academics like her, and what it said about the priorities and financial ties in higher education today. "It was strange to me that his university did nothing about his case until his wife and other academics took it up," Jane told me. "After all this happened, I spoke to leaders at my university and they all dismissed it. I just feel like they're indifferent and I'm only going to make headlines when I'm dead or disappeared."

I asked Jane if she thinks anything so drastic is likely. "The least they could do is a travel ban. The reason they haven't sent the trolls my way is because they don't want to scare me off and want me to come back," she told me. If they are too bold and issue a clear threat, Jane will be able to speak about it while she is still outside the country. "So, they're unsure and don't want to attract public attention to this and cause a diplomatic rift or scandal."

Jane told me she is currently on a visa, but does not have a plan for when the visa, or her passport, expires. If the UAE refuses to renew her passport, then she may have a case for asylum. Until then, everything is up in the air. And she must continue her academic work knowing that if she returns home, at minimum she will likely not be allowed to leave again. "In the past when someone was a dissident they were exiled. Nowadays when you're a dissident you're trapped inside in a prison cell or inside the country." I asked Jane whether she expects the intimidation to continue. "This is a progressing story," she said. "It's not over yet."

What happened to Matthew Hedges should have been a shock to the system of educational expansion into the UAE. But it is possible that Hedges's experience, disturbing as it was, failed to upend the system because it is one that has already seen evidence of troubling developments—and turned away.

The promises for academic freedom then–NYU president John Sexton made in 2007 when announcing the plans for the Abu Dhabi campus are now "largely worthless," according to associate professor of journalism Mohamad Bazzi.[69] Bazzi, who teaches at NYU's main campus, was invited to teach at the UAE venture in 2017. But he could not get there.

Shortly before the semester was set to begin, Emirati officials denied him the requisite security clearances to work in the country. NYU appealed and failed. Years earlier, Bazzi taught a monthslong course at the campus, though his name was not listed publicly on the course, and he worked as a "consultant" while on a tourist visa because NYU officials worried Bazzi's status as a Lebanon-born Shiite Muslim would lead to his denial. He suspects that is exactly what led to his later rejection.

"For two years, various university administrators promised to resolve my case. But the process always stalled, and I was told it was out of their hands," he wrote in *The New York Times*. "I will probably never know exactly what happened, but I suspect that N.Y.U. administrators in Abu Dhabi did not want to expend limited political capital with their Emirati partners on my case, or the 'Shiite problem' in general."

Around the same time, Middle Eastern studies associate professor Arang Keshavarzian, as well as another academic, were also denied access by Emirati authorities and, in turn, NYU's campus. Keshavarzian, also a Shiite Muslim, had to provide information about his "religion and sect" on both the UAE's visa forms *and* NYU Abu Dhabi's human resources form, making clear that "NYU officials are clearly concerned with people's religious background" and aware of the potential consequences associated with it.

But it is not known if his religious background, or his academic pursuits, sealed his fate. He said in the months after the denial, "it's clear to me that some people at NYU—to my face and behind my back—have contemplated or thought that the reason I didn't receive my security clearance or that Professor Bazzi didn't was because of the kind of work, writing, teaching that we do that focuses on Middle East politics."[70] There is reason to believe a professor's politics and academic work would result in his rejection: In 2015, yet another NYU professor, Andrew Ross, was disallowed from boarding an airplane to the UAE for his planned trip to study labor conditions in the country, because of "security concerns." Coincidentally—or not—Ross was also a critic of the treatment of migrant laborers in the UAE.[71] Years later, as protests over Israel and Gaza swept campuses in 2024, NYU Abu Dhabi students and faculty alleged surveillance and censorship from administrators and government officials because of their political speech. New guidelines also banned symbols and scarves at the campus commencement ceremony, reportedly leading to the weeklong detainment and deportation of a student who unveiled a keffiyeh at the event.[72]

"Here's the Heart of It: What Compromises Have to Be Made?"

With Tom Zoellner, a professor of English at Chapman University, I discussed in early 2022 the moral responsibility, if any, of universities operating in unfree countries, and whether they can or should strive to make political change a component of their mission. This issue is personal for Zoellner, who has written a book, and is friends, with Paul Rusesabagina, the man whose work saving lives during the Rwandan genocide was detailed in the film *Hotel Rwanda*. Rusesabagina was essentially kidnapped in 2020 by Rwandan authorities and then sentenced to prison for twenty-five years on terrorism charges for his ties to the National Liberation Forces, an armed coalition accused of violent attacks on Rwanda's border.[73] Prior to his arrest, Rusesabagina was a high-profile critic-in-exile of Rwandan president Paul Kagame. He was ultimately released in 2023.

Kagame is known for aggressive efforts to punish his opponents and critics, and under his leadership, human rights and civil liberties have suffered in Rwanda, a country identified by Freedom House as "not free."[74] But none of that stopped Carnegie Mellon University from opening a campus in Rwanda, CMU-Africa. Rwanda is "a darling of US overseas investment," but "it's an extremely dangerous place for anyone who breathes a word about the dictatorship," Zoellner told me.

When he raised these concerns on Twitter, replying to a tweet from CMU-Africa with a link to a report about human rights in Rwanda, the account simply blocked him, meaning Zoellner could no longer view or reply to the account, and others could not see his comment.

Zoellner told me that he is impressed by what CMU is doing in Rwanda, and the opportunities and services they are offering the region, but there needs to be some accounting of its role there. "The point is not to protest CMU's presence in Rwanda," he said. "I don't want to see it shut down but I do want to see CMU using its influence to say something."

But as Zoellner wrote in an essay on the subject, "CMU has never spoken publicly about [Rusesabagina's arrest] or any other instance of Rwanda's violent authoritarianism." That is not because it has not had opportunities. The CMU campus was

"Kagame's baby," according to one of Kagame's former advisers David Himbara, who said, "This is how he cleans his name: to bring in U.S. institutions to fly his flag. It's how he builds an image for himself." And in 2011, Kagame gave a speech at CMU's campus in Pittsburgh. Protesters demonstrated outside the event, while CMU's then–president Jared Cohon called Kagame a "visionary" and praised his leadership.[75]

"I did not set out to be a bird's eye view on universities in unfree societies, my goal was to get my friend sprung from prison," Zoellner told me. "CMU is one of the institutions, along with the NBA, Goldman Sachs, etc. that do business with Rwanda and promote it as a feel-good thing. Here's a nation that many associate with a redemption story. It looks really good in these glossy brochures. Kagame is eager to get western endorsement. Here's the heart of it: What compromises have to be made?"

While conducting interviews for this book, I spoke to an individual who experienced serious academic freedom violations at a branch campus in China and who believed university expansion deserved extensive scrutiny. His story was disturbing, but because of the personal risk it posed, he was not willing to discuss publicly what he experienced. "In general people cannot talk because of their career," he told me. He suggested that there needs to be some form of compensation or protection for those whose careers may suffer from whistleblowing. Otherwise, many will not feel safe telling their stories. I suspect there are more individuals like him, ones who have been collateral damage in their universities' pursuit of lucrative international expansion, but who fear that discussing that damage will only further limit their careers in a small field.

Of the individuals I have spoken to, over the course of my career and for this book, I have found that they have diverse views about the value of international academic engagement, what can be achieved by it, and how it should be managed. But even if their solutions differ, most tend to agree: The past few decades of academic expansion have been conducted without serious regard for the ethical, legal, and moral realities of planting institutions historically associated with freedom in countries known for their lack of it. In their race to build the most campuses, foster the most global opportunities, and access the deepest funding wells, universities lost their way.

The campuses that universities create in unfree countries are no doubt often freer than the spaces outside their walls. But there is a cost to these lucrative partnerships, both on community members' right to speak freely, and on institutions' principles and ethics generally. How much does a university really value justice and truth if, for its own financial gain, it intentionally avoids stepping on an authoritarian partner's toes?

I spoke with Richard Bensel early in the writing process of this chapter, and his words about Cornell's decision to continue expansion in China stuck with me. He suggested that university leaders who have tolerated the existing human rights violations in China will tolerate further ones. I first began writing this book shortly before Russia's invasion of Ukraine, and as I worked on this chapter, the outlook for Taiwan continued to devolve. It is difficult not to look at universities, often on paper so dedicated to justice at home, and wonder what, exactly, are they *not* willing to tolerate from their partners. A potential invasion of Taiwan would be particularly shocking, of course, but how much more shocking than the mass surveillance and detainment of Uyghurs or the rapid destruction of civil society in Hong Kong?

There is strong disagreement among university communities about when, how, and why their institutions should take what could be perceived as political stances—including, perhaps, opposing or refusing to work with authoritarian governments. That is a rich area for discussion with genuinely strong competing arguments about the role of universities and their purpose in society. But the thing about direct engagement in China is that it is not a detached hypothetical about symbolic protests. When universities decide to pursue certain programs in the country, they willingly choose to work under its laws governing free expression, coordinate with state officials, and perhaps most importantly, moderate their own behavior to avoid upsetting a lucrative partnership. They agree to open a campus in a country conducting human rights violations their community members are not freely allowed to teach or discuss. It is not, then, a question about whether they are silent about such abuses. It may be a question of whether they are complicit in reinforcing that silence.

CHAPTER 6

The Surveilled Classroom

As I discussed in this book's introduction, COVID-19 pushed long simmering free speech fights to the surface and illustrated how the "censors without borders" can turn local censorship laws into international crises. These days, the authoritarians are everywhere, surveilling communities in distant countries, bullying critics abroad, and exporting repressive censorship tactics to freer countries. While this crisis worsened during the pandemic, another seismic societal shift took place: Higher education, like nearly everything else, went online. Suddenly, the basic functions of the college campus were moved wholly onto the internet, prompting a new concern about campus speech suppression in the Zoom era: What happens when the college classroom is *anywhere* and authoritarians can target speech *everywhere*?

Universities are not responsible for the conditions that necessitated online teaching. Like other industries, they were forced to navigate the shifting legal landscape and medical realities that made in-person education and international travel nearly impossible for a time. During the initial spread of COVID-19 and the quick action it required to transplant the college experience onto the internet, it is no surprise that certain other factors—academic freedom and student privacy—were not at the forefront of administrative priorities.

But we are no longer in those early days of the pandemic and its mad dash to accommodate online learning, and there is no excuse to leave vital expressive rights on the backburner. Make no mistake: We are at a crossroads with online learning and higher education. When teaching takes place online, especially during an era of worsening repression, insidious and complex threats to academic freedom and free expression can bloom.

As I will discuss throughout this chapter, the pandemic's push to move education online aggravated existing problems and created new threats to academic freedom and free expression—all while the contemporaneous introduction of a law in Hong Kong introduced fear into classrooms around the world, exposing higher education's vulnerability in an extensively internationalized, and online, world.

The National Security Law

The concept of the "censors without borders" generally applies to governments that use their power to harass and surveil critics abroad or punish citizens for what they have done overseas once they return home—a subtle seeping of censorship across borders and outside of traditional legal structures. But in 2020, the term gained a whole new meaning when China imposed a new law intended to suffocate dissent in Hong Kong. The "national security law," enacted late at night on June 30 with its legislative text kept secret until its passage, marked a new low in China's ongoing campaign to stifle activism in Hong Kong.

The law's targets—separatism, subversion, terrorism, and collusion with foreign countries—are unsurprisingly vague terms that allow Beijing broad authority to control civic life in Hong Kong. The most severe violations of the law can merit life imprisonment. Much can be said about the ways, both terrifying and absurd, that the law now limits expression in Hong Kong.

Since July 2020, dozens of legislators and activists have been arrested for subversive political activity,[1] the Catholic Church has ended its practice of hosting Tiananmen memorial masses,[2] the free press has been mostly decimated,[3] booksellers have cleansed their offerings of potentially illegal material,[4] and new measures have been introduced to sanitize Hong Kong's film industry.[5] Art, culture, politics, journalism, and even the church confessional—nothing is safe from the reaches of the law.

But it does something else too: The law's Article 23 states that it applies to offenses occurring "outside the region by a person who is not a permanent resident of the region." In other words, acts committed by citizens of other countries, in other countries—anyone, anywhere. It is a shockingly blatant attempt to intimidate activists and government critics on a global scale. Authorities have already attempted to make good on this threat. Hong Kong police pressured Israeli web hosting company Wix to take down a website run by overseas activists[6] and threatened the founder of the UK-based Hong Kong Watch with financial penalties and imprisonment.[7] Censors without borders indeed.

What this means is that *you*, reader, can violate this law even if you have never set foot in China or Hong Kong. This may not be perceived as much of a threat by many people, either because they do not plan to visit China, have family in the country that could face repercussions, make statements about political issues in Hong Kong, or think they are important enough to be noticed even if they do. In academia, though, the threat is real. Since its passage, the national security law has sent shockwaves through higher education both in and outside Hong Kong.

Hong Kong's protest movements, from 2014's Umbrella Movement to the local student activists who traveled to Tiananmen Square in 1989, have frequently been defined by their students and student unions. During the city's 2019 protests, universities

The Surveilled Classroom

were not just the home of student activists—they also hosted what would become fierce clashes between protesters and police as demonstrations against the proposed extradition bill swept the city. That November, at campuses including the Chinese University of Hong Kong (CUHK) and Hong Kong Polytechnic University, riot police armed with tear gas and other weapons barreled down upon student protesters' barricades. Nearly 1,100 students were arrested in the aftermath of the days long battles.[8] It is now unthinkable for such mass-scale student activism, even if entirely peaceful, to happen again in Hong Kong's foreseeable future.

Hong Kong's first student union was created just a year after the first institution, the University of Hong Kong (HKU), was founded in 1911.[9] That same student union, 110 years later, would be forced out of HKU, raided by police,[10] and four of its leaders would be arrested under the recently enacted national security law after they appeared to express sympathy for a man who stabbed a police officer before killing himself.[11] That they apologized, resigned from their positions, and retracted the statement did not matter. HKU also banned students who had attended the union's meeting from accessing the campus, alleging their presence would create "serious legal and reputational risks." At the time of their arrest, dozens of civil society organizations had already disbanded across Hong Kong.[12]

Other student unions quickly fell like dominoes. Security Secretary Christopher Tang accused the unions of "wantonly instill[ing] among students improper values and disseminat[ing] false or biased messages in an attempt to incite their hatred against the country."[13] The Chinese University of Hong Kong Student Union disbanded after their administration determined the university would no longer collect student fees for it. CUHK was one of six institutions to announce this penalty.[14] And the Hong Kong Baptist University[15] and Hong Kong Polytechnic University student unions experienced prior restraint and bans against their student publications.[16] Both of their magazines included political content about protest and the rule of law.

Before I began drafting this book, I was in touch with some faculty members in Hong Kong and engaged in preliminary discussions with them about their teaching environment under the national security law. One lecturer at the Chinese University of Hong Kong told me the changes "are very subtle, yet still terrifying" and called it "death by a thousand cuts." She said it was "very challenging to teach critical thinking to students when there is a whole spectrum of issues that they are not allowed to be critical of." The lecturer, "Marie," who asked that her name not be shared for her protection, reported receiving a phone call asking her to censor a student writing project only *four* days after the law's passage.

Marie asked a director at her campus to give her a clear account of what could and could not be said, but was told "it would be dealt with on a case-by-case basis and to just be cautious." She said that "it is exhausting always wondering what could be wrong. We had to revise materials and advise students about what they could and couldn't write about."

When I contacted her again in September 2022 to ask her whether the situation had worsened since we last spoke, she was already gone from Hong Kong.

Perhaps most emblematic of the swift changes in Hong Kong after the national security law's passage was the systematic removal of all physical remembrances of the Tiananmen massacre. Off campus, memorials and candlelight vigils were banned,[17] in part under the guise of pandemic-safety gathering limitations, and individuals were arrested on the anniversary of the massacre for small signs of commemoration like carrying flowers or handing out blank pieces of paper.[18]

The Surveilled Classroom

On campus, administrators quickly set their sights on revered symbols memorializing the killings. The purge began at HKU with Danish artist Jens Galschiøt's "Pillar of Shame," an arresting sculpture of tormented and tortured figures representing those who died that day along with the inscription: "The old cannot kill the young forever." The twenty-six-foot sculpture had stood there for nearly twenty-five years.

In prior years, students would organize an annual cleaning of the statue as an act of remembrance for the dead. That is, until October 2021, when HKU ordered the Hong Kong Alliance in Support of Patriotic Democratic Movements of China, the already disbanded group that organizes Hong Kong's Tiananmen vigils, to remove the statue within a week.[19] HKU alleged that the sculpture's presence posed a "legal risk" to the university and was initially represented in the matter by Chicago-based law firm Mayer Brown, which withdrew from representing the university on this specific legal issue after criticism.[20] Interestingly, this was not Mayer Brown's first foray into art removal efforts. In 2014, the firm represented plaintiffs who unsuccessfully sued to force Glendale, California to take down public art commemorating the "comfort women" forced into sexual slavery by the Japanese army in World War II.[21]

Facing "direct pressure from Beijing's local offices,"[22] under the watch of security guards, and out of sight behind plastic curtains, large barriers, and boarded-up windows, HKU ultimately dismantled and removed the statue in the dead of night just a few days before Christmas. It was loaded into a cargo container and taken away by crane. Weeks later, while students were away on break, HKU would cover up another memorial, this time a slogan painted on a campus bridge: "Souls of martyrs shall forever linger despite the brutal massacre; Spark of democracy shall forever glow for the demise of evils."[23]

Galschiøt said the statue's removal was "a disgrace and an abuse" that "shows that Hong Kong has become a brutal place without laws and regulations." It was "grotesque that they use the Western holiday, Christmas, to carry out the destruction of the artwork." Galschiøt asserted that he owned the statue and should be consulted on its removal, but was ignored by HKU.[24]

If you were hoping for an outcry—or at least a response—from the dozens[25] of American universities that partnered with HKU for study abroad and other programs, you would be disappointed. If these universities have any qualms about sending their students to a region where basic forms of expression and protest are increasingly penalized, they have not been vocal about it. Nor did they speak out when HKU announced a proposal to punish students who "bring disrepute," not defined, to the institution—a laughably vague provision that will surely be used to target students whose political persuasions or administrative criticisms prove a little too uncomfortable for skittish university leaders to tolerate.[26]

As with the student union closures, the removal of the HKU Tiananmen memorial set off a domino effect, with two more occurring that week, also before dawn. Chinese University of Hong Kong took down its "Goddess of Democracy" statue, which stood at the campus for over a decade and mirrored one erected by students at Tiananmen Square, and Lingnan University removed artwork that included depictions of the Goddess of Democracy and "Tank Man," the Chinese protester who famously stood in front of a row of tanks in Tiananmen Square. Lingnan cited "legal and safety risks" and CUHK claimed an "internal assessment" led to the takedown of the "unauthorised statue." A small group of students responded by handing out "missing" flyers asking: "Have you seen her?"[27] The Goddess of Democracy statue at City University of Hong Kong would be next on the chopping block.[28] The office of then–Chief Executive of Hong

Kong Carrie Lam did not offer any comment in response to questions about whether authorities had any involvement in the campus purge.[29]

"The turning point for me and my family was when they took down the Goddess of Democracy statue on Christmas Eve in the middle of the night. That's when I no longer felt safe," Marie told me when I was able to get back in touch with her months after she had left CUHK. Before the law passed, she and her colleagues "openly talked about anything and everything," but "suddenly, it all stopped" in 2020. "That was the scary part—just things changing overnight—nobody really thought it would be that bad."

Forced forgetting, it seems, is to be the future for Hong Kong. This systematic elimination of the symbols and markers of a legacy of protest is an especially cruel punishment for a city whose identity is so firmly intertwined with it. And as the Tiananmen memorials have vanished from campus, something else has taken its place—mandatory education about the very law that has changed the legal and social landscape of Hong Kong.

In fall 2021, the first wave of mandatory national security education began. At Hong Kong Baptist University, in the presence of photographers and CCTV monitoring, students attended a two-hour lecture and 200-page PowerPoint presentation about the national security law's provisions and punishments, followed by a required multiple-choice test. The test included characters like "Ms. Naughty" and "Mr. Breach," illustrating violators of the law.

At one point, the presentation asked, "Is criticizing the government a crime under the national security law?," and answered, "It depends. If the criticism involves any of the four major crimes under the national security law," then "it may be counted as a crime."[30] Similarly, Hong Kong's Polytechnic University incorporated national security education, along with Hong Kong's history and "the humiliation history of China," into a three-hour lecture with a required test for incoming students.[31]

When the 2022–2023 school year started, mandatory education had spread to more campuses. All eight of Hong Kong's publicly funded universities announced trainings—a mix of first-year courses and pre-graduate requirements—that would vary in historical focus and implementation, but would all include lessons about the scope, and consequences, of the national security law.[32] At least one university shared its intent to introduce training for postgraduate students too.

And starting in 2022, in case students were not already being educated enough about their new reality, university campuses across Hong Kong were required to begin holding weekly flag-raising ceremonies for the Hong Kong and Chinese flags. At some ceremonies, local security officials as well as mainland officials were in attendance, and at CUHK, at least, a PhD student alleged that he and other students were required to attend a ceremony by their professors.[33]

An International Security Law

Unsurprisingly, the national security law created new pressures on higher education in Hong Kong, hitting at a time when classroom conversations and lessons took place online rather than in person, greatly increasing the risk that students' and professors' speech could be recorded and surveilled.

Hong Kong University of Science and Technology professor Carsten Holz reported that he and many of his colleagues chose not to take advantage of their universities' lecture recording service, preferring to avoid creating permanent videos of their class commentary. He also said that, in general, academics were growing increasingly fearful of their online footprint. "Most if not all of my colleagues who were active on Twitter or Facebook deleted their accounts around 1 July 2020, or at least deleted selected old posts."[34]

Then–HKU lecturer Jessica R. Valdez also wrote about the complexities of teaching a course about police in literature and culture in the months following the law's passage.[35] Valdez "designed the course to respect students who might be anxious about inadvertently breaking the law," offering one section face-to-face and the other on Microsoft Teams, in acknowledgment of students' "anxiety about Zoom because, while it is a US-based company, its software is developed in China; this connection could make it vulnerable to pressure from the Chinese authorities." (She included a photo of HKU's student union building—a union, like most others, now gone—with a sign on it of Zoom's logo and a warning that "you are now under Chinese surveillance." It was one of two anti-Zoom signs.)

She also sought to protect students by saving "the most sensitive topics for pre-recorded lectures to allow students to absorb the material in privacy" and "offering as many options for participation as possible, including one-on-one consultations . . . to be sensitive to students' anxieties about the new law while also giving them the opportunity to contribute to ongoing discussions."

But as I wrote earlier in this chapter, authorities were not content to limit the law just to Hong Kong's borders. With a global law comes global repercussions, and since the national security law's passage in the summer of 2020, I watched closely as higher education institutions in the United States, Canada, and Europe adjusted, for better or worse, in the face of a law that upended higher education in some communities.

You might be wondering: What are the risks, exactly, to students and academics? To certain individuals, the danger could be severe. For international students from China and Hong Kong, they risk arrest, imprisonment, and other punishment if caught engaging in campus discussions or expression that violates the vague provisions of the law, a fear that hung over them especially during COVID-necessitated online courses. For professors, they must weigh the possibility that teaching freely and openly will introduce legal peril to their international students. And especially for professors and graduate students specializing in sensitive topics in politics, economics, history, and an array of other fields, they run the risk of harming their own careers by engaging in expression that could mean they cannot legally or safely travel to Hong Kong or China to conduct research.

If the law applies to offenses committed outside of the mainland and Hong Kong, that means anything that is said, expressed, written, or researched on campuses around the world can be seized upon by authorities. In short, the law created a perfect storm of fear and uncertainty in higher education. At campuses far from China, both students and professors alike were forced to ask themselves: Should I self-censor? This was not a question they took lightly.

"I have the privilege of tenure and I have decided that I'm not going to Hong Kong or China, so I have the advantage of teaching those courses without too much risk. I understand there are other academics whose careers depend on access to research and to people in Hong Kong and China," University of California, Davis professor Eddy U told me in an interview nearly two and a half years after the law's passage. "I'm almost at the end of my career. I don't have to not be seen as antagonistic to the Hong Kong or Chinese government or violating any element of the law. So that was my position and I'm continuing to teach about China and Hong Kong in the next few years until I decide to retire."

U, decades ago an international student from Hong Kong himself, took both the threats to students and his own academic freedom rights seriously. Rather than shying away from the law, U sought to confront the reality of it. "After the law was passed

The Surveilled Classroom

I immediately proposed to teach about Hong Kong," he told me, planning a class called Democracy and Authoritarianism in Hong Kong. "A year later I taught another first year seminar called Xinjiang and Hong Kong. The idea is to let students know something repressive is going on in those two places, that the Chinese government is using the national security law to try to intimidate academics and students not to talk about those issues."

The students love the classes he has offered, U told me, but acknowledge that "there is a certain known level of danger." Some of his students have understandably balked at it. He knew of at least one student who had signed up for his class, but was then discouraged from taking it by her mother, who was concerned for her daughter's safety. U did not fault her for caring for her child. "What if they say something wrong? What if they're reported to authorities?"

Another student from China told U he intended to drop his course because he believed a fellow student—also from China—was attempting to identify him in class using Airdrop, a tool available on iPhones that is used to transmit files to other nearby Apple products. Using Airdrop, an iPhone user could potentially identify a nearby person if they used their own name on the device—a fellow classmate who did not share his real name in class, for example.

This deeply concerned the student because the class was intentionally devised to allow students anonymity to speak freely about material that was "very critical of the Hong Kong and Chinese governments." U shared with me the special safety section from his syllabus, which warned students that he would be adopting measures to protect student anonymity in light of the national security law.

U advised students to "use an alias to identify yourself in class," and "change your Zoom identification to your alias" if the class was required to move back online. If students had questions or comments to share with the class, U gave them the option to privately email him so he could share their thoughts without their identities being associated with them. He also warned students not to record in-person or online portions of the class, "especially when classmates are speaking."

But, afraid a peer from China was attempting to out him, the student shared that he was dropping the course. "I asked students not to identify others in the class. Someone broke the rule and I can't do anything about that," U told me. Ultimately, though, everything worked out. The student attempting to use Airdrop to identify his peers "was not sympathetic to the course" and chose to drop it—after complaining about it on WeChat, U added. He then reinvited the worried student, who returned and finished the course.

Things likely turned out as well as they could have, given the circumstances, but what happened in U's class offers a glimpse into how precarious teaching about China can be under the law in classrooms thousands of miles away from the authorities enforcing it. Even for a professor dedicated to ensuring students' comfort and safety and a small classroom setting specifically designed to accommodate sensitive conversations, students may feel that true openness is not feasible among their peers.

And that is an impossible problem to solve: In an environment where everyone carries a device that can covertly record you or seek out your identity to share with authorities, can you ever feel free to speak?

Professor U's classroom was far from the only one to adjust in the aftermath of the national security law's passage. During the 2020–2021 academic year, I started tracking how and where these classroom modifications sprung up across the United States, United Kingdom, and other countries. In most cases, when a student-protective policy was enacted in class, it was at the hands of individual professors, not an administrative-led effort. In large part, university administrators were notably silent about the law's passage and what it meant for classrooms.

Administrative acknowledgment of the challenges posed by the law was rare, but in isolated cases, universities stepped up. SOAS University of London, citing its duty of care to its community, issued guidance covering wide ground on student and faculty risks. Professors were advised not to automatically record online classes and to avoid recording student discussion, and warned of the risk of carrying certain information into China or Hong Kong, where authorities could seize it.

The guidance also flagged areas of concern, including student travel to China and collaborations with partners in the region who could be forced to hand over sensitive material. "Self-censoring in order to avoid such risks is, needless to say, unacceptable and should not be contemplated," SOAS made clear.[36] Dartmouth College also shared guidelines recommending that faculty "alert and inform" students of class risks and that students take measures to protect their identities on Zoom and other platforms.[37]

In the classrooms that did see changes, some common themes emerged. Professors who made accommodations usually sought to offer some combination of warnings to students, anonymity in certain settings, code names, blind grading, or options to opt out of sensitive conversations.

Assistant professor Rory Truex, who teaches Chinese politics at Princeton, was one of the initial adopters of such accommodations. In his fall 2020 classes, Truex gave students warnings about potentially illegal material and utilized code names and blind grading so students could submit sensitive work without their names being linked to it. "We cannot self-censor," Truex said at the time. "If we, as a Chinese teaching community, out of fear stop teaching things like Tiananmen or Xinjiang or whatever sensitive topic the Chinese government doesn't want us talking about, if we cave, then we've lost."[38] Months later, he warned students in his Chinese Politics class that "the course contains material that the Chinese government would find sensitive" and "recommend[ed] that students who are currently residing in China should not take the course this year."[39]

Truex was one of a group of professors who put together a set of proposals called "How to Teach China This Fall" as the first semester after the law's passage approached. Among the strategies they recommended were risk disclosures to students, "particularly those who will be taking the course in China and Hong Kong," pledges among students not to record class lectures and conversations, and amnesty or anonymity for students fearful of taking part in class discussions.[40]

I tracked these measures across the academic year at universities throughout the United States, Canada, Europe, and Australia, where I recorded accommodations at universities such as Princeton, Harvard, Amherst College, Yale, the University of California, Irvine, Oxford University, and Warwick University.[41]

Professors like the University of Pennsylvania's Avery Goldstein offered a syllabus warning to students, telling reporters that faculty "have to leave it up to the students whether they enroll, because it is ultimately their lives that are going to be affected." He added that he "will make it clear that there is nothing I can do to protect them."[42]

Warnings are one of the simplest but best ways to handle this challenge and should perhaps continue even long after the peak of the online teaching era. It is a transparent way of notifying students of the risk and letting them make their own decisions without limiting the discussion for *everyone*. Professors should not self-censor in their classes—doing so unacceptably allows authoritarian governments veto power in the classroom and it means students are not receiving the free and open education they deserve.

And international students from Hong Kong and China deserve to have their agency respected. They are adults and know their own situations best. They may decide that their circumstances necessitate that they avoid a certain class or topic for their own safety. Unfortunate, but so be it. They might also, however, believe that they are attending a university with much stronger speech and academic freedom protections than those available in their home country, and that they should take advantage of those freedoms while they have the opportunity to do so. That choice to engage with sensitive material should be respected too. Free universities do not serve students by replicating the censorship their oppressive governments enforce upon them at home.

Weeks after the start of fall 2022 classes, I asked Truex if he had continued his extensive accommodations two years in, or if he had lightened them after in-person classes resumed. Truex confirmed that he had eased them, telling me that he "largely rolled back the accommodations this year, as there is basically no evidence at this stage" that authorities were using the law to prosecute speech that took place in overseas classrooms. "I think being off Zoom has also helped," Truex added.

I talked with University of California, Irvine professor Jeffrey Wasserstrom as well, two years after he had first shared that he was teaching his modern Chinese history fall semester course "sans the Zoom meetings UCI recommends" because of class engagement with material "considered sensitive by Beijing" and "having students all over taking it." Wasserstrom, who emphasized papers and one-on-one conversations, rather than group discussions, stressed that he was "not avoiding sensitive subjects" and was "doing what [he] can to make the class meaningful" with no "self censoring, no avoiding touchy topics."[43] When we spoke over the phone, Wasserstrom told me the questions on accommodations were moot for him at the time, as he was not teaching classes about China this semester. If he were currently teaching about China, though, he "would still feel some of that" concern.

"I'm in the position where I'm fairly reconciled to not going to China or Hong Kong in the foreseeable future and I don't think the national security law is something that makes me worried about what I say. What I always worried about was the position that it put students in who wanted to spend time in Hong Kong or China. That was the concern I had with the online only classes," Wasserstrom explained.

I discussed the future of the law and higher education with him, and Wasserstrom offered an incisive insight. "Early on it seemed that the national security law would be the weapon used generally but it seems that authorities have been quite savvy and are using colonial era sedition laws," he said, citing then–recent jail terms handed down to a group of Hong Kong speech therapists convicted of sedition over their publication of children's books with anti-government messages.[44] Since then, the threat sedition laws pose have crystallized even more, with the 2023 sentencing of a Hong Kong student who posted allegedly seditious posts while studying in Japan.[45] It is not just the national security law that has gone global.

By using a wider selection of tools in its arsenal, Beijing is working to deepen censorship in Hong Kong. The CCP is using the national security law in concert with other repressive laws, not as a replacement for them. Regarding the use of the sedition law in the national security law era, one Hong Kong barrister remarked that the national security law "has re-tooled these old laws that were largely forgotten. You could say we are now drinking bitter, old colonial wine from new, authoritarian bottles."[46]

"It isn't just the national security law," that is just "the only one that claims it could be used about things people did outside of

The Surveilled Classroom

Hong Kong. It's been a clever complicating of the narrative," Wasserstrom says. By shifting some of its repressive efforts onto the sedition laws, authorities may be seeking to take the attention off the national security law. "But overall, it's creating a chilling atmosphere. A lot of the questions people have to consider about Hong Kong are the ones people used to be considering about the mainland."

These questions are being asked by UK academics as well. In 2021, the British Association for Chinese Studies conducted a survey of twenty-five China-focused academics and administrators in the aftermath of the law's passage. Nearly all expressed concerns about the threats to academic freedom posed by online education, but "few, if any," possessed the practical tools to respond to them.[47]

Ultimately, it is unclear whether academic accommodations will persist, fade away entirely, or ebb and flow with the rates of online learning and the degree of threats from the Chinese and Hong Kong governments. But no matter what, for individuals like Eddy U, the existence alone of the law will likely have permanent effects.

I asked U whether it was a difficult decision for him to no longer travel to the place he emigrated from decades earlier, and to which he dedicated his academic career. "For sure. My entire career as a China researcher has been to talk to people and find research and material in China," he told me. "Between choosing to modify my content and worry about the national security law's impact on my personal safety and teaching what I want to teach and believe in, I think at least at this point I have chosen to teach what I believe in. We don't know what the future holds but at this point I'd rather teach what I believe in and take a hit on my productivity than pretend nothing has happened."

The future would hold more bad news. In early 2024, well after I had interviewed U, Hong Kong adopted a new domestic version of the national security law, further tightening its grip on the city's critics. The law made no effort to hide its suppression of speech, targeting acts with "seditious intention," including an intent to evoke "hatred, contempt or disaffection" with Hong Kong or China's government.[48] What criticism of any government, anywhere, would not risk provoking those emotions?

While professors generally worked admirably to protect their rights and their students' safety, there were nevertheless stumbles with censorship and palpable fear among students.

Although academics were largely clear about their intention not to self-censor in the classroom, isolated incidents were reported. At the University of Toronto, a teaching assistant "said he was warned that when moderating online group discussions there will be ethical concerns around teaching students in China" and that "he was advised to steer discussions away from controversial topics that could run students into trouble."[49]

At the United Kingdom's University of Leeds, editor-in-chief and founder of Hong Kong Free Press Tom Grundy announced he withdrew from an invitation to give a class lecture over Zoom at the university's School of Media and Communication after being asked not to touch on a sensitive subject. The lecturer preferred he "not focus on [Hong Kong] protests per se" out of "safety concerns" because over half of the students in the class were from China. Grundy tweeted at the time that he was sympathetic to the pressure Chinese students faced abroad, but did not "think western institutions should bend to it."

In Australia, a lecturer at the University of Sydney anonymously reported that a colleague told him to self-censor when discussing politically sensitive material over Zoom. "You already know what to do. You should cut any materials that could endanger students," he was told.[50] And while it was never made public to staff, an internal working group at the University of Technology Sydney prepared a memo for Vice-Chancellor Shirley Alexander explaining that while "there are no UTS guidelines on this the general advice [is] to avoid topics that could be seen as critical or politically inaccurate eg. regarding territories in China." The memo warned that the university could lose access to online students located in China if teaching material contained prohibited content. Alexander said there "was never any direction to staff to self censor."[51]

Some students, primarily international students from Hong Kong and mainland China, reported feeling fear in online and even in-person classes despite efforts to combat the law's looming presence in higher education. One Dartmouth student from Hong Kong worried that "any slight condemnation or any slight criticism of the government in China," even criticism made at the college's New Hampshire campus, could follow him home in the future. Another Dartmouth student, this one from China, said she felt pressured to be "very careful" about what she said on campus, even before the enactment of the national security law. "The fact that college faculties are worried that they might put students in trouble, it's akin to the Chinese government holding overseas students hostage," the student from Hong Kong said. "They're using those overseas students for putting pressure on U.S. campuses to silence them or to tone them down."[52]

A UC Berkeley student from Hong Kong said that "even if I'm studying in the U.S., I cannot speak freely," explaining that she had previously submitted schoolwork critical of the CCP, but "would hesitate to write that kind of essay now." Further north at UC Davis, a group of Hong Kongers, who would only speak to media through encrypted communications tools, shared that the situation on the ground, and their feeling of safety at home, was swiftly declining. They expressed that they did not feel safe returning.[53]

Once again, the censors without borders infiltrated American campuses thousands of miles from Beijing, ranging from California to Illinois to New Hampshire. But as is so often the case with cross-border censorship, the effects did not just bleed into communities in the United States.

For example, at Monash University in Australia, lecturer Jonathan Benney reported that "some students from the People's Republic of China are indeed concerned about whether the work they submit can be observed by people other than academics—for example, when essays are to be submitted online, some students have checked with me who can see their work." Kevin Carrico, another lecturer at Monash, also said that Hong Kong students feared they would face legal trouble for what they said and did while in Australia.[54]

"The words that you are reading right now could land me in prison for life," a student, "Mark Choi," at Canada's McMaster University wrote in an anonymous op-ed weeks after the law's passage. "This may seem absurd—life imprisonment for writing a political opinion in a newspaper. However, as a Hong Kong international student, this is a very real risk that I face under China's sweeping new Hong Kong security law."

"For Hong Kong international students at McMaster University, this law is terrifying. It severely restricts what we are able to say or do. The law's offenses are intentionally vague, in order to encourage self-censorship," Choi wrote. "Faculty and students at McMaster who are interested in issues deemed politically sensitive by the Chinese government must now choose between permanently avoiding Hong Kong, or dropping such research altogether. In other words, the security law's extraterritorial overreach degrades academic freedom at McMaster."[55]

This is from the same university where the campus CSSA chapter, in an example of sensitivity exploitation, claimed it was "deeply hurt" by the presence of a Uyghur speaker on campus and demanded an investigation of the students who invited her. The events at McMaster offer a window into the breadth and scope of the challenges to students' right to speak freely about authoritarianism. Over the course of just months, students critical of the Chinese government faced disruption of their events, surveillance intended to intimidate dissenters, and demands for their censorship and punishment by the local CSSA chapter, all capped off by the introduction of a law threatening severe consequences for what they say far outside of China's borders.

In this kind of environment, how can any student feel safe to speak their mind about a global superpower? That sense of fear and futility, no doubt, is the intended result.

The Perils of Education in the Internet Age

The national security law was not the only concern to arise as campuses rapidly shifted online in 2020, nor did every threat to academic freedom in digital classrooms tie back to the Chinese government. It should be no surprise that the serious questions global communities have been facing about surveillance and free expression for decades became especially relevant within higher education when nearly every conversation, class, and assignment suddenly had to take place online. Aside from important concerns about how well students can learn in an online-only environment and whether tuition fees should be revised for online-only classes, another serious problem emerged: What new threats materialize when the internet is the only forum available for expression?

As I discussed in chapter 3, the censorship concerns growing in the international higher education community did not arise in a vacuum. In some ways, authoritarian censorship more easily found a foothold on campuses because of the existing restrictions on speech that could offend listeners or harm the university brand. These policies provide a convenient tool for supporters and agents of authoritarian governments to target their critics. And when it comes to the online context, in both policy and practice, universities have long sought to police the way their communities speak on the internet despite their First Amendment obligations or free speech commitments, well before the pandemic shifted life online.

A 2022 speech code report found that 250 of 481 surveyed public and private universities maintained policies that, because of vague wording or overt restrictions, limit student or faculty speech on the internet.[56] The College of the Holy Cross, for example, considers posting "obscene or intolerant language, as well as offensive images" as a policy violation.[57] Tulane University requires its students to agree to be "kind" online[58]—just what the internet is known for. And at Kean University, a public institution in New Jersey that is bound by the First Amendment, its internet use rules ban speech that "is abusive, profane or sexually offensive to the average person," and prohibits students from "sending annoying, threatening, libelous, or sexually, racially, or religiously offensive messages."[59]

And when it comes to punishing what students and professors say on social media, email, and in other formats, universities have retaliated against a wide swath of speech over the past two decades. In that time, student groups and individual community members have been punished for online speech—including social media posts calling Islam "not a religion of peace,"[60] a tweet calling for the National Rifle Association CEO's "head on a stick,"[61] a student's email to peers joking about obtaining "ANTIFA and ISIS hunting permits,"[62] a medical student's topless Instagram photos from a European beach supporting the #freethenipple campaign,[63] anonymous Instagram parody posts advocating "building a wall" between rival universities,[64] a professor's joke on Facebook that she "had a good day today, DIDN'T want to kill even one student: -),"⁶⁵ and a professor's sarcastic tweet about wanting "white genocide" as a Christmas gift.⁶⁶

In one particularly absurd case, a professor at New Jersey's Bergen Community College was put on leave and required to undergo psychiatric review after posting on Google+ a picture of his daughter wearing a T-shirt featuring a quote from Game of Thrones, "I will take what is mine with fire & blood." Yes, there was a censorship case even on the short-lived Google+. Bergen called the post, a picture of a child and a quote from an immensely popular television show, "threatening."

So when the move online took place, advocates had reason to worry about how universities might handle the expressive rights of their communities when they already made clear their willingness to investigate and punish online speech. But, as it turned out, there was yet another reason to worry about the preservation of free expression and academic freedom in the online teaching age: The policies of the tools and platforms universities used to conduct online education, especially Zoom.

When universities switched to online learning, it was a major change in ways too few people realized. Because when universities moved to Zoom, that meant a communications technology company—one susceptible to legislative and public pressure over its moderation decisions and without obligations to academic freedom—suddenly became an intermediary in the classroom. No longer were professors speaking directly and unencumbered to students. Now there were screens, and a company worth billions, standing between them.

The first shot across the bow did not take long. As I discussed in chapter 1, activists running Tiananmen memorial events spoke out when Zoom closed their accounts, which were managed by users outside mainland China, for violating laws applicable *within* China. Though Zoom changed its policies so that Chinese government requests would no longer dictate moderation decisions made outside the country, details would later emerge revealing that a China-based executive at the company worked directly with Chinese officials to censor activists. And in 2023, the US Attorney's Office in the Eastern District of New York announced charges against defendants who allegedly "weaponized" an American telecommunications company—presumably referring to Zoom—"to intimidate and silence dissenters, and enforce PRC law to the detriment of Chinese activists in New York" and elsewhere.[67]

Along with a group of other free speech advocates, I wrote to Zoom after the global moderation policy change, asking the company to answer a series of questions about how Zoom will address concerns about CCP interference in the academic context. Among other questions, we asked whether users would be notified if other participants are removed from meetings based on the content expressed, if Zoom would provide detailed reports of why users are removed from meetings so that educators can know what would disrupt student access to class, and if all government requests would be made publicly available.[68] We were not given an answer.

Months after the Tiananmen memorial dustup, Zoom found itself at the center of a new controversy much closer to home when it announced it would not allow two San Francisco State University (SFSU) faculty members to host a September 2020 roundtable discussion and Q&A, "Whose Narratives? Gender, Justice and Resistance," with Leila Khaled.[69] Khaled is best known for being the first woman to hijack an airplane, which she did in 1969 in support of the Popular Front for the Liberation of Palestine,[70] a group deemed a foreign terrorist organization by the US Department of State.

Ahead of the decision, protesters demonstrated outside of Zoom headquarters demanding the company intervene so the event could not go forward. One of the event organizers, Lawfare Project, issued a statement that "communications platforms have been put on notice: block terrorism and cancel anti-Semitism, or you will be canceled,"[71] and even demanded the US Department of Justice "take appropriate action" against the organizers.[72] A coalition of over eighty groups incorrectly alleged that the event would violate California statutes concerning election campaigns and the use of university names at events supporting or opposing a boycott or any "political, religious, sociological, or economic movement, activity, or program."[73] Colorado Representative Doug Lamborn also accused SFSU of "aiding the dissemination of terrorist propaganda."[74]

Zoom suggested anti-terrorism laws were the basis of the cancellation of the SFSU event, as well as the company's decision not to allow a series of similar online seminars organized at other universities in solidarity with the SFSU event.[75] "In light of the speaker's reported affiliation or membership in a U.S. designated foreign terrorist organization, and SFSU's inability to confirm otherwise, we determined the meeting is in violation of Zoom's Terms of Service and told SFSU they may not use Zoom for this particular event," Zoom spokesperson Andy Duberstein said after the cancellations. As free speech advocates like FIRE argued at the time, it is difficult to see how an academic event featuring Khaled would constitute "material support for terrorism" in violation of US law.[76] Notably, Duberstein added that Zoom has the authority to ban or cancel any events or users from the service, for any reason.

Khaled, to put it mildly, is a controversial figure. But while she is not a sympathetic case study to many—as is the case in many important free speech precedents—I encourage readers to focus not on Khaled's views or history, but on what it means for Zoom or other tech companies to determine what campus discussions can take place when in-person events are impossible.

The purpose of a university is for its community to freely research, debate, and learn. The purpose of a business is to protect its earnings and brand. Zoom's goals and incentives are not the same as those of the academic communities it serves, and as a corporation, it is much more likely to accede to the demands of political figures, outraged consumers, or advocacy groups than to stand by expressive values.

Given Khaled's especially divisive status, some readers may not be particularly troubled to see her critics' campaign succeed. But that is a dangerous standard to accept for our online campuses, and one that we should be uncomfortable with should online teaching return in force again. We should fully think through the various ways moderation could inhibit the online classroom or quad.

As individual states pass varying abortion laws that sometimes include restrictions on *speech* about abortion in the aftermath of the overturning of *Roe v. Wade*, Zoom may decide it risks liability if it allows academic events about abortion to proceed. The company might also be pressured by lawmakers to moderate professors' discussions of "critical race theory" in light of state laws seeking to limit so-called CRT in the classroom. Or, perhaps seeking to mitigate public anger, the company could respond to campaigns demanding it moderate "misinformation" or "hate" by limiting which groups or speakers it will allow to be hosted on campus Zoom events. The list goes on.

This is the risk of the online campus, whether it is one facilitated by Zoom or another company: Some ideas are simply not good for business. Corporations unmoored by legal and moral obligations to the First Amendment could get the final say over who can speak, and what can be said, in higher education.

Some faculty bodies realized this too. In late 2020, Georgetown University's Main Campus Executive Faculty passed a nearly unanimous motion asking Georgetown to "develop and publicize alternatives to Zoom so that it no longer enjoys a monopoly as on-line classroom platform and meeting platform at Georgetown." The resolution called for a Zoom contract with academic freedom protections with "teeth," due to "repeated cases of the Zoom Corporation violating freedom of speech and academic freedom," including Khaled and the Tiananmen memorial incidents.[77]

Around the same time, a faculty body at the Academic Senate of the University of California's Committee on Academic Freedom pointed out that Zoom's terms of service ban "posting or sending hateful imagery," including those of hate groups, "any material that is . . . indecent," "gory media," "impersonat[ing] anyone," and nudity, with some educational or medical exceptions. The committee wrote:

> From swastikas portrayed in history classes to nudity in art studios, from clinical training in the medical schools to impersonation by our theater clubs, mock trial teams, and school mascots, members of the University of California routinely violate Zoom's terms and standards in the course of regular instruction, research, and extracurricular activities. Of course, Zoom may never enforce its terms and standards to the absurdly broad extent that their vague language would allow. . . . Under our current contract, however, the power to decide what content to allow lies with Zoom, not the University. This is an astonishingly open-ended threat to the University's ability to carry out its fundamental mission.[78]

To its credit, Zoom heard these valid concerns and in April 2021 announced that for events hosted by higher education institutions, the company's Trust and Safety team would not act on non-hosts' reports of violations unless "the report alleges an immediate threat to the physical safety of any person" or "Zoom determines that there is legal or regulatory risk to Zoom if it does not act."⁷⁹ The statement recognized that "academic freedom and freedom of speech are defining commitments for many of our higher education users, both inside the classroom and on the broader campus." This was an important step and meant that academics had less reason to fear certain potential terms of service violations posed by basic academic discussions.

But Zoom's mention of acting on "legal or regulatory risk" in the statement leaves open the possibility that the company would still grant even clearly unconstitutional legislative or political demands, whether they originate from politicians looking to moderate hate speech or governors attempting to eliminate CRT in higher education. And notably, Zoom did not address the Leila Khaled events in its statement on academic freedom.

So it was no surprise that when SFSU faculty once again attempted to host Khaled just weeks later, in an event titled "Whose Narratives? What Free Speech for Palestine?," both Zoom and Eventbrite removed the event from their platforms.⁸⁰

The Future of Online Ed

For most readers, the worst of the COVID-19 pandemic is behind us. Students are meeting in person—Zoom is an option, but not a necessity—and the associated academic freedom threats posed by third party companies and foreign laws have somewhat diminished. It may be tempting to dismiss the concerns I discussed earlier in this chapter under the assumption that, with pandemic life mostly back to normal, we are no longer going to be bound by the challenges of online learning. But complacency would be a mistake for a few reasons.

For one, online teaching remains more prevalent than readers may realize. A spring 2022 report from the Institute of International Education of over 550 higher education institutions in the United States found that while only four of the surveyed schools were virtual only and about one-fourth reported being in-person only, the remaining 71 percent reported a hybrid mode of mixed online and in-person education.[81]

Second, we cannot predict what new COVID-19 variants—or worse, other viruses—will emerge in the coming months and years, and how viral or deadly future stages of the pandemic could be. It remains well within the realm of possibility that mass-scale online education and limited international travel will bring these threats to academic freedom to the forefront once again.

Finally, we have opened doors that are difficult to completely close. With online education now a widespread option, we should not be surprised to see more students and institutions turn to it for a variety of purposes. For valid reasons, online education may be the model that makes sense for people who cannot or do not want to relocate or commute to receive in-person education. And certain other unexpected urgent factors—like energy shortages, air quality alerts, heat waves, wildfire seasons, or other climate-related disruptions—could emerge that push universities back online. While I worked on this book, two Polish institutions, the University of Bialystok[82] and Jagiellonian University, the country's oldest university,[83] announced a significant number of operations would go online, not because of the pandemic, but in response to soaring electric and heating costs. I would not be surprised to see more follow, especially as the climate of the future looks increasingly volatile.

If COVID-19 taught us anything, it should be that we cannot predict how global events will shake out, or what our world will look like even six months away. I think it is a safe bet that we will experience more turmoil that will invite some degree of a return to online education in the coming years. It will likely ebb and flow, but it is here to stay. So there is no excuse for us to ignore the ways it creates new strains on fundamental rights in some of our most important institutions. Online education is likely in our future, and we cannot allow it to make academic freedom a thing of the past.

CHAPTER 7

A Free World Needs Free Campuses

In January 2021, a federal court barred the University of Florida from enforcing its controversial conflict of interest policy, which allowed university officials to govern professors' off-campus activities. Faculty members sued after administrators used the policy to prevent them from offering testimony in a voting rights lawsuit—testimony that would undermine the state's official position in court.[1]

The opening words of the order laid bare the stakes for intellectual freedom, unfavorably comparing Florida's arguments to the deterioration of freedom in Hong Kong. In his order enjoining enforcement of the policy, Mark E. Walker, chief judge of the US District Court for the Northern District of Florida, opened by lamenting the University of Hong Kong's removal of its Tiananmen memorial, Jens Galschiøt's Pillar of Shame. "In many ways, the Pillar's demise was emblematic of the demise of academic freedom in Hong Kong," Walker wrote.[2]

Walker assessed the decline of academic freedom in Hong Kong, laying the blame not just on the Chinese government, but also at the feet of the university administrations willing to do its dirty work. "Much of the pressure on students and professors comes not from Beijing, but from university administrators," he said. Walker suggested a similar form of pressure was at play at the University of Florida when administrators blocked faculty from engaging in testimony that angered politicians running the state of Florida.

"Some might say, 'that's China, it could never happen here,'" Walker wrote. "But Plaintiffs contend it already has."

While Walker's opinion gave the University of Florida a well-earned shellacking, it also spoke to two deeper and broader concerns applicable across higher education around the world—and brought home a reminder that American campuses should not take their relative freedom for granted. The first concern is that the line between freedom and tyranny is thinner and more permeable than we may want to admit. Because of the protections universities in freer nations enjoy, it can be tempting to shrug at occasional rights violations as minor hiccups.

But such nonchalance about our rights is a mistake. An erosion of freedom on campus will reverberate off campus, as the second concern—about the fundamental role universities play in the maintenance of free societies—makes clear. When universities' constituents or leadership neglect their responsibilities for political or financial ends, there is more at risk than individual students' or professors' liberties, though those matter on their own too.

Universities are a building block of free societies, not an adornment on them. If they falter, other institutions and freedoms are at greater risk of crumbling as well.

Globally, we are growing less free, and as I have discussed throughout this book, higher education is not responding well to the challenge. A significant number of international students operate under the knowledge that their home countries' surveillance follows them wherever they go. Administrators ignore or, worse, exacerbate the threats these students face, while knowingly pursuing ethically questionable partnerships with some of the world's worst human rights offenders, and evading questions about the mismatch between university values and local law. Tenure is one of the few protections allowing professors the ability to speak freely about their universities' dealings, but it is growing increasingly inaccessible to large scores of faculty members working at institutions that often look more like corporations than universities. For many, silence is the safest option—an outcome that suits authoritarians well.

In this concluding chapter, I will address where we are going wrong—from administrators to academic communities to politicians—amid the fight against authoritarian influence in higher education, as well as what changes we can make to protect free expression on campus as avenues for dissent are otherwise closing off around the world. There will be no permanent, one-and-done solutions, because this is a problem that cannot be "solved," only mitigated. Authoritarians will continue to try to violate speech rights as long as they exist. The responsibility of university community members and leadership, politicians, and those concerned about our rights on and off campus, is to push back and adjust to these threats as they evolve.

Where We Go Wrong

One of the biggest challenges posed by authoritarian influence is that the severity of the threat it poses can tempt its opponents to respond in kind, to the point that they violate their own professed values in an attempt to combat their subversion. Fighting fire with fire will not ultimately protect a free country's values, but it may very well incinerate them.

As I have written throughout this book, I am deeply concerned about the state of authoritarianism in higher education, including the role that some student groups, primarily Chinese Students and Scholars Association chapters, play in demanding censorship of the CCP's critics. It is a real problem that universities need to wise up to swiftly by recognizing when students are pressing for censorship of dissenters under the rationale of anti-hate or bias policies. But that does not mean that students from China or other authoritarian nations should be held responsible for the actions of some of their peers, or their government, because of their country of origin.

Unfortunately, that is exactly what some US politicians have advocated. Texas House candidate Shelley Luther tweeted, "Chinese students should be BANNED from attending all Texas universities," and "No more Communists!" during her 2022 campaign.[3] Arkansas Senator Tom Cotton has pursued legislation that would ban Chinese students from pursuing certain areas of study at US campuses. "If Chinese students want to come here and learn Shakespeare and the Federalist Papers—that's what they need to learn from America; they don't need to learn quantum computing and artificial intelligence from America," he said.[4]

And in 2018, Stephen Miller, senior advisor to then–President Trump, reportedly advocated banning all Chinese nationals from obtaining visas to study in the United States, citing espionage concerns. Miller allegedly argued that the proposal would also conveniently serve as a way to cut off a funding source for liberal universities that were opposed to the Trump administration.[5] Ultimately, President Trump, citing the potential for spying or intellectual property theft, would issue a proclamation restricting the granting of visas to certain individuals who studied or researched at universities linked to the Chinese government's "military-civil fusion strategy"[6] and revoking the visas of over 1,000 Chinese nationals.[7] Upon taking office, President Joe Biden kept the Trump-era restrictions in place.[8]

In 2019, along with a coalition of civil liberties advocates, I wrote to then–US Secretary of State Michael Pompeo in response to reports that the Trump administration was considering a new round of measures for Chinese students seeking to study in the United States. The measures included "checks of student phone records and scouring of personal accounts on Chinese and U.S. social media platforms for anything that might raise concerns about students' intentions in the United States."[9]

While our coalition acknowledged the national security concerns at play, we wrote that "this kind of phone and social media surveillance would surely chill the speech of Chinese students, many who are already under strict surveillance in their home country." Prospective students could very well self-censor out of fear that political discussion about China or the United States would harm their academic prospects. And that surveillance could affect *Americans* too. After all, their communications with these students could also be under the microscope.

That illiberal policy would also embolden censorship abroad by undermining America's ability to lead by example. As we wrote in our letter, instituting

> a surveillance policy against foreign students may inspire other countries to do the same against American students studying abroad. A policy that we would not wish to see enforced against American students is not one that we should consider employing against foreign students planning to study here. Free societies are best served when we extend to others the protections we wish to preserve for ourselves.[10]

But months later, the State Department launched a new policy that required *all* visa applicants—not only those from China—to submit any social media handles they had used in the past five years.[11] Previously, such disclosures were voluntary. At the time, advocates warned that the policy change would raise free speech concerns on multiple fronts. Not only would some applicants likely choose to self-censor legal speech out of fear it could harm their visa applications, but it would also create more opportunities for officials to deny applicants on the basis of their viewpoints.

Advocates, particularly those in higher education, had good reason to be concerned. In the weeks prior to the decision, at least two well-known Palestinian figures were among those denied entry to the United States ahead of campus speaking engagements. In April 2019, Omar Barghouti, co-founder of the Boycott, Divestment and Sanctions movement, alleged that he was stopped in Israel's Ben Gurion International Airport ahead of speeches at NYU and Harvard and told he would not be allowed into the United States despite holding valid travel documents.[12] State Department officials generally refuse to discuss reasons for denials, citing confidentiality, but Barghouti alleged his political views led to the decision. The next month, Palestinian politician and negotiator Hanan Ashrawi wrote that her visa was also rejected with no reason given.[13] Ashrawi had intended to speak at campuses on her trip to the United States. Then, in August 2019, nine Chinese students heading for Arizona State University, some who were close to graduation, were stopped in Los Angeles' airport and sent back without explanation, though immigration officials reportedly looked at their devices.[14]

Around the same time, Ismail B. Ajjawi, an incoming Harvard student and Palestinian resident living in Lebanon, was stopped at Boston's Logan International Airport, where he was searched and questioned for several hours—and then deported. While State Department officials refused to publicly comment on his case, Ajjawi offered a disturbing reason for his visa cancellation: *other people's* political views.

Ajjawi alleged that immigration officers questioned him about his faith and religious practices and, when they obtained access to the devices they asked him to unlock, interrogated him about his friends' social media activities. "When I asked every time to have my phone back so I could tell them about the situation, the officer refused and told me to sit back in [my] position and not move at all," Ajjawi said. "After the 5 hours ended, she called me into a room, and she started screaming at me. She said that she found people posting political points of view that oppose the US on my friend[s] list."[15] He told them that he did not promote or share the views shared by others on his friends list, but it did not matter. He was sent back home. Ajjawi ultimately made it back to campus in time to start classes after Harvard officials, working with advocates, appealed to immigration authorities.[16] But it is unclear how many other students or speakers have faced similar roadblocks with less public attention to pressure officials to reverse course.

If viewpoint-based reasoning is employed to decide who can and cannot enter the United States, that ultimately means the range of views and voices expressed on (and off) our campuses could be skewed to fit the preferences of immigration officials, who operate under murky standards that are unclear to the American public—and to immigrants. This is not conducive to viewpoint diversity, and it will hinder our understanding of the world we live in.

Critics have also contended that efforts to combat national security threats posed by professors' ties to China have led to prosecutorial excesses. The Justice Department's China Initiative, launched during the Trump administration, specifically targeted espionage and intellectual property theft in higher education. It earned some convictions, like the verdict against Harvard chemist Charles Lieber, found guilty of making false statements to the FBI about his participation in a Chinese government program for foreign scientists and failure to disclose bank accounts and financial earnings in China.[17] But it also prompted valid fears from faculty about racially motivated and overreaching investigations into professors of Asian descent.

Take, for example, University of Tennessee professor Anming Hu, a naturalized citizen of Canada. Hu was accused of hiding ties with the Chinese government and was placed on house arrest for over a year, put on trial (which resulted in a mistrial), and suspended from his job without pay. He was ultimately acquitted. Part of the investigation originated from an FBI agent's "open source" investigation—meaning an online search—into Hu. The agent found a flier written in Chinese that he roughly translated through Google showing Hu had a teaching contract at the Beijing University of Technology.[18] Hu had failed to list this teaching position on one form. The agent later admitted that he showed UT leadership a presentation accusing Hu of being a member of the Chinese military. But "based on my summary translations, my reports and my outline, no, Hu wasn't involved in the Chinese military," he said at the trial.

"I lost two years of my life," Hu, now back to his job, said of the ordeal.

Similarly, Massachusetts Institute of Technology professor and naturalized US citizen Gang Chen was arrested for allegedly failing to disclose funding from Chinese groups in early 2021 in what Chen called "a politically and racially motivated prosecution" that was "riddled with basic factual errors."[19] His colleagues at MIT were similarly outraged—170 of them signed a letter asserting that the "complaint against Professor Chen vilifies what would be considered normal academic and research activities."[20] A year later, prosecutors dropped the charges against Chen.[21]

"As a nation, we can be more true to our ideals—and a better world leader—by acknowledging our wrongdoings and learning from our mistakes rather than blindly pressing forward," Chen wrote about his case in *The Boston Globe*. "While acknowledging mistakes can be painful, history shows that it is the best way forward."

In February 2022, the Justice Department announced a reworking—and renaming—of the China Initiative that would expand beyond threats from China to include those posed by countries like North Korea and Russia, and that would also adjust some of its methods. "By grouping cases under the China Initiative rubric, we helped give rise to a harmful perception that the department applies a lower standard to investigate and prosecute criminal conduct related to that country or that we in some way view people with racial, ethnic or familial ties to China differently," official Matthew G. Olsen explained about the policy change.[22] Olsen said the Initiative led to a narrative "that the Justice Department treats people from China or of Chinese descent differently."

The shift helped to reassure critics of the China Initiative, but some remain wary that the department can capably strike the appropriate balance between investigating national security threats and understanding the complexities of cross-border research and collaboration.[23] At a University of Michigan event in late 2022, FBI Director Christopher Wray reaffirmed that "it's part of our responsibility to work with universities" to protect against the Chinese government's "international talent war to try to leverage and steal intellectual property and sensitive research and data from countries all over the world."

Wray went on to argue that the Initiative's failed cases were a sign of the program's strength, not a weakness. "The fact that we sometimes lose cases actually speaks volumes about the integrity and independence of our justice system," Wray said. "I actually think it's a mark in our favor as a country that the government loses cases. I'd be willing to bet you that our counterparts over in China don't lose very many cases, and it ain't because they're better than we are."[24] The targets of those failed cases, like Hu and Chen, may not agree that they are proof of the Initiative's integrity.

The China Initiative serves as another reminder that we still have a responsibility to respond with wisdom, restraint, and care when faced even with valid concerns, like those regarding potential foreign interference in the American higher education system. We will not protect our universities or the knowledge they produce by making them less free.

The Threat of Off-Campus Speech Restrictions

It is not just the China Initiative that prompts fears about how the American government oversteps at home. More broadly, American officials must stop pushing legislative and policing efforts that would be more at home in authoritarian countries. We cannot effectively repel interference in Americans' free expression rights without combating homegrown threats too. Yet these threats seem to multiply by the day, with legislators across the country pushing bills and threatening measures that would unconstitutionally limit Americans' First Amendment rights, in the name of fighting what public officials deem unwanted speech.

Why bother to fight foreign governments' efforts to import harmful censorship if we are willing to manufacture it here as well?

Alongside the flurry of anti-CRT bills put forward in the past few years that I discussed in chapter 3, other attempts to restrict speech have grown similarly popular. These are just a sample of incidents that took place across one year: In 2022, two Virginia politicians sought a rarely used state law to quite literally *sue books* for alleged obscenity in order to censor them from stores and libraries and force their authors and publishers to defend them in court.[25] Then, legislators in South Carolina introduced a bill that would make it a felony punishable by up to twenty-five years in prison to "knowingly or intentionally aid, abet, or conspire" with another person to obtain an abortion, which would effectively criminalize a wide range of protected speech.[26] In Texas, Hood County constable Chad Jordan announced the launch of an "active and pending criminal investigation" after complaints about the presence of some books in a high school library—launching a two-year investigation into three school librarians, which ended only when the statute of limitations finally expired.[27] The nationwide rush to pull any and all school library books with the potential to offend a parent has been a particularly ascendent and shameful trend in recent years, and unlikely to stay cabined to the confines of school libraries.

Other kinds of unpopular expression have faced political attention too. Under the guise of endeavoring to reduce violent online imagery, New York Attorney General Letitia James released a set of internet recommendations in the aftermath of a deadly shooting in Buffalo. But the recommendations, which included a required "tape delay" for unverified livestreams, would violate the First Amendment.[28] Her suggestions for livestreaming restrictions unwittingly echoed some of those called for by China's Ministry of Culture and Tourism just weeks earlier.[29]

As Walker's ruling against the University of Florida warned, efforts to censor or curtail speech do not originate only from authoritarian countries like China and can spring up in freer countries as well. The first step to combating interference and censorship from oppressive regimes is ensuring we do not tolerate such efforts here at home from our own leaders. Advocacy for censorship *should* be poisonous to the chances of electoral-hopefuls in the United States, but politicians usually do not lose votes by grandstanding on unpopular speech or speakers. And Americans unfortunately will regularly defend their own right to speak with one hand, while clawing away at their opponents' rights with the other.

When it comes to campus, universities' acquiescence to censorship attempts in the United States suggests that they will not have the spine to stand up to other countries' pressures either. After all, public universities are bound by the First Amendment, and benefit from well-staffed legal teams that exist to ensure universities' actions match their legal responsibilities. Yet, in the wake of recent legislative measures, some have been willing to throw out these considerations to satisfy more expedient political concerns. In 2021, Boise State University suddenly suspended *dozens* of classes in response to a rumor that a student's beliefs were insulted in class.[30] The suspensions also followed the Idaho Joint Finance-Appropriations Committee's suggested budget cuts related to CRT on campus. Then, Oklahoma City Community College temporarily canceled a class, "Race and Ethnicity in the United States," after the state passed a bill banning the teaching of "divisive concepts"—in *K–12* public schools.[31]

Months later, Iowa State adamantly argued that a new state law governing the teaching of "divisive concepts" in "mandatory staff or student training" actually applied to classroom discussion and instructed faculty to avoid coverage of this material in class if it could be considered "mandatory." Iowa State's instruction went beyond the demands of the law, and into academic freedom violations.[32] And after Florida passed the "Stop WOKE Act," administrators did not insist on preserving intellectual freedom. Instead, they uniformly acquiesced, issuing guidance warning faculty to avoid sharing opinions unless they were approved by state officials. North Florida College released guidance to faculty offering warnings, among others, that they should not assign blame for Jim Crow laws to "any particular race."[33]

If a university unlawfully censors campus expression to appease factions within the United States, why would it not do the same for those located abroad?

American legislators and public officials go very wrong when they violate the First Amendment and our core expressive freedoms. But universities also go wrong when they are eager to go above and beyond to assist them. To trust that universities can reject authoritarian censorship efforts abroad, we must first know that they can resist them at home.

Universities' Role in the Growth of Campus Authoritarianism

Universities bear at least some responsibility for the poor state of free expression and academic freedom in the international higher education sphere. As I discussed in chapter 3, universities have frequently failed to appropriately manage their legal and moral obligations to their community members' rights. This has resulted in a multitude of free speech issues in American higher education: Polling shows that students struggle with understanding First Amendment norms, illiberal and unconstitutional campus speech codes have limited the expression of a wide range of views, and a bloated bureaucracy that prioritizes brand management has bloomed, while faculty feel less free to speak as tenure declines and the presence of less protected part-time professors grows.

And these failures invite downstream effects that largely remain unaccounted for in higher education. "Sensitivity exploitation" flourishes as universities employ restrictive speech policies against controversial or unpopular expression, creating models that could be used against critics of authoritarian governments. Universities act more like large corporations than institutions of learning, and risk making the same concessions other industries have made to authoritarian regimes. Faculty, often first in line in objecting to ethically dicey university program expansions, fear doing so will imperil their careers.

Universities' mistakes have expanded beyond their application of institutional policy and practice on free speech and academic freedom. Too often, university leaders treat their international student population as a revenue source to preserve, rather than as a community whose speech rights face unique threats. It is an unfortunate truth that protecting institutional access to revenue from international students does not necessarily coincide with protecting their right to speak. Sometimes they can openly conflict and if faced with a choice between the two, it is no mystery which path many administrations would choose.

Universities have pursued engagement in deeply unfree countries, courting governments that commit serious human rights violations, while claiming such partnerships would not imperil their academic freedom commitments or institutional values despite copious evidence to the contrary. And some have even *actively* censored their communities when they have spoken out against oppressive governments. It is difficult to fully assess how deeply universities damage not only their own credibility, but public discourse as well, when they intervene in such an illiberal manner in favor of authoritarians.

Like corporate brands, universities say they are doing their best to provide a useful service while still following local law in the countries in which they operate. To some extent, this is true in the case of satellite campuses abroad: They generally do provide greater pockets of freedom in their host countries. But universities have not sufficiently investigated these questions: Have they been honest and truthful with their communities about the chasm between their values and the law? Does their voluntary submission to oppressive laws aid the authoritarians who enforce them? And is the service they are providing worth the harm they are committing to their institutional values?

What Must Change

Universities must engage in a radical change of their understanding of their role in the world today. Thus far, they have operated as if they can reap the rewards of international engagement, while remaining immune from the pressures and compromises other global industries face. That is not the case. And in some ways, these pressures hit higher education even harder than other trades, given its status as a values-driven industry. This standard of expansion in higher education—where universities leap into international growth while touting its benefits and downplaying or ignoring its costs—may prove lucrative for universities' finances and their leaders' reputations as global figures, but it leaves vulnerable students and faculty out in the cold and inhibits the conversation around human rights and authoritarian regimes.

Universities want to be active participants in the global stage when it suits them and cast themselves as impartial observers when it does not. They advertise their values and their principles when convenient and appeal to the limitations of local law and business realities when it is not.

If an institution's core values recede to suit other goals, they were never really meaningful commitments; they were just branding slogans. But they do not have to be.

Reevaluating How Universities Currently Operate

First, university leaders can do something very simple: They can ask questions and, more importantly, *listen* to the answers. Higher education is full of experts on authoritarianism and global politics, as well as academic freedom advocacy groups, like FIRE, Scholars at Risk, and the United Kingdom's Academic Freedom and Internationalisation Working Group. Leaders should seek out their counsel, not just to check a box to confirm that their input has been recorded and can subsequently be disregarded, but to learn how institutional behavior falls short of its values and what administrators can do differently as they adapt as global institutions in an unfree world. This includes reassessing their campuses and programs abroad and conducting meaningful inquiries into the academic freedom conditions on the ground and whether local and international conditions have worsened the prospects for campus rights since these programs were initiated. They do not have to wait until there is a controversy, tragedy, or PR mess. They can proactively begin that reassessment now.

And, unlike institutions such as Cornell University, they can seriously consider community concerns, as Wesleyan University did in 2019 when it canceled plans to pursue a joint venture campus in partnership with Chinese corporation Hengdian Group and the Shanghai Theatre Academy, in part because of "issues of academic freedom and the implications for our home campus."[34] This is especially important not just for reevaluating existing university programs, but for considering prospective ones too.

Saudi Arabia, for example, is signaling an interest in opening its doors to international branch campuses.[35] The human rights and free expression limitations are obvious. But so are the financial opportunities. Will universities be able to resist the allure? Other major American institutions have certainly not—just look at the PGA Tour, which long decried the human rights violations in Saudi Arabia during its legal and PR battle with the Saudi-funded LIV Golf, and then suddenly merged with it.[36] And in early 2024, Arizona State University decided to try its chances in Saudi Arabia, announcing a joint memorandum of understanding for a new university in Riyadh and answering the question of whether universities could resist the country's draw.[37] They could not. The announcement came only six years after Saudi officials ordered the secret execution and dismemberment of US-based journalist Jamal Khashoggi.

The environment that may have beckoned universities to expand overseas a decade ago may no longer be the one they operate in today. Countries across the world have grown increasingly repressive in recent years, and students and academics have often been the first to feel those effects. While this does not mean universities should simply cut off engagement with unfree countries, they should carefully and thoughtfully tailor engagement to limit opportunities for rights violations and interference, and fully inform all participants in their programs of the risks. This means honest and upfront communication about local law and university limitations, not vague platitudes about commitments to free expression and academic freedom.

In recent years, there has been much vague talk from administrators about "bright lines" on academic freedom that cannot be crossed, and very little discussion of the realities of local law or what will happen if those lines are crossed. University leaders should commit to transparent inquiries that include public conditions for what findings would necessitate that the university remove itself from the partnership. The problem is that if universities spell out in clear terms how severely local laws limit speech rights, it may be hard to justify having programs there in the first place. Universities should not pursue programs with limitations they are unwilling to discuss in public transparently and truthfully.

During a continuously uneasy time of budget cuts and financial mismanagement, universities will undoubtedly be resistant to make decisions that could potentially alienate current or future funding from foreign governments or wealthy partners. But not every university is under strain, and institutions that have the resources to weather temporary financial setbacks should be pressured to set the standard here. Harvard and Yale have nearly 100 *billion* dollars in their combined endowments, followed by Stanford and Princeton, both of which have nearly 40 billion each.[38]

And yet an administrator at Harvard, which boasts an endowment larger than the GDP of dozens of countries,[39] interfered with a Chinese human rights activist's event so that it would not disturb the university's projects in China. This is unacceptable, and we must demand better. Students, faculty, and alumni should pressure Harvard and other wealthy universities to use their endowments as shields for free expression against the pressures and threats of authoritarianism. They have no colorable excuse to do otherwise.

Combatting Censorship in Old and New Ways

More broadly, universities need to reconsider not just how their existing programs should be reformed or what policies must be revised, but what new ideas they can pursue to protect basic freedoms in their institutions and around the world. They do not need to only play defense.

After the removal of the Tiananmen memorials at Hong Kong's universities, Chinese University of Hong Kong students placed small versions of the "Goddess of Democracy" statue around campus ahead of the massacre's anniversary, in defiance of university staff.[40] Activists created online versions of memorial statues that could not be so easily taken apart by the censors.[41] And Jens Galschiøt, sculptor of the Pillar of Shame, released the copyright of the sculpture and offered a free blueprint so others could create their own 3D printed versions. "They have made a big mistake," Galschiøt said. "Now, instead of one, they're getting hundreds of Pillars of Shame."[42]

This same spirit should guide universities. They should, of course, adjust university policy to protect against incursions on speech and academic freedom rights. But they should also consider how they cannot just protect against present and future censorship, but also preserve the expression that authoritarians wish to silence.

In 2021, UC Berkeley PhD student and Hong Kong Democracy Council Board Chair Alex Chow co-wrote a *New York Times* essay calling the rapid degradation of free speech and academic freedom in Hong Kong a "warning for global academia."[43] Universities around the world should "set up Hong Kong studies programs and offer haven to scholars and students who hope to study Hong Kong from afar," he wrote. Higher education does not simply have to weather growing oppression—it can actively challenge it by ensuring the information and scholars authoritarians wish to silence find a new venue.

A year after his essay, I spoke to Chow about whether universities have stepped up to the plate. He told me there has been some progress to find homes for Hong Kong's displaced scholars and studies, but it is an uphill battle. "There's definitely an effort to try to create a space where Hong Kong and China can be discussed freely with the awareness that there's shrinking space in China and Hong Kong to talk about public affairs and history in a free way," he told me. But a major problem remains: How will it be funded?

As universities' financial crises continue, Chow says, it is difficult to see how strong foundations for these studies will be built. These programs "need more financial and intellectual infrastructure and support. Right now, they don't have an endowment. It seems to be something that is still a struggle," Chow explained. And even private donors and funding are complicated by a simple reality, one I have discussed throughout the book: money and China. Wealthy patrons may simply not want to be seen challenging the Chinese government. "Big donors might also have reservations whether these programs would be seen as too political. For big donors who might be able to provide financial support, they may still have to go back to China or Hong Kong. Their support could be seen as hostile."

No matter the difficulties, though, Chow believes there is real value in universities being aware that political oppression in China and Hong Kong can impact teaching and research.

Ching Kwan Lee, a sociology professor at UCLA, is involved in one of the efforts Chow recommends, the University of California's Global Hong Kong Studies program. When we spoke, Lee told me it is important for academics to use their limited power to ensure that censored material is still discussed in freer universities, but was careful to note that this is not a problem that professors alone can fix. "It's tricky," Lee told me. Giving a venue to Hong Kong's censored academics was one of her objectives, but experience has shown her it is often not simple.

"Our colleagues who are still in Hong Kong are still reluctant for good reason. They're inclined to self-censor because their jobs, families, and whole lives are still there," she said. She provides a platform for them, but "fear of reprisal" is often a more powerful motivator. "I think it's kind of romantic from our side. It's not always as simple as that. It's not the lack of venue, it's how pervasive the surveillance machine is and how broad their influence. My experience is that it's not a solution to the problem of censorship."

Academics should use the tools available to them—and Lee does, creating a space for scholarly and empirically based discussions on Hong Kong and one that protects attendees' identities—but they can't do this alone. Lee singled out higher education ranking companies—the QS World University Rankings is one example—as one of the institutions that must evolve to address these challenges and begin to account for campus climate and academic freedom threats in their rankings.

Other scholars and activists have made similar calls in recent years, including those at the V-Dem Institute, the Global Public Policy Institute, and Scholars at Risk, who worked with researchers to produce a global Academic Freedom Index, which provides important information about countries' on-the-ground treatment of academic freedom.[44] But ranking companies have thus far generally ignored how free or unfree universities are, meaning that students and professors could face retaliation, arrest, and censorship, and it would not make a difference to how that university is ranked. The incentives to protect community rights and resist censorship simply are not there—but they could be if authoritarian leaders see consequences in the highly coveted global rankings.

Giving Students the Tools to Speak Freely

Universities also need to assess how they are failing their international students. Reconsidering their partnerships with oppressive regimes can ameliorate this problem. By showing students that their universities will not carelessly look away from human rights concerns and free speech restrictions in authoritarian countries that can nevertheless improve institutions' reach and finances, these students may be able to trust that if they choose to speak out against their governments, their universities will not censor, punish, or put them in harm's way to protect university interests.

Administrators must also find more hands-on ways to protect their at-risk international students' speech rights. A good start would be conducting anonymous, private surveys of international students to discern whether they feel safe speaking online or on campus, while ensuring and reassuring them that their anonymity will be protected. They could give a name to what students are experiencing—transnational repression—and make clear that it is unwelcome and will be combatted to the fullest extent possible at the university level. From there, they should coordinate orientation programming for international students—and perhaps even all students—about how they can speak safely, freely, and legally. Teach them what their rights are on campus, and what recourse is available to them if they fear that they cannot speak because of consequences awaiting them at home. This is especially necessary for international students who are accustomed to vastly different legal systems and may not know their expressive rights abroad.

And, importantly, they must educate students about how to safeguard themselves while speaking freely online. Universities should provide students with materials on encryption, anonymity, data security, and privacy settings. Even students' anodyne political statements made online can leave a permanent trail of evidence that could follow them when they return home—and students have found themselves behind bars at home for social media they have posted abroad. So why not ensure they know at least the basics of protecting themselves on the internet? Universities do not have the means to defang authoritarian governments, but they can help arm students with tools to defend their rights online.

Universities can also work with students and faculty to create recommended best practices and plans for the entire community to follow when it comes to free expression and privacy. What should students do when they travel abroad to unfree countries? How will administrators respond to foreign police or security forces' requests for student data? Do professors have sufficient protections on devices carrying sensitive information when they cross borders? How will administrators respond when they receive censorship requests from government officials? These are all questions leaders should be able to answer *before* they have to answer them.

"It would be helpful for faculty, students, and administrators to talk about those issues and come up with policies that sustain a safe environment for students to speak up," Chow told me. "Right now, the support is fragmented and there is no systemic or collective effort."

Students, and especially student press, have a role to play too. As local, off-campus media organizations wither away, student journalists—like those who have tracked the satellite campuses and programs at Duke, NYU, and Cornell—are uniquely suited to cast a light on the often wealthy and powerful institutions whose conduct can escape notice from national press. There are few groups and individuals better equipped to understand and access administrative decision-makers and university communities in order to cover important stories like student self-censorship, ethically questionable partnerships, and the presence of authoritarianism in higher education. A purpose of the press is to serve as a check on power—including institutions of higher education.

Expecting Better from Our Institutions

Pressure from authoritarian actors requires a counterweight. We can ask more of our universities, and we have the power to do so. Faculty bodies can push for reforms protecting them in overseas programs and campuses, and they can organize to broaden academic freedom protections. Students and student groups can expand their activism to focus on the rights of their peers from other nations, and ask what university officials are doing to keep them safe and free. Donors can withhold donations to universities that fail to update their protocols to reflect today's new threats to free expression or that refuse to investigate the conditions for expression in their global programs.

While this book focuses on the problems in higher education, it is not just campuses that have missed the mark or failed to live up to their potential. As I discussed in earlier chapters, universities have often followed in the footsteps of corporate counterparts who, in their international dealings, have been all too willing to distance themselves from free expression and follow the dictates of authoritarian governments. While acquiescence in higher education is a uniquely serious concern—given its role in the production and distribution of knowledge and research, as well as the molding of future leaders and generations—Americans are still right to be worried about what happens when authoritarian pressures seep into institutions across the corporate world.

It is not just a hypothetical, and we know what the end result of that pressure can be—it looks like movies rewritten for entire global audiences in order to protect a studio's interests in China; perhaps a sports association that normally embraces political expression, but rejects it when it is critical of the CCP; maybe a telecommunications tool that applies a country's censorship policies outside its borders; or maybe an AI image generating company that intentionally exempts Xi Jinping from users' satirical images.[45] These stories could fill their own book.

Businesses operating internationally have to walk a fine line around the conflicting legal requirements they encounter across different borders, but they do not have to automatically consent to every unfounded censorship demand they receive, and they are certainly not required to change their operations in America to satisfy authoritarian impulses abroad. Yet that has sometimes been the case. Norms that develop in business matter not just for the sake of the changes they will engender within the corporate world, but for their potential to spread to other institutions as well.

We can ask more of our institutions. We can urge them not to choose the path of least resistance, to reject illiberal demands when possible, and to transparently notify the public when they are facing pressure to engage in self-censorship or violate their values. It is especially important that we ask this when the institutions in question are ones that carry weight in moderating or creating public discourse, knowledge, and culture—whether they are media organizations, tech firms, or entertainment conglomerates.

Corporations will argue that we live in an interconnected world and must sometimes make compromises to maintain cross-border business operations. That is no doubt true. But it is also true that in such an interconnected world, decisions to censor or avoid certain topics necessarily have more far-reaching consequences than in a more isolated one, and we should encourage corporations against carelessly using such power.

Rejecting Governmental Censorship Across the Board

Every day, it seems, there is a new legislative proposal in a different state pressing for some new restriction on expression, from critical race theory to protest to online speech. For a country that correctly considers its protections of the right to speak one of its strongest offerings and proudest achievements, the United States is home to a shameful spate of frequent efforts to restrict expression—efforts which are regularly cheered on by various segments of the population.

This must stop. Americans need to learn the basics of the First Amendment, and not just what it protects, but *why* it protects speech we find distasteful or immoral. With every new bill we cheer on for punishing our ideological opponents, we help create the standards that will be used to punish our own speech—and perhaps the speech of the world's dissidents and dissenters too. It is not just morally wrong. It is a tactical failure too.

When it comes to combating the threat of authoritarian censorship on campus, it is vital that we simultaneously work to discourage speech restrictions emerging from within the United States. Not only do such restrictions offer authoritarian governments tools with which to silence dissenters abroad, they also help to weaken the protections that make the United States a unique haven for free expression. Global freedom is currently in a downturn, and the worst thing the United States could do is help contribute to its spiral.

Freer Campuses, and a Freer World, Are Possible

When I began working on this book, sparse protests against the 2022 Beijing Olympics were taking place in some countries and campuses, but it looked, for the most part, as if the Chinese government would succeed in drowning out its critics and shifting focus from its human rights abuses to the spectacle of the games.

Later that year, it was impossible to avoid the sense that something changed. Beginning in late November, demonstrations swept China in record numbers as protesters, echoing the words of a lone individual who courageously hung protest banners over a Beijing bridge the month before, expressed anger about a deadly fire in Xinjiang (which protesters say was worsened by lockdowns), zero-COVID rules more generally, and sometimes, Xi Jinping himself.

Those protests sparked on campuses as well, as Chinese and other students in countries around the world joined to make their voices heard about what was taking place within China's borders. Unsurprisingly, some acts of censorship and violence

A Free World Needs Free Campuses

took place. At Carnegie Mellon University, when students painted messages critical of China's government, their messages were defaced with words like "idiots," "shit," and "colonized people."[46] A Xinjiang fire vigil created by students was set ablaze at UC Berkeley.[47] A protester at a rally at Columbia University was attacked while speaking and punched in the face. She was knocked unconscious and had to be taken to the hospital.[48]

In an even more troubling incident, the FBI was prompted to arrest Berklee College of Music student and People's Republic of China citizen Xiaolei Wu in Boston on charges of stalking a pro-democracy activist. Wu threatened to report the victim to Chinese authorities and implied her family would be punished for her behavior in the United States. He also made comments directed to the victim on WeChat, email, and Instagram, including a threat that if she posted more pro-democracy flyers on Berklee's campus, he would "chop [her] bastard hands off."[49]

That our campuses can be at the forefront of protest movements against oppressive governments, as well as primary targets of censorship attempts against authoritarianism's critics, is a testament to their importance in the global debate and the need to ensure they remain open and free. Yet too often, universities treat their academic freedom and free expression obligations as problems to overcome or unpleasant realities to be acknowledged.

Here, a change in thinking is in order. University leaders should view these obligations and commitments as a lodestar for how they can better serve their communities in the United States and abroad. With some courage and dedication, universities can be one of the remaining open places to speak in a world growing less free by the day. That is not a burden. It is an opportunity and a privilege.

There may be temporary repercussions for universities that reject authoritarian interference by protecting dissident students and scholars' rights, terminating partnerships that imperil expressive rights, and transparently and publicly announcing their refusal to tolerate pressure to censor. But the consequences of allowing our most important centers of academic debate and knowledge production to dim amid an ever-darkening world are more severe and permanent.

Censorship has global repercussions, and we cannot wish it away by treating it as someone else's problem. Activists, scholars, students, and dissidents around the world have shown tremendous bravery in pushing back against the horrors of authoritarianism. It is on us to ensure that our universities aid them—and not their oppressors.

A free world cannot exist without free universities.

Acknowledgments

I am deeply grateful to everyone who believed the story of *Authoritarians in the Academy* is worth telling and who helped make this work possible.

First, I would like to thank my colleagues at the Foundation for Individual Rights and Expression for their principled work and assistance in producing this book. I pestered many of them with questions while writing, and they all responded helpfully and graciously. I owe gratitude to each of them, but especially to Greg Lukianoff (whose initial encouragement is the reason why I undertook this project), Will Creeley (who generously provided valuable feedback in the early writing stages), and Alisha Glennon and Ronnie London (who ensured this book stayed on track).

My agent, Scott Mendel, was vital in guiding me through the publishing process as a first-time author and I could not have done this without his generosity, assistance, and patience. I sent Scott many stressed-out emails over the past couple of years, and he responded to each with kindness.

I am also grateful to Johns Hopkins University Press and Editorial Director Gregory Britton for working with me to find the best ways to tell this story. I must also thank Helen Wheeler at Westchester Publishing Services, along with Jennifer D'Urso, Kris Lykke, Phoebe Peter Oathout, Charles Dibble, and the many others at Johns Hopkins University Press who shepherded this book to publication.

I cannot thank enough the students, scholars, advocates, and activists who made time to speak to me about their experiences with authoritarian censorship and the state of global higher education today. I would also especially like to thank those who needed to remain anonymous out of fear of retaliation, but nevertheless courageously shared their stories with me. It is an unfortunate reality that the individuals who have experienced the most egregious forms of censorship, threats, and abuse—and whose stories most need to be told—are often those who risk the most by speaking out about it. My thanks also go to Nadine Strossen, Anthony Hennen, Rory O'Connor, and more who are too many to name for their feedback, input, and encouragement as I worked on the proposal, ideas, and writing of the book.

Lastly, I would like to thank the friends and family who have supported me and reserved a space for me on their bookshelves, especially my parents. They not only encouraged and facilitated my lifelong love of books, but also raised me to be troubled by the kinds of injustices I write about in this one. And, finally, my love and gratitude to my husband, Adam. Even on his busiest days, he always found time to make me a cup of tea while I wrote.

Notes

Introduction

1. US Department of Justice, "Five Individuals Charged Variously with Stalking, Harassing and Spying on U.S. Residents on Behalf of the PRC Secret Police," news release, March 16, 2022, www.justice.gov/opa/pr/five-individuals-charged-variously-stalking-harassing-and-spying-us-residents-behalf-prc-0.
2. Tom Grundy, "Security Chief: Google Refused to Change Search Results for Hong Kong Anthem, 'Hurt the Feelings' of Citizens," *Hong Kong Free Press*, December 13, 2022, https://hongkongfp.com/2022/12/13/security-chief-google-refused-to-change-search-results-for-hong-kong-anthem-hurt-the-feelings-of-citizens.
3. "Coronavirus: The Information Heroes China Silenced," *RSF*, accessed January 13, 2022, rsf.org/en/coronavirus-information-heroes-china-silenced.

Chapter 1. American Campuses, Red Lines

1. Josh Butler, "China's Threat to 'Punish' Olympic Athletes for Free Speech 'Very Concerning,' Australia Says," *Guardian* (international edition), January 21, 2022, www.theguardian.com/sport/2022/jan/21/china-threat-punishment-beijing-winter-olympics-athletes-political-statements-free-speech-very-concerning-australia-says.
2. Jon Werthheim, "Chinese Artist Badiucao: Drawing Truth to Power," *CBS News*, December 26, 2021, www.cbsnews.com/news/badiucao-60-minutes-2021-12-26/.
3. Sarah McLaughlin, "George Washington University Recants Promise to Uncover Chinese Government Critics After Artist's Satirical Olympics Posters Appear on Campus," *FIRE*, February 7, 2022, www

.thefire.org/news/george-washington-university-recants-promise-uncover-chinese-government-critics-after-artists.

4. Jessica Martin, "Washington University First North American Member of the University Alliance of the Silk Road," *Newsroom*, April 12, 2016, https://source.wustl.edu/2016/04/washington-university-first-north-american-member-of-chinese-university-consortium/.

5. James McBride, Noah Berman, and Andrew Chatzky, "China's Massive Belt and Road Initiative," Council on Foreign Relations, last updated February 2, 2023, https://www.cfr.org/backgrounder/chinas-massive-belt-and-road-initiative.

6. Jordan S. West, email response to bias incident submission, accessed March 1, 2022. On file with author.

7. George Washington University, "Message Regarding Posters Displayed on Campus," February 2, 2022, https://president.gwu.edu/message-regarding-posters-displayed-campus.

8. Sheng Zhang and Haining Bao, "Freedom of Speech as the Last Refuge of Racist Hater: GWU Asylum for Racism Reflects Double Standard of US Society," *Global Times*, February 10, 2022, https://www.globaltimes.cn/page/202202/1251952.shtml.

9. Joe Tsai (@joe.tsai.3781), "Open letter to all NBA fans," Facebook, October 6, 2019, https://www.facebook.com/100001583307192/posts/2653378931391524?sfns=mo.

10. "China Center Receives $30 Million Gift in Honor of Dr. Paul Tsai," Yale Law School, March 21, 2016, https://law.yale.edu/yls-today/news/china-center-receives-30-million-gift-honor-dr-paul-tsai.

11. Miya Shay, "Rockets GM Daryl Morey's Tweet Sparks Backlash from Chinese Basketball," *ABC 13*, October 7, 2019, https://abc13.com/daryl-morey-hong-kong-houston-rockets-tilman-fertitta/5599623/.

12. Patrick Brzeski, "NBA's Apology to China Draws Outrage Across Political Spectrum," *Hollywood Reporter*, October 6, 2019, https://www.hollywoodreporter.com/news/general-news/nbas-apology-china-draws-outrage-political-spectrum-1245772/.

13. Steve Fainaru and Mark Fainaru-Wada, "ESPN Investigation Finds Coaches at NBA China Academies Complained of Player Abuse, Lack of Schooling," *ESPN*, July 29, 2020, https://www.espn.com/nba/story

/_/id/29553829/espn-investigation-finds-coaches-nba-china-academies-complained-player-abuse-lack-schooling.

14. "Who Are the Uyghurs and Why Is China Being Accused of Genocide?," *BBC News*, May 24, 2022, https://www.bbc.com/news/world-asia-china-22278037.

15. Bethany Allen-Ebrahimian, "Chinese Students at Cornell 'Taunt' Uyghur Classmate During Event," *Axios*, May 15, 2022, https://www.axios.com/chinese-students-cornell-taunt-uyghur-classmate-3d2b1046-dd17-41de-a69d-59ec116da8bb.html.

16. Elissa Slotkin (@RepSlotkin), "In response, a group of Chinese international students got up and walked out," Twitter, March 15, 2022, https://twitter.com/RepSlotkin/status/1503806198902140937.

17. "BREAKING: Recent Cornell Graduate Allegedly Attacked While Putting Up Pro-Democracy Posters," *Cornell Review*, June 8, 2022, https://www.thecornellreview.org/breaking-recent-cornell-graduate-attacked-while-putting-up-pro-democracy-posters/.

18. "International Students in the United States," College Choice, January 21, 2023, https://www.collegechoice.net/choosing-a-college/popular-us-colleges-for-international-students/.

19. Sarah McLaughlin, "Apology for Anti-Asian Bigotry Statement at Carnegie Mellon Highlights Difficulty of Discussing China on Campus," *FIRE*, March 30, 2021, https://www.thefire.org/apology-for-anti-asian-bigotry-statement-at-carnegie-mellon-highlights-difficulty-of-discussing-china-on-campus/.

20. Sebastian Rotella, "Even on U.S. Campuses, China Cracks Down on Students Who Speak Out," *ProPublica*, November 30, 2021, https://www.propublica.org/article/even-on-us-campuses-china-cracks-down-on-students-who-speak-out.

21. Anastasya Lloyd-Damnjanovic, "A Preliminary Study of PRC Political Influence and Interference Activities in American Higher Education," Wilson Center, accessed February 3, 2022, https://www.wilsoncenter.org/sites/default/files/media/documents/publication/prc_political_influence_full_report.pdf.

22. "COVID 'Hate Crimes' Against Asian Americans on Rise," *BBC News*, May 21, 2021, https://www.bbc.com/news/world-us-canada-56218684.

23. Will Aiken, "CSA and College Republicans Go to SA over Tibet and Uighur Dispute," *Campus Times*, October 3, 2019, http://www.campustimes.org/2019/10/03/csa-and-college-republicans-go-to-sa-over-tibet-and-uighur-dispute/.

24. Efua Agyare-Kumi, "Painting War Brings International Controversy to Tunnel," *Campus Times*, November 25, 2019, http://www.campustimes.org/2019/11/25/painting-war-brings-international-controversy-to-tunnel/.

25. Editorial Board, "The Painted Tunnel Provides a Primer in Dialogue," *Campus Times*, November 27, 2019, http://www.campustimes.org/2019/11/27/the-painted-tunnel-provides-a-primer-in-dialogue/.

26. Alexander Bowe, "China's Overseas United Front Work: Background and Implications for the United States," U.S.-China Economic and Security Review Commission, August 24, 2018, https://www.uscc.gov/sites/default/files/Research/China%27s%20Overseas%20United%20Front%20Work%20-%20Background%20and%20Implications%20for%20US_final_0.pdf.

27. Bethany Allen-Ebrahimian, "China's Long Arm Reaches into American Campuses," *Foreign Policy*, March 7, 2018, https://foreignpolicy.com/2018/03/07/chinas-long-arm-reaches-into-american-campuses-chinese-students-scholars-association-university-communist-party/.

28. Miles Kenyon, "WeChat Surveillance Explained," Citizen Lab, May 7, 2020, https://citizenlab.ca/2020/05/wechat-surveillance-explained/.

29. Jeanne Whalen, "Chinese Censorship Invades the U.S. via WeChat," *Washington Post*, January 7, 2021, https://www.washingtonpost.com/technology/2021/01/07/wechat-censorship-china-us-ban/.

30. James Millward (@JimMillward), "Coordinated disruption of Brandeis webinar on Xinjiang: a thread," Twitter, November 15, 2020, https://twitter.com/JimMillward/status/1327980009055789057.

31. Sarah McLaughlin, "Brandeis Panel on Uyghur Muslims Faces Calls for Cancellation, Zoombombing," *FIRE*, November 24, 2020, https://www.thefire.org/brandeis-panel-on-uyghur-muslims-faces-calls-for-cancellation-zoombombing/.

32. Gilda Geist, "University President Responds to Zoom-Bombing Incident," *Justice*, February 2, 2022, https://www.thejustice.org/article/2022/01/university-president-responds-to-zoom-bombing-incident-brandeis.

33. Sarah McLaughlin, "Pressure Continues Against Campus Critics of China," *FIRE*, May 24, 2021, https://www.thefire.org/pressure-continues-against-campus-critics-of-china/.
34. Clark Kovacs, "Investigate the CSSA," *Chicago Maroon*, August 19, 2021, https://www.chicagomaroon.com/article/2021/8/19/investigate-cssa/.
35. Shizheng Tie, "Canceling Joshua Wong and Nathan Law, In the Name of Democracy," Change.org, February 3, 2020, https://www.change.org/p/johns-hopkins-school-board-stopping-an-event-that-divides-and-infuriates.
36. Emily McDonald and Greta Maras, "Hong Kong Activists Spark Controversy at FAS," *Johns Hopkins News-Letter*, February 27, 2020, https://www.jhunewsletter.com/article/2020/02/hong-kong-activists-spark-controversy-at-fas.
37. Austin Tong (@comrademeow), "Don't tread on me. #198964," Instagram, accessed July 20, 2020, https://archive.is/eBooc.
38. "Fordham Student Punished for Holding Gun in Instagram Photo Memorializing Tiananmen Square Massacre," *FIRE*, July 17, 2020, https://www.thefire.org/fordham-student-on-campus-probation-for-instagram-photo-holding-a-gun-memorializing-tiananmen-square-massacre/.
39. "10 Worst Colleges for Free Speech: 2021," *FIRE*, February 17, 2021, https://www.thefire.org/10-worst-colleges-for-free-speech-2021/.
40. William Gilligan, Email to Emerson College Student Body, September 30, 2021, https://www.thefire.org/research-learn/email-emerson-interim-president-william-gilligan-student-body-september-30-2021.
41. Sean Salai, "Conservative Student Group Blackballed by Massachusetts College for 'Anti-China Hate,'" *Washington Times*, February 18, 2022, https://www.washingtontimes.com/news/2022/feb/18/emerson-college-disavows-student-conservative-grou/.
42. "Sticker Shock: Emerson College Doubles Down on Censorship, Denies TPUSA Chapter's Appeal of 'Bias' Charge for Distributing Stickers Criticizing China's Government," *FIRE*, November 16, 2021, https://www.thefire.org/sticker-shock-emerson-college-doubles-down-on-censorship-denies-tpusa-chapters-appeal-of-bias-charge-for-distributing-stickers-criticizing-chinas-government/.

43. Adam Steinbaugh, "Emerson College Pooh-Poohs Free Speech: Deflecting Criticism over Censorship of 'China Kinda Sus' Stickers, Emerson Hides Tweets Critical of China's Government," *FIRE*, October 8, 2021, https://www.thefire.org/emerson-college-pooh-poohs-free-speech-deflecting-criticism-over-censorship-of-china-kinda-sus-stickers-emerson-hides-tweets-critical-of-chinas-government/.
44. Mario Cacciottolo, "The Streisand Effect: When Censorship Backfires," *BBC News*, June 15, 2012, https://www.bbc.com/news/uk-18458567.
45. Sarah Jackson-Han, "Student: Apology Was Fake," *Radio Free Asia*, April 18, 2008, https://web.archive.org/web/20210329055300/https://www.rfa.org/english/news/chinese_tibet-04182008142055.html.
46. Grace Wang, "The Old Man Who Lost His Horse," *China Digital Times*, May 11, 2008, https://chinadigitaltimes.net/2008/05/grace-wang-the-old-man-who-lost-his-horse-video-added/.
47. "Discourse Gone Awry," *Duke Chronicle*, April 16, 2008, https://www.dukechronicle.com/article/2008/04/discourse-gone-awry.
48. Wang, "Old Man."
49. *Global Times* (@globaltimesnews), "Chinese student Yang Shuping shamed and accused of slander by Chinese netizens," Twitter, May 22, 2017, https://twitter.com/globaltimesnews/status/866601636382167040.
50. Tom Phillips, "Chinese Student Abused for Praising 'Fresh Air of Free Speech' in US," *Guardian* (UK edition), May 23, 2017, https://www.theguardian.com/world/2017/may/23/china-yang-shuping-free-speech-university-of-maryland-us-student.
51. Ken Shepherd, "Yang Shuping, Univ. of Maryland Graduate, Apologizes for Offending China in Pro-Free Speech Address," *Washington Times*, May 24, 2017, https://www.washingtontimes.com/news/2017/may/24/yang-shuping-univ-of-maryland-graduate-apologizes-/.
52. Lloyd-Damnjanovic, "PRC Political Influence and Interference Activities."
53. Bethany Allen-Ebrahimian, "University of Minnesota Student Jailed in China over Tweets," *Axios*, January 22, 2020, https://www.axios.com/china-arrests-university-minnesota-twitter-e495cf47-d895-4014-9ac8-8dc76aa6004d.html.

54. Rotella, "China Cracks Down on Students."
55. Bethany Allen-Ebrahimian, "Zoom Closed Account of U.S.-Based Chinese Activist 'to Comply with Local Law,'" *Axios*, June 10, 2020, https://www.axios.com/zoom-closes-chinese-user-account-tiananmen-square-f218fed1-69af-4bdd-aac4-7eaf67f34084.html.
56. "Improving Our Policies as We Continue to Enable Global Collaboration," Zoom, June 11, 2020, https://blog.zoom.us/improving-our-policies-as-we-continue-to-enable-global-collaboration/.
57. Aruna Viswanatha and Aaron Tilley, "Zoom Executive in China Charged with Disrupting Tiananmen Memorials," *Wall Street Journal*, December 18, 2020, https://www.wsj.com/articles/zoom-executive-in-china-charged-with-disrupting-tiananmen-memorials-11608326277.
58. Rotella, "China Cracks Down on Students."
59. "President Daniels Responds to Chinese Student's Harassment," *Purdue Exponent*, December 15, 2021, https://www.purdueexponent.org/campus/article_aa3e67de-5de9-11ec-9246-af6384980cbb.html.
60. Charlie Parker, "Kazakhs Studying in UK Forced to Reveal Passwords," *Times* (UK), October 3, 2020, https://www.thetimes.co.uk/article/kazakhs-studying-in-uk-forced-to-reveal-passwords-q3t3v2bht.
61. Eric Fish, "End of an Era? A History of Chinese Students in America," *China Project*, May 12, 2020, https://thechinaproject.com/2020/05/12/end-of-an-era-a-history-of-chinese-students-in-america/.
62. Wilma Fairbank, *America's Cultural Experiment in China 1942–1949* (Department of State, 1976).
63. Fish, "End of an Era?"
64. Henry J. Kellermann, *Cultural Relations as an Instrument of U.S. Foreign Policy: The Educational Exchange Program Between the United States and Germany 1945–1954* (Department of State, 1978).
65. Yale Richmond, *Cultural Exchange & the Cold War: Raising the Iron Curtain* (Pennsylvania State University Press, 2003).

Chapter 2. The Censorship Bureaucracy and Its Victims

1. "Dalai Lama Arrives for Tour of U.S.," *New York Times*, September 4, 1979, https://www.nytimes.com/1979/09/04/archives/dalai-lama-arrives-for-tour-of-us.html.

2. James Nashold, "The Meeting of East and West: The Dalai Lama's First Trip to the United States," *Tibet Journal* 5, no. 1/2 (Spring/Summer 1980): 34–41, http://www.jstor.org/stable/43299969.
3. Shannon Tiezzi, "Obama Walks Tightrope with Dalai Lama Meeting," *Diplomat*, February 22, 2014, https://thediplomat.com/2014/02/obama-walks-tightrope-with-dalai-lama-meeting/.
4. Roberta Rampton and Sui-Lee Wee, "Obama Meets with Dalai Lama Despite China Warnings," *Reuters*, February 20, 2014, https://www.reuters.com/article/us-usa-china-tibet/obama-meets-with-dalai-lama-despite-china-warnings-idUSBREA1K01P20140221.
5. Valerie Strauss, "China Frowns on Dalai Lama's U.S. Visit," *Washington Post*, April 5, 1991, https://www.washingtonpost.com/archive/politics/1991/04/05/china-frowns-on-dalai-lamas-us-visit/b94ddf58-f050-465c-b884-c2196ffa9f7c/?utm_term=.660abf.
6. "On Partnerships with Foreign Governments: The Case of Confucius Institutes," American Association of University Professors, June 2014, https://www.aaup.org/report/confucius-institutes.
7. "Confucius Institute Inaugurated in San Diego," *China.org.cn*, March 27, 2009, http://www.china.org.cn/international/2009-03/27/content_17513402.htm.
8. University of Texas at Dallas, "A Texas First: Confucius Institute," news release, September 30, 2007, https://news.utdallas.edu/campus-community/a-texas-first-confucius-institute/.
9. Marco Rubio, "Rubio Joins Blackburn and Colleagues in Introducing Bill to Ensure Confucius Institutes Abide by Standards of Transparency," press release, March 13, 2020, https://www.rubio.senate.gov/public/index.cfm/2020/3/rubio-joins-blackburn-and-colleagues-in-introducing-bill-to-ensure-confucius-institutes-abide-by-standards-of-transparency.
10. U.S. Senate Permanent Senate Subcommittee on Investigations, *China's Impact on the U.S. Education System* (Government Printing Office, 2019).
11. Jamie P. Horsley, "It's Time for a New Policy on Confucius Institutes," Brookings Institution, April 1, 2021, https://www.brookings.edu/articles/its-time-for-a-new-policy-on-confucius-institutes/.

12. Ethan Epstein, "How China Infiltrated U.S. Classrooms," *Politico*, January 16, 2018, https://www.politico.com/magazine/story/2018/01/16/how-china-infiltrated-us-classrooms-216327/.

13. Rachelle Peterson, "Outsourced to China," National Association of Scholars, April 5, 2017, https://www.nas.org/reports/outsourced-to-china/full-report.

14. "Confucius Institutes: Vehicles of CCP Propaganda?," Stanford Center on China's Economy and Institution, updated April 1, 2022, https://sccei.fsi.stanford.edu/china-briefs/confucius-institutes-vehicles-ccp-propaganda.

15. U.S. Senate, *China's Impact*.

16. Janet Lorin and Brandon Kochkodin, "Harvard Leads U.S. Colleges That Received $1 Billion from China," *Bloomberg News*, February 6, 2020, https://www.bloomberg.com/news/articles/2020-02-06/harvard-leads-u-s-colleges-that-received-1-billion-from-china.

17. U.S. Department of Education, "U.S. Department of Education Launches Investigation into Foreign Gifts Reporting at Ivy League Universities," press release, February 12, 2020, https://www.pressreleasepoint.com/us-department-education-launches-investigation-foreign-gifts-reporting-ivy-league-universities.

18. Marshall Sahlins, *Confucius Institutes: Academic Malware* (Prickly Pear Press, 2014).

19. Marshall Sahlins, "Confucius Institutes: Academic Malware and Cold Warfare," *Inside Higher Ed*, July 25, 2018, https://www.insidehighered.com/views/2018/07/26/confucius-institutes-function-propaganda-arms-chinese-government-opinion.

20. Sahlins, *Confucius Institutes*.

21. Epstein, "How China Infiltrated U.S. Classrooms."

22. Editorial Board, "The Price of Confucius Institutes," *Washington Post*, June 21, 2014, https://www.washingtonpost.com/opinions/the-price-of-confucius-institutes/2014/06/21/4d7598f2-f7b6-11e3-a3a5-42be35962a52_story.html.

23. Isaac Stone Fish, "The Other Political Correctness," *New Republic*, September 4, 2018, https://newrepublic.com/article/150476/american-elite-universities-selfcensorship-china.

24. Bethany Allen-Ebrahimian, "How China Managed to Play Censor at a Conference on U.S. Soil," *Foreign Policy*, May 9, 2018, https://foreignpolicy.com/2018/05/09/how-china-managed-to-play-censor-at-a-conference-on-u-s-soil/.

25. "How Many Confucius Institutes Are in the United States?," National Association of Scholars, updated June 22, 2023, https://www.nas.org/blogs/article/how_many_confucius_institutes_are_in_the_united_states.

26. Marco Rubio, "Rubio Warns of Beijing's Growing Influence, Urges Florida Schools to Terminate Confucius Institute Agreements," press release, February 5, 2018, https://www.rubio.senate.gov/rubio-warns-of-beijing-s-growing-influence-urges-florida-schools-to-terminate-confucius-institute-agreements/.

27. Elizabeth Redden, "Closing Confucius Institutes," *Inside Higher Ed*, January 8, 2019, https://www.insidehighered.com/news/2019/01/09/colleges-move-close-chinese-government-funded-confucius-institutes-amid-increasing.

28. Michael McCaul, "McCaul, Cuellar Send Letter to Texas Universities Hosting Confucius Institutes," press release, April 5, 2018, https://mccaul.house.gov/media-center/press-releases/mccaul-cuellar-send-letter-to-texas-universities-hosting-confucius.

29. Elizabeth Redden, "Closing a Confucius Institute, at Congressmen's Request," *Inside Higher Ed*, April 8, 2018, https://www.insidehighered.com/news/2018/04/09/texas-am-cuts-ties-confucius-institutes-response-congressmens-concerns.

30. Connor O'Brien, "Senate Sends $717B Defense Bill to Trump," *Politico*, August 1, 2018, https://www.politico.com/story/2018/08/01/senate-defense-bill-trump-717791.

31. U.S. Department of State, "'Confucius Institute U.S. Center' Designation as a Foreign Mission Fact Sheet," fact sheet, August 13, 2020, https://2017-2021.state.gov/confucius-institute-u-s-center-designation-as-a-foreign-mission/index.html.

32. Yojana Sharma, "Taiwan Fills Gap Left by Confucius Institute Closures," *University World News*, December 2, 2021, https://www.universityworldnews.com/post.php?story=20211202125025734.

33. Rachelle Peterson, Ian Oxnevad, and Flora Yan, "After Confucius Institutes," National Association of Scholars, June 15, 2022,

https://www.nas.org/reports/after-confucius-institutes/full-report.

34. Anastasya Lloyd-Damnjanovic, "A Preliminary Study of PRC Political Influence and Interference Activities in American Higher Education," Wilson Center, accessed February 3, 2022, https://www.wilsoncenter.org/sites/default/files/media/documents/publication/prc_political_influence_full_report.pdf.

35. "Op-Ed: Why I Won't Accept the Dalai Lama as a Commencement Speaker," *UCSD Guardian*, February 7, 2017, https://ucsdguardian.org/2017/02/07/op-ed-why-i-wont-accept-the-dalai-lama-as-a-commencement-speaker/.

36. Elizabeth Redden, "Chinese Students vs. Dalai Lama," *Inside Higher Ed*, February 15, 2017, https://www.insidehighered.com/news/2017/02/16/some-chinese-students-uc-san-diego-condemn-choice-dalai-lama-commencement-speaker.

37. "English Translation of Chinese Students and Scholars Association Statement," UCSD Chinese Students and Scholars Association, February 26, 2017, https://docs.google.com/document/d/18kX-g2BAgmozWIc1iu1dBJQkurvXElkXiB8un35rASk/edit.

38. Lloyd-Damnjanovic, "Preliminary Study of PRC Political Influence."

39. Steven A. Cook, (@stevenacook), "Disappointed to learn that @Columbia's Provost effectively canceled this panel two days before the event," Twitter, April 3, 2019, https://twitter.com/stevenacook/status/1113428939303583744.

40. PEN America, "PEN America Response to the Canceled Panel at Columbia University," press release, April 3, 2019, https://pen.org/press-release/columbia-university-panel/.

41. Karen DeYoung, "Columbia University's Cancellation of Forum on Turkey Draws Criticism," *Washington Post*, April 4, 2019, https://www.washingtonpost.com/world/national-security/columbia-universitys-cancellation-of-forum-on-turkey-draws-criticism/2019/04/04/edb33654-5705-11e9-9136-f8e636f1f6df_story.html.

42. Arsen Ostrovsky (@Ostrov_A), "This delusional and fase accusation is nothing but a modern-day antisemitic blood libel," X, August 13, 2023, https://x.com/Ostrov_A/status/1690788248535089152.

43. Graham Piro, "Princeton Passes First 'Principles' Test, Declines Calls to Remove Book on Israeli-Palestinian Conflict from Course," *FIRE*,

August 31, 2023, https://thefire.org/news/princeton-passes-first
-principles-test-declines-calls-remove-book-israeli-palestinian
-conflict.

44. Sarah Cascone, "Beijing Attempted to Shut Down This Artist's International Art Exhibition. Here's How He and a Small Italian City Fought Back," *Artnet News*, November 15, 2021, https://news.artnet.com/art-world/italy-anti-chinese-government-badiucao-show-2034812.

45. Elisabetta Povoledo, "The Show Goes On, Even After China Tried to Shut It Down," *New York Times*, November 12, 2021, https://www.nytimes.com/2021/11/12/arts/design/badiucao-brescia-china.html.

46. Lloyd-Damnjanovic, "Preliminary Study of PRC Political Influence."

47. Elizabeth Redden, "The Blacklist Academic Leaders Ignore," *Inside Higher Ed*, July 13, 2008, https://www.insidehighered.com/news/2008/07/14/blacklist-academic-leaders-ignore.

48. Edward Wong, "China Denies Entry to an American Scholar Who Spoke Up for a Uighur Colleague," *New York Times*, July 7, 2014, https://www.nytimes.com/2014/07/08/world/asia/us-scholar-who-supported-uighur-colleague-is-denied-entry-to-china.html.

49. James A. Millward, "Being Blacklisted by China, and What Can Be Learned from It," *Medium*, December 28, 2017, https://jimmillward.medium.com/being-blacklisted-by-china-and-what-can-be-learned-from-it-faf05eb8e1e2.

50. Sheena Chestnut Greitens and Rory Truex, "Repressive Experiences Among China Scholars: New Evidence from Survey Data" (paper, University of Missouri and Princeton University, 2018), http://dx.doi.org/10.2139/ssrn.3243059.

51. Perry Link, "China: The Anaconda in the Chandelier," *ChinaFile*, April 11, 2002, https://www.chinafile.com/library/nyrb-china-archive/china-anaconda-chandelier.

52. Motion to Dismiss by Defendant Audrey Truschke, Hindu Am. Found. v. Viswanath, No. 1:21-cv-01268 (D.D.C. Aug. 27, 2021) (quoting Dr. Audrey Truschke [@AudreyTruschke], Twitter, April 8, 2021), https://static1.squarespace.com/static/5fd8d19b84774a17d4cd0bf7/t/612cc1df832e7a3f853d0525/1630323168007/Truschke+Motion+to+Dismiss+HAF+case+August+2021.pdf.

53. "Select Timeline of Hindutva Harassment of Scholars," Hindutva Harassment Field Manual, last updated June 2023, https://www.hindutvaharassmentfieldmanual.org/timeline.
54. "Delhi HC Bars 3 Historians from Publishing Defamatory Material on Vikram Sampath," *Times of India*, February 20, 2022, https://timesofindia.indiatimes.com/life-style/books/features/delhi-hc-bars-3-historians-from-publishing-defamatory-material-on-vikram-sampath/articleshow/89698944.cms.
55. Matteo N. Wang, "The End of the Harvard Century," *Harvard Crimson*, April 23, 2020, https://www.thecrimson.com/article/2020/4/23/harvard-china-scrutiny/.
56. Yuichiro Kakutani, "Harvard Canceled Human Rights Event as Its President Met with Xi Jinping," *Free Beacon*, May 4, 2020, https://freebeacon.com/national-security/harvard-canceled-human-rights-event-as-its-president-met-with-xi-jinping/.
57. Megan Zahneis, "Columbia U. Canceled an Event on Chinese Human-Rights Violations. Organizers See a University Bowing to Intimidation.," *Chronicle of Higher Education*, November 19, 2019, https://www.chronicle.com/article/columbia-u-canceled-an-event-on-chinese-human-rights-violations-organizers-see-a-university-bowing-to-intimidation.
58. Ishaan Parmar and Alexandria Johnson, "Pro-Hong Kong, Pro-China Protesters Clash Ahead of NYU Law Human Rights Panel," *Washington Square News*, November 18, 2019, https://nyunews.com/news/2019/11/19/students-rally-at-hong-kong-panel/.
59. Zahneis, "Columbia U. Canceled an Event on Chinese Human-Rights Violations."
60. "Love Overseas Students, Pass on Love for Studying Abroad," trans. Google Translate, Consulate General of the People's Republic of China in New York, September 14, 2022, http://newyork.china-consulate.gov.cn/lghd/202209/t20220914_10766133.htm.
61. "Made in Hollywood, Censored by Beijing," PEN America, accessed March 31, 2022, https://pen.org/report/made-in-hollywood-censored-by-beijing/.
62. Isaac Stone Fish, *America Second: How America's Elites Are Making China Stronger* (Alfred A. Knopf, 2022).

63. Zach Sharf, "Judd Apatow Calls Out Hollywood Censorship in China: 'They've Bought Our Silence with Money,'" *IndieWire*, September 16, 2020, https://www.indiewire.com/2020/09/judd-apatow-hollywood-censoring-films-china-1234586770/.

64. Ian Stewart, "Netflix Drops Hasan Minhaj Episode in Saudi Arabia at Government's Request," *NPR*, January 1, 2019, https://www.npr.org/2019/01/01/681469011/netflix-drops-hasan-minhaj-episode-in-saudi-arabia-at-governments-request.

65. Alex Marshall, "Netflix Expands into a World Full of Censors," *New York Times*, October 31, 2019, https://www.nytimes.com/2019/10/31/arts/television/netflix-censorship-turkey-india.html.

66. L.A. Larkin, "Caving to Insidious Chinese Censorship," *ABC News*, April 3, 2014, https://www.abc.net.au/news/2014-04-04/larkin-caving-to-insidious-chinese-censorship/5367068.

67. Oliver Telling, "British Publishers Censor Books for Western Readers to Appease China," *Financial Times*, March 14, 2022, https://www.ft.com/content/63cbf209-656f-4f99-9ee3-722755c228ed.

Chapter 3. How Did We Get Here?

1. "American University Launches Bogus Harassment Investigation into Students who Criticized Leaked Supreme Court Abortion Ruling in Private Group Chat," *FIRE*, June 24, 2022, https://www.thefire.org/american-university-launches-bogus-harassment-investigation-into-students-who-criticized-leaked-supreme-court-abortion-ruling-in-private-group-chat/.

2. "American University Students' GroupMe Transcript re: Abortion Rights, May 2, 2022" *FIRE*, https://www.thefire.org/american-university-students-groupme-transcript-re-abortion-rights-may-2-2022/.

3. Vimal Patel, "A Lecturer Showed a Painting of the Prophet Muhammad. She Lost Her Job," *New York Times*, January 8, 2023, https://www.nytimes.com/2023/01/08/us/hamline-university-islam-prophet-muhammad.html.

4. Scott Jaschik, "Academic Freedom vs. Rights of Muslim Students," *Inside Higher Ed*, January 2, 2023, https://www.insidehighered.com/news/2023/01/03/debates-whether-academic-freedom-includes-images-offensive-muslims.

5. Adam Steinbaugh, "Hamline University President Triples Down in Defending Instructor's Nonrenewal for Showing Muhammad Painting," *FIRE*, January 12, 2023, https://www.thefire.org/news/hamline-university-president-triples-down-defending-instructors-nonrenewal-showing-muhammad.

6. Council on American-Islamic Relations, "CAIR Announces Official Position on Hamline University Controversy, Islamophobia Debate," press release, January 13, 2023, https://www.cair.com/press_releases/cair-announces-official-position-on-hamline-university-controversy-islamophobia-debate/.

7. "Public University Rejects Animal Rights Club, Citing 'Emotional Risk' to Students," *FIRE*, December 10, 2019, https://www.thefire.org/public-university-rejects-animal-rights-club-citing-emotional-risk-to-students/.

8. Azhar Majeed, "Read a Book, Harass a Co-Worker at IUPUI," *FIRE*, March 5, 2008, https://www.thefire.org/read-a-book-harass-a-co-worker-at-iupui/.

9. Hannan Adely, "Rutgers Clears Professor Who Said He 'Hates White People,'" *NorthJersey*, November 15, 2018, https://www.northjersey.com/story/news/2018/11/15/no-punishment-rutgers-university-professor-over-white-people-comments-facebook/2016377002/.

10. Adam Steinbaugh, "Essex County College Tells The Intercept Its Termination of Lisa Durden is Being Mischaracterized," *FIRE*, January 26, 2018, https://www.thefire.org/news/essex-county-college-tells-intercept-its-termination-lisa-durden-being-mischaracterized.

11. Adam Steinbaugh, "After FIRE Lawsuit, Essex County College Finally Turns Over Documents About Firing of Black Lives Matter Advocate," *FIRE*, January 23, 2018, https://www.thefire.org/after-fire-lawsuit-essex-county-college-finally-turns-over-documents-about-firing-of-black-lives-matter-advocate.

12. "Scholars Under Fire Database," FIRE, accessed May 12, 2022, https://www.thefire.org/research/scholars-under-fire-database/#home/.

13. "FIRE, NCAC Call on Fordham to Recognize Students for Justice in Palestine," *FIRE*, January 25, 2017, https://www.thefire.org/fire-ncac-call-on-fordham-to-recognize-students-for-justice-in-palestine/.

14. "Nursing Student Expelled After Writing Assignment About a Shooting Labeled 'Insensitive,'" *FIRE*, September 9, 2021, https://

www.thefire.org/nursing-student-expelled-after-writing-assignment-about-a-shooting-labeled-insensitive.

15. "FIRE Tells Rocky Mountain College to Rescind Ban on 'Divisive' Displays, Including Crosses," *FIRE*, November 7, 2019, https://www.thefire.org/news/fire-tells-rocky-mountain-college-rescind-ban-divisive-displays-including-crosses/.

16. "Syracuse Slams Students with Multi-Year Suspensions for Satirical Fraternity Roast," *FIRE*, June 8, 2018, https://www.thefire.org/syracuse-slams-students-with-multi-year-suspensions-for-satirical-fraternity-roast.

17. Sarah McLaughlin, "Does Linfield College Respect Freedom of Expression? We Asked—and Linfield Didn't Answer," *FIRE*, June 30, 2017, https://www.thefire.org/news/does-linfield-college-respect-freedom-expression-we-asked-and-linfield-didnt-answer.

18. Ryne Weiss, "Trinity College Administration Recognizes 'Churchill Club,' Even as Student Government Votes to Deny Recognition," *FIRE*, May 1, 2019, https://www.thefire.org/trinity-college-administration-recognizes-churchill-club-even-as-student-government-votes-to-deny-recognition.

19. "Pro-Israel Group Denied Recognition by Williams College Student Government, administration's response falls short," *FIRE*, May 15, 2019, https://www.thefire.org/pro-israel-group-denied-recognition-by-williams-college-student-government-administrations-response-falls-short.

20. "Wichita State Student Government Refuses to Recognize Libertarian Student Group Because of First Amendment Advocacy," *FIRE*, April 7, 2017, https://www.thefire.org/news/wichita-state-student-government-refuses-recognize-libertarian-student-group-because-first.

21. "Citing the 'Harm' of Open Discussion, Emory Law's Student Government Denies Recognition to Student Free Speech Group," *FIRE*, January 10, 2022, https://www.thefire.org/news/citing-harm-open-discussion-emory-laws-student-government-denies-recognition-student-free.

22. Katlyn Patton, "Worcester State Stands Idle as Student Government Violates First Amendment," *FIRE*, April 21, 2020, https://www.thefire

.org/news/worcester-state-stands-idle-student-government-violates-first-amendment.

23. Ari Cohn, "Students, Faculty, and Administrators Launch Attack on Texas State University Newspaper," *FIRE*, December 13, 2017, https://www.thefire.org/students-faculty-and-administrators-launch-attack-on-texas-state-university-newspaper/.

24. Sarah McLaughlin, "Wesleyan Student Assembly Strikes Again," *FIRE*, March 23, 2016, https://www.thefire.org/wesleyan-student-assembly-strikes-again.

25. "2021 College Free Speech Rankings," FIRE, September 21, 2021, https://www.thefire.org/research-learn/2021-college-free-speech-rankings.

26. Adam Steinbaugh, "Bias Response Teams and the Distinction Between Protected and Unprotected Speech," *FIRE*, February 8, 2017, https://www.thefire.org/bias-response-teams-and-the-distinction-between-protected-and-unprotected-speech.

27. "Spotlight on Speech Codes 2017," FIRE, accessed November 5, 2022, https://www.thefire.org/research-learn/spotlight-speech-codes-2017.

28. "COVID on Campus: The Pandemic's Impact on Student and Faculty Speech Rights," FIRE, February 16, 2021, https://www.thefire.org/research/publications/one-mans-vulgarity-art-censorship-on-american-campuses/one-mans-vulgarity-art-censorship-on-american-campuses-full-text.

29. "LAWSUIT: A History Professor Advocated for Removing Confederate Statues. Then His College Fired Him," *FIRE*, March 8, 2022, https://www.thefire.org/lawsuit-a-history-professor-advocated-for-removing-confederate-statues-then-his-college-fired-him.

30. Susan Kruth, "After Backlash, Skyline College Apologizes for 'Badly Worded' Media Policy," *FIRE*, March 25, 2014, https://www.thefire.org/after-backlash-skyline-college-apologizes-for-badly-worded-media-policy.

31. Greg Lukianoff and Ryne Weiss, "Catching Up with 'Coddling' Part Twelve: Protecting the Brand and Apolitical Censorship—the 'Big Middle' of FIRE's Cases," *FIRE*, March 12, 2021, https://www.thefire.org/catching-up-with-coddling-part-twelve-protecting-the-brand-and-apolitical-censorship-the-big-middle-of-fires-cases.

32. Marieke Tuthill Beck-Coon, "FIRE Lawsuit Against Iowa State University Administrators Ends with Nearly $1 Million in Damages and Fees," *FIRE*, March 23, 2018, https://www.thefire.org/fire-lawsuit-against-iowa-state-university-administrators-ends-with-nearly-1-million-in-damages-and-fees.

33. Adam Steinbaugh, "Nine Years Later, UCLA Complains—Again—About Online Critic," *FIRE*, November 2, 2018, https://www.thefire.org/nine-years-later-ucla-complains-again-about-online-critic.

34. Adam Steinbaugh, "As Los Angeles City Council Demands Cancellation of Students for Justice in Palestine Conference, UCLA Backs Down on Spurious Trademark Threat," *FIRE*, November 8, 2018, https://www.thefire.org/as-los-angeles-city-council-demands-cancellation-of-students-for-justice-in-palestine-conference-ucla-backs-down-on-spurious-trademark-threat.

35. Nicolaus Mills, "The Corporatization of Higher Education," *Dissent*, Fall 2012, https://www.dissentmagazine.org/article/the-corporatization-of-higher-education.

36. Editorial Board, "Editorial: Colleges' Overreliance on Adjunct Faculty Is Bad for Students, Instructors and Academic Freedom," *Los Angeles Times*, November 28, 2021, https://www.latimes.com/opinion/story/2021-11-28/editorial-colleges-overreliance-on-adjunct-faculty-is-bad-for-students-instructors-and-academic-freedom.

37. Adam Steinbaugh, "Babson Falsely Claimed It Was 'Cooperating' with Massachusetts State Police over Professor's 'Threatening' Facebook Post," *FIRE*, February 17, 2020, https://www.thefire.org/babson-falsely-claimed-it-was-cooperating-with-massachusetts-state-police-over-professors-threatening-facebook-post.

38. Tamar Lewin, "Gap Widens for Faculty at Colleges, Report Finds," *New York Times*, April 8, 2013, https://www.nytimes.com/2013/04/08/education/gap-in-university-faculty-pay-continues-to-grow-report-finds.html.

39. Sarah Kendzior, "Academia's Indentured Servants," *Al Jazeera*, April 11, 2013, https://www.aljazeera.com/opinions/2013/4/11/academias-indentured-servants.

40. "Northwestern Risks Academic Freedom (Again) by Censoring Bioethics Journal with 'Bad Girls' Theme," *FIRE*, June 16, 2015,

https://www.thefire.org/northwestern-risks-academic-freedom-again-by-censoring-bioethics-journal-with-bad-girls-theme.

41. Adam Steinbaugh, "Linfield University Sued over Process-Free Termination of Tenured Professor, Daniel Pollack-Pelzner," *FIRE*, July 16, 2021, https://www.thefire.org/linfield-university-sued-over-process-free-termination-of-tenured-professor-daniel-pollack-pelzner.

42. Adam Steinbaugh, "Why Did a Bellevue College Administrator Censor an Art Installation Memorializing Japanese-American Internment Camps? Public Records Suggest a Motive," *FIRE*, May 19, 2020, https://www.thefire.org/why-did-a-bellevue-college-administrator-censor-an-art-installation-memorializing-japanese-american-internment-camps-public-records-suggest-a-motive.

43. "No Comment: Public Universities' Social Media Use and the First Amendment," FIRE, accessed September 10, 2022, https://www.thefire.org/research/publications/miscellaneous-publications/social-media-use-and-the-first-amendment/no-comment-public-universities-social-media-use-and-the-first-amendment.

44. Elizabeth Paton, "Versace, Givenchy and Coach Apologize to China After T-Shirt Row," *New York Times*, August 12, 2019, https://www.nytimes.com/2019/08/12/fashion/china-donatella-versace-t-shirt.html.

45. Isaac Stone Fish, "How China Gets American Companies to Parrot Its Propaganda," *Washington Post*, October 11, 2019, https://www.washingtonpost.com/outlook/how-china-gets-american-companies-to-parrot-its-propaganda/2019/10/11/512f7b8c-eb73-11e9-85c0-85a098e47b37_story.html.

46. Vincent Ni, "John Cena 'Very Sorry' for Saying Taiwan Is a Country," *Guardian* (UK edition), May 25, 2021, https://www.theguardian.com/world/2021/may/26/john-cena-very-sorry-for-saying-taiwan-is-a-country.

47. Rhoda Kwan, "Kodak Deletes Xinjiang Photo from Instagram, Vows to 'Respect Chinese Gov't,'" *Hong Kong Free Press*, July 21, 2021, https://hongkongfp.com/2021/07/21/kodak-deletes-xinjiang-photo-from-instagram-vows-to-respect-chinese-govt.

48. Christian Schneider, "Syracuse U. Dean Apologizes for Email Calling Tibet a Country Separate from China," *College Fix*, February 11, 2022,

https://www.thecollegefix.com/syracuse-u-dean-apologizes-for-email-calling-tibet-a-country-separate-from-china.

49. Christian Schneider, "Duke Mum on Whether It Apologized for Calling Tibet a Country," *College Fix*, February 3, 2022, https://www.thecollegefix.com/duke-mum-on-whether-it-apologized-for-calling-tibet-a-country.

50. Dan Patrick (@Dan Patrick), "I will not stand by and let looney Marxist UT professors poison the minds of young students with Critical Race Theory," Twitter, February 15, 2022, https://twitter.com/DanPatrick/status/1493694009600053250.

51. Dan Patrick, "Statement on Plans for Higher Education and Tenure," statement, February 18, 2022, https://www.ltgov.texas.gov/2022/02/18/lt-gov-dan-patrick-statement-on-plans-for-higher-education-and-tenure.

52. "Victory: After FIRE Lawsuit, Court Halts Enforcement of Key Provisions of the Stop WOKE Act Limiting How Florida Professors Can Teach About Race, Sex," *FIRE*, November 17, 2022, https://www.thefire.org/news/victory-after-fire-lawsuit-court-halts-enforcement-key-provisions-stop-woke-act-limiting-how.

53. Adam Steinbaugh, "Doubling Down: Iowa State Again Insists New 'Critical Race Theory' Law Applies to Its Faculty and Classes," *FIRE*, July 29, 2021, https://www.thefire.org/doubling-down-iowa-state-again-insists-new-critical-race-theory-law-applies-to-its-faculty-and-classes.

54. Kenneth Stern, "Will Campus Criticism of Israel Violate Federal Law?," *New York Times*, December 12, 2016, https://www.nytimes.com/2016/12/12/opinion/will-campus-criticism-of-israel-violate-federal-law.html.

55. Felicia Somnez and Anjuman Ali, "House Votes for Legislation to Combat Islamophobia Abroad After Republican Falsely Accuses Rep. Omar of Being 'Affiliated With' Terrorist Organizations," *Washington Post*, December 14, 2021, https://www.washingtonpost.com/politics/islamophobia-omar-house-democrats/2021/12/14/dc2beda4-5c61-11ec-8665-aed48580f911_story.html.

56. Jessica Moore, "Cornell Students Shocked by Arrest of Fellow Student Patrick Dai for Antisemitic Threats," *CBS News*, November 1, 2023, https://www.cbsnews.com/newyork/news/cornell-students-shocked-by-arrest-of-fellow-student-patrick-dai-for-antisemitic-threats/.

57. Claire O. Finkelstein, "To Fight Antisemitism on Campuses, We Must Restrict Speech," *Washington Post*, December 10, 2023, https://www.washingtonpost.com/opinions/2023/12/10/university-pennsylvania-president-magill-resigns-antisemitism-speech/.

58. Art Haywood, "Senator Art Haywood to Introduce Legislation to Combat Hate Speech," news release, December 12, 2023, https://www.senatorhaywood.com/senator-art-haywood-to-introduce-legislation-to-combat-hate-speech.

59. Letter from the State University System of Florida Chancellor Ray Rodrigues on the deactivation of Students for Justice in Palestine, October 24, 2023, https://www.thefire.org/research-learn/letter-state-university-system-florida-chancellor-ray-rodrigues-deactivation.

60. Jordan Howell, "Free Speech Promises Be Damned, Brandeis Bans Students for Justice in Palestine," *FIRE*, November 7, 2023, https://www.thefire.org/news/free-speech-promises-be-damned-brandeis-bans-students-justice-palestine.

61. Jennifer Schuessler, "Hunter College Pulls Screening of Film Critical of Israel," *New York Times*, November 16, 2023, https://www.nytimes.com/2023/11/16/arts/israel-documentary-hunter-cancel.html.

62. Columbia University (@Columbia), "What is Columbia doing to address antisemitism on campus and what is Columbia's reaction to calls for genocide against Jews?," Twitter, December 7, 2023, https://twitter.com/columbia/status/1732931212568641545?s=21&t=sfN64h5sWd2lFfss5HT0rA.

63. Michael Karlis, "Protesters Say UTSA Restricted Their Speech at March Calling for Gaza Ceasefire," *San Antonio Current*, April 24, 2024, https://www.sacurrent.com/news/utsa-students-say-school-restricted-speech-at-protest-calling-for-gaza-ceasefire-34379435.

Chapter 4. The Global Threat of Authoritarian Censorship in Academia

1. Sophie Richardson, "Numbers Tell the Story of Hong Kong's Human Rights," *Human Rights Watch*, December 6, 2019, https://www.hrw.org/news/2019/12/06/numbers-tell-story-hong-kongs-human-rights.

2. Amanda Coletta (@a_coletta), "Here is an email from the VP of the CSSA to the president of the university's student's union and equity and inclusion office," Twitter, accessed March 16, 2021, https://web

.archive.org/web/20210316201120/https://twitter.com/a_coletta/status/1371916994371551235.

3. Justin Mowat, "McMaster Student Government Bans Chinese Students' Group from Campus," *CBC News*, September 26, 2019, https://www.cbc.ca/news/canada/hamilton/mcmaster-china-student-association-ban-1.5298882.

4. Gerry Shih and Emily Rauhala, "Angry over Campus Speech by Uighur Activist, Chinese Students in Canada Contact Their Consulate, Film Presentation," *Washington Post*, February 14, 2019, https://www.washingtonpost.com/world/angry-over-campus-speech-by-uighur-activist-students-in-canada-contact-chinese-consulate-film-presentation/2019/02/14/a442fbe4-306d-11e9-ac6c-14eea99d5e24_story.html.

5. Joanna Chiu, *China Unbound: A New World Disorder* (House of Anansi Press, 2021).

6. Alex Joske, "The Party Speaks for You," Australian Strategic Policy Institute, June 9, 2020, https://www.aspi.org.au/report/party-speaks-you.

7. Matthew Fisher, "Canadian Universities Rely on Foreign Students. What If China Called Its Students Home?," *Global News*, June 15, 2020, https://globalnews.ca/news/7057654/china-students-canada.

8. Canadian Coalition on Human Rights in China, "Harassment & Intimidation of Individuals in Canada Working on China-related Human Rights Concerns: An Update as of March 2020," Amnesty Canada, May 12, 2020, https://www.amnesty.ca/human-rights-news/human-rights-defenders-increasingly-face-threats-intimidation-over-china-advocacy-report/.

9. Canadian Coalition on Human Rights in China, "Harassment & Intimidation."

10. "China Denies Role in Backlash Against Tibetan Student's Election at U of T," *CBC News*, February 15, 2019, https://www.cbc.ca/news/canada/toronto/china-denies-role-in-backlash-against-tibetan-student-s-election-at-u-of-t-1.5021226.

11. Canada (Minister of Citizenship and Immigration) v. Qu, 2001 FCA 399, [2001] 3 F.C. 3.

12. Samantha Craggs, "McMaster Cuts Chinese Institute, Worried by Discrimination," *CBC News*, February 11, 2013, https://www.cbc.ca

/news/canada/hamilton/headlines/mcmaster-cuts-chinese-institute-worried-by-discrimination-1.1321862.

13. "U of C Offends Chinese Government," *CBC News*, February 4, 2010, https://www.cbc.ca/news/canada/calgary/u-of-c-offends-chinese-government-1.898139.

14. Doug Lederman, "China Again Recognizes U. of Calgary," *Inside Higher Ed*, April 4, 2011, https://www.insidehighered.com/quicktakes/2011/04/05/china-again-recognizes-u-calgary.

15. Lydia Gall, "Hungary's Hypocritical War on Universities," *Human Rights Watch*, November 6, 2018, https://www.hrw.org/news/2018/11/06/hungarys-hypocritical-war-universities.

16. Nick Thorpe, "Hungary Broke EU Law by Forcing Out University, Says European Court," *BBC News*, October 6, 2020, https://www.bbc.com/news/world-europe-54433398.

17. Lydia Gall, "Hungary Renews Its War on Academic Freedom," *Human Rights Watch*, July 2, 2019, https://www.hrw.org/news/2019/07/02/hungary-renews-its-war-academic-freedom.

18. "Hungary: Anti-LGBT Law Reaches Children's Booksellers," *Deutsche Welle*, August 7, 2021, https://www.dw.com/en/hungary-orders-restrictions-on-childrens-books-with-gay-themes/a-58788814.

19. Szabolcs Panyi, "The Fight Over Fudan: A Chinese University in Budapest Sparks Reckoning for Sino-Hungarian Relations," *China Observers*, June 7, 2021, https://chinaobservers.eu/the-fight-over-fudan-a-chinese-university-in-budapest-sparks-reckoning-for-sino-hungarian-relations/.

20. "Change to Chinese University's Charter Dropping 'Freedom of Thought' Stirs Debate," *Reuters*, December 18, 2019, https://www.reuters.com/article/china-university/change-to-chinese-universitys-charter-dropping-freedom-of-thought-stirs-debate-idUKL4N28S2F3.

21. "Budapest Protest Against China's Fudan University Campus," *BBC News*, June 5, 2021, https://www.bbc.com/news/world-europe-57372653.

22. "Budapest Roads Renamed in Protest Against Chinese University," *BBC News*, June 2, 2021. https://www.bbc.com/news/world-europe-57333270.

23. "China Defends Hungary University Plan Following Budapest Protest," *Al Jazeera*, June 7, 2021, https://www.aljazeera.com/news/2021/6/7/china-defends-hungary-university-plan-following-budapest-protest.

24. Agence France-Presse, "Top Hungarian Court Bars Referendum on Chinese University Plan," *South China Morning Post*, May 18, 2022, https://www.scmp.com/news/china/diplomacy/article/3178264/top-hungarian-court-bars-referendum-chinese-university-plan.

25. Elizabeth Redden, "Censorship at China Studies Meeting," *Inside Higher Ed*, August 5, 2014, https://www.insidehighered.com/news/2014/08/06/accounts-confucius-institute-ordered-censorship-chinese-studies-conference.

26. Yojana Sharma, "Spanish University Caught in China-Taiwan Crossfire," *University World News*, August 30, 2018, https://www.universityworldnews.com/post.php?story=20180830173445642.

27. Yojana Sharma, "New Row over Confucius Institutes' Role on Campuses," *University World News*, October 29, 2021, https://www.universityworldnews.com/post.php?story=20211029094715105.

28. Sophie Hogan, "Chinese Students Signing 'Loyalty' Pledges Before Arrival in Sweden," *PIE News*, January 16, 2023, https://thepienews.com/news/chinese-students-signing-loyalty-pledges-arrival-sweden/.

29. Larissa Rhyn and Katrin Büchenbacher, "A Tweet Cost Him His Doctorate: The Extent of China's Influence on Swiss Universities," *Neue Zürcher Zeitung*, August 4, 2021, https://www.nzz.ch/english/swiss-phd-students-dismissal-spotlights-chinas-influence-ld.1638771.

30. "Translation: Indictment of Activists Huang Xueqin and Wang Jianbing," *Human Rights in China*, September 27, 2023, https://new.hrichina.org/press-work/translation-indictment-of-activists-huang-xueqin-and-wang-jianbing-1.

31. "China: 'Malicious' Conviction of #MeToo and Labour Activists Shows Beijing's Growing Fear of Dissent," *Amnesty International*, June 14, 2024, https://www.amnesty.org/en/latest/news/2024/06/china-malicious-conviction-of-metoo-and-labour-activists-shows-beijings-growing-fear-of-dissent/.

32. Jessie Lau, "China's Silenced Feminist: How Sophia Huang Xueqin Went Missing," *BBC News*, May 18, 2022, https://www.bbc.com/news/av/world-asia-china-61467135.

33. Steerpike, "Revealed: Huawei's Oxbridge Millions," *Spectator* (UK), December 30, 2021, https://www.spectator.co.uk/article/revealed-huawei-s-oxbridge-millions.

34. Lucy Fisher, "Jesus College Accepted £155,000 Contribution from Huawei," *Times* (UK), September 15, 2020, https://www.thetimes.co.uk/article/jesus-college-accepted-155-000-contribution-from-huawei-53rr7qmcf.

35. Amy Howell and Elizabeth Haigh, "Jesus College Professor Calls for Discussions of Uighur Human Rights to Have 'Both Views Represented,'" *Varsity*, June 5, 2021, https://www.varsity.co.uk/news/21616.

36. Sam Dunning, "The CCP Training Programme at the Heart of Cambridge," *Spectator* (UK), February 5, 2022, https://www.spectator.co.uk/article/the-ccp-training-programme-at-the-heart-of-cambridge.

37. Ben Ellery and Sam Dunning, "Jesus College Cambridge to Rename Its China Centre in Funding Shake-Up," *Times* (UK), May 31, 2022, https://www.thetimes.co.uk/article/jesus-college-cambridge-to-rename-its-china-centre-in-funding-shake-up-9z2dcmkl8.

38. Ben Chu, "Why Are Chinese Students So Keen on the UK?," *BBC News*, March 5, 2022, https://www.bbc.com/news/uk-scotland-60587499.

39. "Chinese Money Is Pouring into British Universities," *Economist*, March 12, 2022, https://www.economist.com/britain/2022/03/12/chinese-money-is-pouring-into-british-universities.

40. Tena Prelec, Saipira Furstenberg, John Heathershaw, and Catarina Thomson, "Is Academic Freedom at Risk from Internationalisation? Results from a 2020 Survey of UK Social Scientists," *International Journal of Human Rights* 26, no. 10 (2022): 1698–1722, https://www.tandfonline.com/doi/full/10.1080/13642987.2021.2021398.

41. Samantha Hoffman, "The Hong Kong National Security Law and UK Academic Freedom" (report, British Association for Chinese Studies, July 2021), http://bacsuk.org.uk/wp-content/uploads/2021/08/BACS-HK-SSL-report-HoffmanS.pdf.

42. "'Badge of Honour' - China Sanctions UK Politicians for Xinjiang 'Lies,'" *Reuters*, March 25, 2021, https://www.reuters.com/article/uk-china-uk-xinjiang/china-sanctions-uk-entities-individuals-over-xinjiang-lies-idUSKBN2BH3LK.

43. Donald Clarke, "Statement by Sanctioned Scholar Jo Smith Finley," *China Collection*, March 27, 2021, https://thechinacollection.org/statement-sanctioned-scholar-jo-smith-finley.

44. "Durham Students Warned by Chinese Embassy Not to Say Anything Negative," *Northern Echo*, December 5, 2014, https://www.thenorthernecho.co.uk/news/11649218.durham-students-warned-chinese-embassy-not-say-anything-negative.

45. Jim Waterson, "The Chinese Embassy Told Durham University's Debating Society Not to Let This Former Miss World Contestant Speak at a Debate," *Buzzfeed News*, February 10, 2017, https://www.buzzfeed.com/jimwaterson/the-chinese-embassy-told-durham-universitys-debating-society.

46. "Hong Kong Protests: Sheffield University Students Clash," *BBC News*, October 2, 2019, https://www.bbc.com/news/uk-england-south-yorkshire-49914304.

47. "Sheffield Hong Kong Protest Clash: Student Arrested," *BBC News*, October 8, 2019, https://www.bbc.com/news/uk-england-south-yorkshire-49980427.

48. David Leask, "Hong Kong Security Law: Students Demand Closure of Confucius Institutes," *Times* (UK), July 17, 2020, https://www.thetimes.co.uk/article/hong-kong-security-law-students-demand-closure-of-confucius-institutes-n6fk5k07z.

49. Jack Power, "Concern over Proposed Changes to UCD's Academic Freedom," *Irish Times*, April 9, 2020, https://www.irishtimes.com/news/education/concern-over-proposed-changes-to-ucd-s-academic-freedom-1.4225393.

50. Colm Keena, "UCD Staff Say College Institute Teaching Chinese Studies 'Devalues' Reputation," *Irish Times*, August 7, 2021, https://www.irishtimes.com/news/education/ucd-staff-say-college-institute-teaching-chinese-studies-devalues-reputation-1.4641042.

51. Jack Power, "UCD President Slates 'Misguided' Criticism of Beijing-Linked Institute," *Irish Times*, February 22, 2022, https://www.irishtimes.com/news/ireland/irish-news/ucd-president-slates-misguided-criticism-of-beijing-linked-institute-1.4809489.

52. University College Dublin (@ucddublin), "University statement on Ukraine," Twitter, February 28, 2022, https://twitter.com/ucddublin/status/1498315306825138178.

53. Katherine Donnelly and Alan Caulfield, "UCD 'Clarifies' Its Stance to 'Condemn' Ukraine Invasion After Professor Ben Tonra Resigns Position," *Irish Independent*, March 1, 2022, https://www.independent.ie/irish-news/ucd-clarifies-its-stance-to-condemn-ukraine-invasion-after-professor-ben-tonra-resigns-position/41398114.html.

54. Noel Baker, "Professor Resigns from Senior Role over UCD Response to Invasion of Ukraine," *Irish Examiner*, March 1, 2022, https://www.irishexaminer.com/news/arid-40819389.html.

55. Ronan McGreevy and Carl O'Brien. "Second UCD Statement on Ukraine Invasion 'Late and Grudging,'" *Irish Times*, March 2, 2022, https://www.irishtimes.com/news/ireland/irish-news/second-ucd-statement-on-ukraine-invasion-late-and-grudging-1.4816863.

56. John Brumby, "Foreign Students Are Our Fourth Largest Export, Even with the Pandemic," *Sydney Morning Herald*, February 19, 2021, https://www.smh.com.au/national/foreign-students-are-our-fourth-largest-export-even-with-the-pandemic-20210218-p573pz.html.

57. Nick McKenzie, Richard Baker, Sashka Koloff, and Chris Uhlmann, "The Chinese Communist Party's Power and Influence in Australia," *ABC News* (Australia), June 3, 2017, https://www.abc.net.au/news/2017-06-04/the-chinese-communist-partys-power-and-influence-in-australia/8584270.

58. Shashank Bengali and Maria Petrakis, "An Australian Student Denounced His University's Ties to China. Then He Became a Target," *Los Angeles Times*, December 21, 2020, https://www.latimes.com/world-nation/story/2020-12-21/student-australia-china-xi-jinping-uighurs-muslims.

59. Fergus Hunter, "Universities Must Accept China's Directives on Confucius Institutes, Contracts Reveal," *Sydney Morning Herald*, July 25, 2019, https://www.smh.com.au/politics/federal/universities-must-accept-china-s-directives-on-confucius-institutes-contracts-reveal-20190724-p52ab9.html.

60. "UQ Vice-Chancellor Receives Confucian Award from China's Vice-Premier," University of Queensland, December 7, 2015, https://www.uq.edu.au/news/article/2015/12/uq-vice-chancellor-receives-confucian-award-china%E2%80%99s-vice-premier.

61. Damien Cave, "Chinese Nationalists Bring Threat of Violence to Australia Universities," *New York Times*, July 30, 2019, https://www.nytimes.com/2019/07/30/world/australia/hong-kong-china-queensland-protests.html.
62. "They Don't Understand the Fear We Have," report, Human Rights Watch, June 30, 2021, https://www.hrw.org/report/2021/06/30/they-dont-understand-fear-we-have/how-chinas-long-reach-repression-undermines.
63. John Power, "University of Queensland Faces Heat for Naming Chinese Diplomat Xu Jie as Faculty Member," *South China Morning Post*, July 26, 2019, https://www.scmp.com/week-asia/geopolitics/article/3020168/university-queensland-faces-heat-naming-chinese-diplomat.
64. Australian Associated Press, "Queensland Court Dismisses Student Activist Drew Pavlou's Case Against Chinese Diplomat," *Guardian* (UK), August 9, 2020, https://www.theguardian.com/australia-news/2020/aug/10/queensland-court-dismisses-student-activist-drew-pavlous-case-against-chinese-diplomat.
65. Ben Smee, "University of Queensland Takes Disciplinary Action Against Pro-Hong Kong Student Activist," *Guardian* (UK), April 16, 2020, https://www.theguardian.com/australia-news/2020/apr/16/university-of-queensland-takes-disciplinary-action-against-pro-hong-kong-student-activist.
66. Keyue Xu, "Australian University Students Support Anti-China Rioter Expulsion," *Global Times*, April 24, 2020, https://www.globaltimes.cn/content/1186614.shtml.
67. Aaron Patrick, "The War Against Drew Pavlou, UQ's Rebel Senator," *Financial Review*, May 31, 2020, https://www.afr.com/work-and-careers/education/the-war-against-drew-pavlou-uq-s-rebel-senator-20200531-p54y1j.
68. Bethany Hiatt, "Leading Academics Slam UWA Student Guild for Putting 'Cultural Sensitivities' Above Free Speech," *PerthNow*, April 4, 2018, https://www.perthnow.com.au/news/wa/leading-academics-slam-uwa-student-guild-for-putting-cultural-sensitivities-above-free-speech-ng-b88795876z.
69. Richard Ferguson, "Victoria University Stops Anti-China Communist Party Film After Query," *Australian*, November 30, 2018, https://www

.theaustralian.com.au/higher-education/victoria-university-stops-antichina-communist-party-film-after-query/news-story/2cd94f68c4b6b32725ca576b271dde3e.

70. Lisa Visentin, "'Targeted Attack': Artist Abused as ANU-Based Gallery Takes Down Artwork Critical of Chinese Government," *Sydney Morning Herald*, March 26, 2021, https://www.smh.com.au/politics/federal/targeted-attack-artist-abused-as-anu-based-gallery-takes-down-artwork-critical-of-chinese-government-20210326-p57egh.html.

71. Ben Smee, "UNSW Faces Backlash After Deleting Twitter Post Critical of China's Crackdown in Hong Kong," *Guardian*, August 2, 2020, https://www.theguardian.com/australia-news/2020/aug/03/unsw-faces-backlash-after-deleting-twitter-post-critical-of-chinas-crackdown-in-hong-kong.

72. Yusha Zhao, "Australian University Under Attack for Article 'Interfering' HK Affairs," *Global Times*, August 1, 2020, https://www.globaltimes.cn/content/1196340.shtml.

73. Naaman Zhou, "University of NSW Vice-Chancellor Apologises for Removal of Tweet Criticising China's Human Rights Abuses," *Guardian*, August 5, 2020, https://www.theguardian.com/australia-news/2020/aug/05/university-of-nsw-vice-chancellor-apologises-for-removal-of-tweet-criticising-chinas-human-rights-abuses.

74. Naaman Zhou, "UNSW Criticised for Letter in Chinese with No Mention of Freedom of Speech," *Guardian*, August 6, 2020, https://www.theguardian.com/australia-news/2020/aug/07/unsw-criticised-for-letter-in-chinese-with-no-mention-of-freedom-of-speech.

75. Laura Walters, "AUT Scraps Tiananmen Square Event," *Newsroom*, July 30, 2019, https://www.newsroom.co.nz/2019/07/30/705870/aut-scraps-tiananmen-square-event.

76. "'Dismayed' Academics Rally Behind Anne-Marie Brady Over China Research Paper," *Stuff*, October 9, 2020, https://www.stuff.co.nz/national/300128923/dismayed-academics-rally-behind-annemarie-brady-over-china-research-paper.

77. Jamie Smyth, "New Zealand University Dismisses Complaints Against China Expert," *Financial Times*, December 11, 2020, https://www.ft.com/content/2b4f5f99-8c3c-477d-b7f1-447966e5cce5.

78. Joyce Lau and John Ross, "China Influence Case Tests Academic Freedom in New Zealand," *Times Higher Education*, November 2,

2020, https://www.timeshighereducation.com/news/china-influence-case-tests-academic-freedom-new-zealand.

79. International expert community letter in support of Professor Anne-Marie Brady, October 7, 2020, https://europeanvalues.cz/en/international-expert-community-letter-in-support-of-professor-anne-marie-brady.

80. Smyth, "New Zealand University Dismisses Complaints."

Chapter 5. Compromised Campuses

1. Carter Forinash, "Duke Plans for 'Close to Normal' Fall Semester, Administrators Tell Faculty," *Duke Chronicle*, March 18, 2021, https://www.dukechronicle.com/article/2021/03/duke-university-campus-restrictions-summer-fall-coronavirus-travel-conduct.

2. "Welcome to Duke Kunshan University," Duke Kunshan University, accessed June 30, 2022, https://www.dukekunshan.edu.cn/about/welcome-to-duke-kunshan-university.

3. Editorial Board, "More Questions About DKU," *Duke Chronicle*, September 17, 2013, https://web.archive.org/web/20150210170929/https://www.dukechronicle.com/articles/2013/09/17/more-questions-about-dku#.VNo7T-zP32c.

4. Chris Buckley, "China Warns Officials Against 'Dangerous' Western Values," *New York Times*, May 13, 2013, https://www.nytimes.com/2013/05/14/world/asia/chinese-leaders-warn-of-dangerous-western-values.html.

5. Lara Farrar, "China Bans 7 Topics in University Classrooms," *Chronicle of Higher Education*, May 20, 2013, https://www.chronicle.com/article/china-bans-7-topics-in-university-classrooms.

6. Steve Inskeep, "Pushing for Academic Freedom in China," *NPR*, June 3, 2019, https://www.npr.org/2019/06/03/729191914/a-foot-in-both-worlds-pushing-for-academic-freedom-in-china.

7. US Government Accountability Office, *U.S. Universities in China Emphasize Academic Freedom but Face Internet Censorship and Other Challenges*, GAO-16-757 (Washington, DC, 2016), accessed July 30, 2022, https://www.gao.gov/assets/gao-16-757.pdf.

8. Inskeep, "Pushing for Academic Freedom in China."

9. Charlie Colasurdo, "Q&A: Denis Simon Reflects on Five Years at DKU, Looks to Future at Duke," *Duke Chronicle*, July 17, 2020, https://www.dukechronicle.com/article/2020/07/duke-university-kunshan-denis-simon-five-years-dku.

10. Isaac Stone Fish, "No Academic Freedom for China," *Daily Beast*, July 13, 2017, https://www.thedailybeast.com/no-academic-freedom-for-china.

11. Peter Hessler, "A Teacher in China Learns the Limits of Free Expression," *New Yorker*, May 9, 2022, https://www.newyorker.com/magazine/2022/05/16/a-teacher-in-china-learns-the-limits-of-free-expression.

12. "Academics Speak Out on Rising Tensions at UK-China Branch Campuses," *Times Higher Education*, August 19, 2021, https://www.timeshighereducation.com/news/academics-speak-out-rising-tensions-uk-china-branch-campuses.

13. Emily Feng, "China Tightens Party Control of Foreign University Ventures," *Financial Times*, July 1, 2018, https://www.ft.com/content/4b885540-7b6d-11e8-8e67-1e1a0846c475.

14. Joe Wilensky, "Ethics Guidelines for International Engagement Developed," *Cornell Chronicle*, November 14, 2019, https://news.cornell.edu/stories/2019/11/ethics-guidelines-international-engagement-developed.

15. Elizabeth Redden, "Cutting Ties," *Inside Higher Ed*, October 28, 2018, https://www.insidehighered.com/news/2018/10/29/cornell-ends-partnership-chinese-university-over-academic-freedom-concerns.

16. Javier C. Hernández, "Cornell Cuts Ties with Chinese School After Crackdown on Students," *New York Times*, October 29, 2018, https://www.nytimes.com/2018/10/29/world/asia/cornell-university-renmin.html.

17. Alec Giufurta, "Faculty Slam Proposed Partnership with Chinese University Over Human Rights, Academic Freedom Violations," *Cornell Daily Sun*, February 26, 2021, https://cornellsun.com/2021/02/26/faculty-slam-proposed-partnership-with-chinese-university-over-human-rights-academic-freedom-violations.

18. Sara Javkhlan, "Faculty Senate Opposes Proposed Partnership with Peking University," *Cornell Daily Sun*, April 2, 2021, https://

cornellsun.com/2021/04/02/faculty-senate-opposes-proposed-partnership-with-peking-university.

19. "S.A. Resolution #39 Calling upon Cornell to Uphold Its Ethical Guidelines for International Engagements" (Cornell University Student Assembly, March 24, 2021), https://assembly.cornell.edu/sites/default/files/sa_r39_-_calling_upon_cornell_to_uphold_its_ethical_guidelines_for_international_engagements_0.pdf.

20. Yuichiro Kakutani, "China-Backed Student Group Pressures Cornell on Educational Partnership," *Washington Free Beacon*, April 15, 2021, https://freebeacon.com/national-security/china-backed-student-group-pressures-cornell-on-educational-partnership.

21. Tom Fleischman, "Hotel School, Peking University Green-Lighted to Launch Dual-Degree program," *Cornell Chronicle*, May 28, 2021, https://news.cornell.edu/stories/2021/05/hotel-school-peking-university-green-lighted-launch-dual-degree-program.

22. Bill Bostock, "Secretary of State Antony Blinken Says He Stands by Mike Pompeo's Designation That China Committed Genocide Against the Uighurs," *Business Insider*, January 28, 2021, https://www.businessinsider.com/antony-blinken-agrees-china-uighur-genocide-pompeo-designation-2021-1.

23. "China & Academic Freedom Teach In, Cornell University," posted May 9, 2022, by edf286, YouTube, https://www.youtube.com/watch?v=Ji-iN5Mpi_E.

24. Theo Wayt, "NYU Shanghai Quietly Added Pro-Government Course at Behest of Chinese Government," *VICE*, November 20, 2019, https://www.vice.com/en/article/43k9jn/nyu-shanghai-quietly-added-pro-government-course-at-behest-of-chinese-government.

25. Elizabeth Redden, "Who Controls NYU Shanghai?," *Inside Higher Ed*, August 24, 2021, https://www.insidehighered.com/news/2021/08/25/question-nyus-control-over-nyu-shanghai-sits-center-faculty-suit.

26. Isabella Farr, "Censored Book Incidents at NYU Shanghai," *On Century Avenue*, March 21, 2016, https://web.archive.org/web/20160420190136/http://oncenturyavenue.org/2016/03/censored-book-incident-at-nyu-shanghai/.

27. "About," Kean University, accessed August 3, 2022, https://www.kean.edu/about.

28. Nic Corbett, "Kean University Gets Approval from Chinese Government to Build Degree-Granting Campus," *NJ.com*, December 21, 2011, https://www.nj.com/news/2011/12/kean_university_gets_approval.html.

29. Elizabeth Redden, "Is Kean Giving Control of Its Overseas Faculty to Chinese Government?," *Inside Higher Ed*, November 15, 2018, https://www.insidehighered.com/news/2018/11/16/faculty-kean-u-china-campus-wont-be-kean-employees-much-longer.

30. Elizabeth Redden, "Chinese Communists Preferred," *Inside Higher Ed*, July 22, 2015, https://www.insidehighered.com/news/2015/07/23/hiring-materials-kean-us-campus-china-raise-questions-about-whether-institution.

31. John Kean Jr., "Kean University: Our China Campus Is Thriving, in Part, Because We Treat Our Teachers Right," *NJ.com*, December 11, 2018, https://www.nj.com/opinion/2018/12/kean-university-our-china-campus-is-thriving-in-part-because-we-treat-our-teachers-right.html.

32. Liam Knox, "Is There a Future for U.S. Campuses in China?," *Inside Higher Ed*, July 6, 2023, https://www.insidehighered.com/news/global/us-colleges-world/2023/07/06/challenges-compound-us-branch-campuses-china.

33. Alexander Cornwell, "U.S. University in Qatar Cancels Lebanese Band Talk After Anti-Gay Backlash," *Reuters*, February 3, 2020, https://www.reuters.com/article/us-qatar-society/u-s-university-in-qatar-cancels-lebanese-band-talk-after-anti-gay-backlash-idUSKBN1ZX1UY?mc_cid=4b83ee5d76&mc_eid=92eff05184.

34. Alexander Cornwell, "Qatar Foundation Rejects U.S. University's Reason for Scrapping Event After Anti-Gay Backlash," *Reuters*, February 5, 2020, https://www.reuters.com/article/us-qatar-society/qatar-foundation-rejects-u-s-universitys-reason-for-scrapping-event-after-anti-gay-backlash-idUSKBN1ZZ1IA.

35. Patrick Jack, "Will the World Cup Be an Own Goal for Qatar University Campuses?," *Times Higher Education*, November 28, 2022, https://www.timeshighereducation.com/news/will-world-cup-be-own-goal-qatar-university-campuses.

36. "Rights and Responsibilities of the Northwestern Community," Northwestern University in Qatar, accessed February 10, 2020,

https://my.qatar.northwestern.edu/student-life/code-of-conduct/student-rights.html.

37. "Northwestern University Faculty Handbook," Northwestern University, last updated August 5, 2021, https://www.northwestern.edu/provost/docs/faculty_handbook_aug2021.pdf.

38. "Rights and Responsibilities of the Northwestern Community," accessed August 5, 2022.

39. Nick Anderson, "In Qatar's Education City, U.S. Colleges Are Building an Academic Oasis," *Washington Post*, December 6, 2015, https://www.washingtonpost.com/local/education/in-qatars-education-city-us-colleges-are-building-an-academic-oasis/2015/12/06/6b538702-8e01-11e5-ae1f-af46b7df8483_story.html.

40. Sama Abduljawad, "Education City Universities Face Book Censorship," *NUQ Views* (formerly *Daily Q*), accessed August 22, 2022, https://qviews.qatar.northwestern.edu/3909/uncategorized/education-city-universities-face-book-censorship/.

41. Christopher M. Davidson, "US University Campuses in the Gulf Monarchies," in *The Political Economy of Education in the Arab World*, ed. Hicham Alaoui and Robert Springborg (Lynne Reinner, 2021), 125–46.

42. "Welcome to Georgetown University in Qatar," Georgetown University Qatar, accessed August 22, 2022, https://www.qatar.georgetown.edu/.

43. Kristina Bogos, "American Universities in a Gulf of Hypocrisy," *New York Times*, December 15, 2016, https://www.nytimes.com/2016/12/15/opinion/american-univisities-nyu-georgetown-in-a-gulf-of-hypocrisy.html.

44. "Code of Conduct," Georgetown University Qatar, accessed August 29, 2022, https://www.qatar.georgetown.edu/current-students/policies-and-procedures/code-conduct.

45. "Georgetown Qatar Cancels 'God Is Woman' Event After Social Media Backlash," *Al Bawaba*, October 9, 2018, https://www.albawaba.com/loop/georgetown-qatar-cancels-god-woman-event-after-social-media-backlash-1197458.

46. Menatalla Ibrahim and Saad Ejaz, "Georgetown Cancels Religious Debate After Backlash," *NUQ Views* (formerly *Daily Q*), updated October 10, 2018, https://qviews.qatar.northwestern.edu/9003/uncategorized/georgetown-cancels-religious-debate-after-backlash/.

47. Georgetown University in Qatar (@GUQatar), "Since the event was not sanctioned by the University and did not follow the appropriate policies," Twitter, October 8, 2018, https://twitter.com/GUQatar/status/1049446012975280129.
48. Ibrahim, "Georgetown Cancels Religious Debate."
49. "10 Worst Colleges for Free Speech: 2019," *FIRE*, February 12, 2019, https://www.thefire.org/news/10-worst-colleges-free-speech-2019.
50. Catriona Kendall, "Georgetown in Qatar Ranks Poorly on Free Speech," *Georgetown Hoya*, February 15, 2019, https://thehoya.com/news/gu-q-ranks-poorly-free-speech.
51. Kendall, "Georgetown in Qatar Ranks Poorly."
52. "Speech and Expression Policy," Georgetown University Qatar, accessed August 29, 2022, https://www.qatar.georgetown.edu/current-students/policies-and-procedures/speech-and-expression-policy.
53. "United Arab Emirates' Experiments with Branch Campuses Have Mixed Results," *Al-Fanar Media*, October 13, 2014, https://www.al-fanarmedia.org/2014/10/uaes-experiments-branch-campuses-mixed-results.
54. "UAE: Jailed British Academic Denied Rights," *Human Rights Watch*, October 21, 2018, https://www.hrw.org/news/2018/10/21/uae-jailed-british-academic-denied-rights.
55. Matthew Hedges, "An Ally Held Me as a Spy—and the West Is Complicit," *Atlantic*, January 25, 2019, https://www.theatlantic.com/international/archive/2019/01/matthew-hedges-uae-held-me-spy-west-complicit/581200.
56. "UAE Appeals Court Sentences Matthew Hedges to Life in Prison," *Al Jazeera*, November 21, 2018, https://www.aljazeera.com/news/2018/11/21/uae-appeals-court-sentences-matthew-hedges-to-life-in-prison.
57. Nazia Parveen and Patrick Wintour, "Matthew Hedges: Pardoned Academic Returns to UK," *Guardian* (UK), November 27, 2018, https://www.theguardian.com/uk-news/2018/nov/27/matthew-hedges-jailed-academic-returns-to-uk-after-uae-pardon.
58. David Batty, "Two More UK Universities Cut Ties with UAE over Hedges Jailing," *Gulf Times*, November 25, 2018, https://www.gulf-times.com/story/614102/Two-more-UK-universities-cut-ties-with-UAE-over-He.

59. John Archer et al., "NYU Hedges Petition," November 22, 2018, https://docs.google.com/document/u/1/d/e/2PACX-1vQe5AohCyz C2lUgNP_s7ZiUfL6BjEZqdYaSksc56y4JiyrMvXzSzGUj0bQuwwIuE pe1CglVxMkTg6dU/pub.
60. NYU President Andrew Hamilton, letter of response to faculty petition November 2018, November 25, 2018, https://www.nyu.edu /about/leadership-university-administration/office-of-the-president /communications/letter-of-response-to-faculty-petition-november -2018.html.
61. Editorial Board, "NYU Has an Abu Dhabi Problem," *Washington Square News*, November 26, 2018, https://nyunews.com/2018/11/26 /nyuad-uae-hedges-academic-freedom.
62. Meghna Maharishi, "Faculty Discuss NYU's Ties to Abu Dhabi," *Washington Square News*, December 4, 2018, https://nyunews.com /2018/12/03/faculty-forum-uae-academic-freedom/.
63. "Hamilton, in Interview with WSN, Says NYU Should Not Be Democratic," *Washington Square News*, May 14, 2019, https://nyunews.com /news/2019/05/14/nyu-president-hamilton-says-nyu-should-not-be -democratic.
64. Sally Weale, "Cambridge University Accused of Faustian Pact in Planned £400m Deal with UAE," *Guardian*, July 7, 2021, https:// www.theguardian.com/education/2021/jul/07/cambridge -university-accused-of-faustian-pact-in-planned-400m-deal-with -uae.
65. Weale, "Cambridge University Accused of Faustian Pact."
66. Ben Ellery, Sam Dunning, and Oliver Wright, "Huawei 'Infiltrates' Cambridge University Research Centre," *Times* (UK), September 13, 2021, https://www.thetimes.co.uk/article/huawei-infiltrates -cambridge-university-research-centre-kn6m5lnhc.
67. "Principles for Managing International Risks," University of Cambridge, accessed August 31, 2022, https://www.strategic-partnerships .admin.cam.ac.uk/managing-risks-international-engagement /principles-managing-international-risks.
68. "Cambridge University Pauses £400m UAE Deal over Spyware Claim," *BBC News*, October 15, 2021, https://www.bbc.com/news/uk -england-cambridgeshire-58926039.

69. Mohamad Bazzi, "N.Y.U. in Abu Dhabi: A Sectarian Bargain," *New York Times*, September 26, 2017, https://www.nytimes.com/2017/09/26/opinion/nyu-abu-dhabi.html.

70. Josh Varlin, "Interview with Arang Keshavarzian, NYU Professor Barred from the UAE," *World Socialist Web Site*, February 26, 2018, https://www.wsws.org/en/articles/2018/02/26/kesh-f26.html.

71. Stephanie Saul, "N.Y.U. Professor Is Barred by United Arab Emirates," *New York Times*, March 16, 2015, https://www.nytimes.com/2015/03/17/nyregion/nyu-professor-is-barred-from-the-united-arab-emirates.html.

72. Dharma Niles and Krish Dev, "'Extremely Disturbing': Concerns over Academic Freedom at NYU Abu Dhabi Surface Following Policies Restricting Attire at Graduation," *Washington Square News*, June 9, 2024, https://nyunews.com/news/2024/06/09/nyu-abu-dhabi-free-speech/.

73. Abdi Latif Dahir, "The 'Hotel Rwanda' Hero Is on Trial. Here's What We Know," *New York Times*, February 16, 2021, https://www.nytimes.com/2021/02/16/world/africa/rwanda-paul-rusesabagina-trial.html.

74. "Rwanda," Freedom House, accessed September 6, 2022, https://freedomhouse.org/country/rwanda/freedom-world/2022.

75. Madelyn Glymour, "Kagame's Visit Sparks Protest, Controversy," *Tartan*, September 19, 2011, https://thetartan.org/2011/9/19/news/local_protest_kagame.

Chapter 6. The Surveilled Classroom

1. "Hong Kong: 47 Lawmakers, Activists Face Unfair Trial," *Human Rights Watch*, August 22, 2022, https://www.hrw.org/news/2022/08/22/hong-kong-47-lawmakers-activists-face-unfair-trial.

2. Theodora Yu, "Hong Kong Catholic Church Cancels Tiananmen Memorial Mass," *Washington Post*, May 24, 2022, https://www.washingtonpost.com/world/2022/05/24/hong-kong-catholic-church-tiananmen.

3. Sum Lok-kei, "A Year on from Apple Daily's Closure, What's Left of Hong Kong's Free Press?," *Guardian* (UK), June 24, 2022, https://www.theguardian.com/global-development/2022/jun/24/year-on-from-pro-democracy-apple-daily-closure-whats-left-of-hong-kongs-free-press.

Notes to Pages 200–201

4. Katie Tam, "Hong Kong Book Fair Sees Self-Censorship and Fewer Books," *Associated Press*, July 14, 2021, https://apnews.com/article/business-lifestyle-entertainment-health-hong-kong-1df873d75789b96bd4ebdb9eff4789b1.

5. Tony Cheung, "Hong Kong Passes Bill to Ban Films Deemed Threats to National Security, Increase Penalty for Unauthorised Screenings," *South China Morning Post*, October 27, 2021, https://www.scmp.com/news/hong-kong/politics/article/3153857/hong-kong-passes-bill-ban-films-deemed-threats-national.

6. Kang-chung Ng, "Hong Kong National Security Law Used to Briefly Shut Down Website Run by Opposition Activists Overseas," *South China Morning Post*, June 3, 2021, https://www.scmp.com/news/hong-kong/law-and-crime/article/3135963/hong-kong-national-security-law-used-briefly-shut-down.

7. "Security Bureau Threatens UK-Based Hong Kong Watch Founder with Life Imprisonment; NGO Says It Won't Disband," *Hong Kong Free Press*, March 14, 2022, https://hongkongfp.com/2022/03/14/security-bureau-threatens-uk-based-hong-kong-watch-founder-with-life-imprisonment-ngo-says-it-wont-disband.

8. K. K. Rebecca Lai, "How Universities Became the New Battlegrounds in the Hong Kong Protests," *New York Times*, November 19, 2019, https://www.nytimes.com/interactive/2019/11/18/world/asia/hong-kong-protest-universities.html.

9. Timothy McLaughlin, "The Anger of Hong Kong's Youth," *Atlantic*, September 22, 2019, https://www.theatlantic.com/international/archive/2019/09/hong-kongs-students-continue-fight/598183.

10. Nadia Lam, Clifford Lo, and Jeffie Lam, "Hong Kong National Security Police Raid University Student Union as Part of Investigation into Stabbed Officer Motion," *South China Morning Post*, July 16, 2021, https://www.scmp.com/news/hong-kong/politics/article/3141386/hong-kong-national-security-police-raid-university-student.

11. Tiffany May, "Hong Kong Police Arrest Students over 'Advocating Terrorism,'" *New York Times*, August 18, 2021, https://www.nytimes.com/2021/08/18/world/asia/hong-kong-university-arrests.html.

12. Mimi Leung, "University Student Union Disbands Amid Civil Society Meltdown," *University World News*, October 7, 2021, https://www.universityworldnews.com/post.php?story=20211007140203859.

13. Thomas Chan, "The Death of Hong Kong's University Student Unions," *Diplomat*, April 14, 2022, https://thediplomat.com/2022/04/the-death-of-hong-kongs-university-student-unions.

14. Mimi Leung, "University Student Union Disbands amid Civil Society Meltdown," *University World News*, October 7, 2021, https://www.universityworldnews.com/post.php?story=20211007140203859.

15. "HKBU Students' Union Editorial Board Resigns en Masse Slamming School Intervention," *Standard* (Hong Kong), January 29, 2022, https://www.thestandard.com.hk/breaking-news/section/4/186600/HKBU-students%E2%80%99-union-editorial-board-resigns-en-masse-slamming-school-intervention.

16. Chan Ho-him, "National Security Law: Hong Kong's PolyU Tells Student Union to Take Magazine off Shelves over 'Inappropriate' Content," *South China Morning Post*, August 24, 2021, https://www.scmp.com/news/hong-kong/education/article/3146237/national-security-law-hong-kongs-polyu-tells-student-union.

17. "Hong Kong: Activists Jailed for Joining Banned Tiananmen Vigil," *BBC News*, September 15, 2021, https://www.bbc.com/news/world-asia-china-58568349.

18. "Hong Kong: Tiananmen Anniversary Arrests an Insult to Memory of Victims," *Amnesty International*, June 4, 2022, https://www.amnesty.org/en/latest/news/2022/06/hong-kong-tiananmen-anniversary-vigil.

19. Candice Chau, "University of Hong Kong Orders Removal of Tiananmen Massacre Statue After 24 Years, Artist 'Shocked,'" *Hong Kong Free Press*, October 8, 2021, https://hongkongfp.com/2021/10/08/breaking-university-of-hong-kong-orders-removal-of-tiananmen-massacre-statue-after-24-years.

20. Adam Taylor and Shibani Mahtani, "U.S. Law Firm Mayer Brown to Cease Work for University of Hong Kong in Dispute over Tiananmen Memorial's Removal," *Washington Post*, October 15, 2021, https://www.washingtonpost.com/world/2021/10/15/mayer-brown-hku/.

21. Chase Scheinbaum, "Firm's Involvement in Flap Over 'Comfort Women' Statue Raising Eyebrows," *Daily Journal*, April 23, 2014, https://www.dailyjournal.com/article/266149-firm-s-involvement-in-flap-over-comfort-women-statue-raising-eyebrows.

22. Elizabeth Lawrence, "China Removes Famous Tiananmen Square Massacre Monument in Middle of the Night," *American Military*

News, December 23, 2021, https://americanmilitarynews.com/2021/12/china-removes-famous-tiananmen-square-massacre-monument-in-middle-of-the-night.

23. Hillary Leung, "University of Hong Kong Covers Up 33-Year-Old Tiananmen Tribute Painted on Bridge, Weeks After Removing Statue," *Hong Kong Free Press*, January 29, 2022, https://hongkongfp.com/2022/01/29/university-of-hong-kong-covers-up-33-year-old-tiananmen-slogan-painted-on-bridge-weeks-after-removing-statue.

24. Tom Grundy, "University of Hong Kong Removes Tiananmen Massacre Monument in Dead of Night," *Hong Kong Free Press*, December 23, 2021, https://hongkongfp.com/2021/12/23/breaking-fears-for-condemned-tiananmen-massacre-monument-as-university-of-hong-kong-erects-barricades-around-statue-overnight.

25. "Partner List," International Affairs Office, accessed September 16, 2022, https://intlaffairs.hku.hk/partner-list.

26. William Yiu, "University of Hong Kong Proposes Disciplining Students for 'Bringing Disrepute' to Institution, Fueling Concerns over Freedom of Speech," *South China Morning Post*, April 26, 2022, https://www.scmp.com/news/hong-kong/education/article/3175599/university-hong-kong-proposes-disciplining-students.

27. Sara Cheng and Jessie Pang, "Two More Tiananmen Monuments Removed from Hong Kong Universities," *Reuters*, December 24, 2021, https://www.reuters.com/world/asia-pacific/two-more-tiananmen-monuments-removed-hong-kong-university-campuses-2021-12-24.

28. Hillary Leung, "Hong Kong's City University Demands Removal of Tiananmen Massacre Statue as Campus Crackdown Continues," *Hong Kong Free Press*, December 27, 2021, https://hongkongfp.com/2021/12/27/hong-kongs-city-university-demands-removal-of-tiananmen-massacre-statue-as-campus-crackdown-continues.

29. Cheng and Pang, "Two More Tiananmen Monuments Removed."

30. Sara Cheng and Jessie Pang, "Exclusive - New Hong Kong University Classes Set Out Dangers of Breaking Security Law," *Reuters*, November 5, 2021, https://www.reuters.com/world/china/exclusive-new-hong-kong-university-classes-set-out-dangers-breaking-security-law-2021-11-05.

31. Chan Ho-him, "Hong Kong's PolyU to Teach National Security Law and History of 'Humiliation' of China in Course on Leadership

Qualities," *South China Morning Post*, September 20, 2021, https://www.scmp.com/news/hong-kong/education/article/3149472/hong-kongs-polyu-teach-national-security-law-and-history.

32. Mimi Leung, "National Security Education Compulsory for Undergraduates," *University World News*, August 17, 2022, https://www.universityworldnews.com/post.php?story=20220817081736131.

33. Mimi Leung and Yojana Sharma, "Campus Flag-Raising Ceremonies May Become 'New Flashpoint,'" *University World News*, September 16, 2022, https://www.universityworldnews.com/post.php?story=20220916105029847.

34. Pola Lem, "'Discreet' Chats to Quiet Defiance: Tactics on Hong Kong Campuses," *Times Higher Education*, January 12, 2022, https://www.timeshighereducation.com/depth/discreet-chats-quiet-defiance-tactics-hong-kong-campuses.

35. Jessica R. Valdez, "Learning in a Time of Crisis: Reimagining Global Policing in the Literary Classroom," *Nineteenth-Century Gender Studies* 17.1 (Spring 2021), http://ncgsjournal.com/issue171/valdez.html.

36. Nicola Woolcock, "Wipe References to China to Protect Students, SOAS Lecturers Told," *Times* (UK), May 7, 2021, https://www.thetimes.co.uk/article/wipe-references-to-china-to-protect-students-soas-lecturers-told-9bjwlwwvm.

37. Kyle Mullins, "Dartmouth Encourages Faculty to Safeguard Students as Chinese Law Targets Free Speech Globally," *Dartmouth*, September 24, 2020, https://www.thedartmouth.com/article/2020/09/dartmouth-encourages-faculty-to-safeguard-students-as-chinese-law-targets-free-speech-globally.

38. Lucy Craymer, "China's National-Security Law Reaches into Harvard, Princeton Classrooms," *Wall Street Journal*, August 19, 2020, https://www.wsj.com/articles/chinas-national-security-law-reaches-into-harvard-princeton-classrooms-11597829402.

39. Marie-Rose Sheinerman, "Amid Digital Crackdown, Chinese Politics Professor Recommends Students in China Avoid His Class," *Daily Princetonian*, January 15, 2021, https://www.dailyprincetonian.com/article/2021/01/princeton-china-digital-national-security-law-american-universities.

40. Dimitar D. Gueorguiev, Xiaobo Lü, Kerry Ratigan, Meg Rithmire, and Rory Truex, "How to Teach China This Fall," *China File*, August 20, 2020, https://www.chinafile.com/reporting-opinion/viewpoint/how-teach-china-fall.

41. "Tracker: University Responses to Chinese Censorship," *FIRE*, accessed September 26, 2022, https://www.thefire.org/research-learn/tracker-university-responses-chinese-censorship.

42. Lucy Craymer, "China's National-Security Law Reaches into Harvard, Princeton Classrooms," *Wall Street Journal*, August 19, 2020, https://www.wsj.com/articles/chinas-national-security-law-reaches-into-harvard-princeton-classrooms-11597829402.

43. Jeff Wasserstrom (@jwassers), "Thread on my modern Chinese history fall quarter class," Twitter, October 10, 2020, https://twitter.com/jwassers/status/1314961845044690949.

44. Theodora Yu, "Hong Kong Therapists Guilty of Sedition over Cartoons of Sheep and Wolves," *Washington Post*, September 7, 2022, https://www.washingtonpost.com/world/2022/09/07/hong-kong-childrens-book-sedition-cartoon.

45. Jessie Pang, "Hong Kong Student Jailed for 2 Months Under Sedition over Social Media Posts in Japan," *Reuters*, November 3, 2023, https://www.reuters.com/world/asia-pacific/hong-kong-student-jailed-2-months-under-sedition-over-social-media-posts-japan-2023-11-03/.

46. Greg Torode and James Pomfret, "Insight: 'Colonial Wine from New, Authoritarian Bottles': Hong Kong Re-Tools Sedition Law," *Reuters*, January 11, 2022, https://www.reuters.com/world/asia-pacific/colonial-wine-new-authoritarian-bottles-hong-kong-re-tools-sedition-law-2022-01-11.

47. Will Nott, "UK Academics Fear Reprisals for Speaking Out on Sensitive Issues," *PIE News*, August 18, 2021, https://thepienews.com/news/uk-academics-fear-reprisals-for-speaking-out-on-sensitive-chinese-issues.

48. "Hong Kong: New Security Law Full-Scale Assault on Rights," *Human Rights Watch*, March 19, 2024, https://www.hrw.org/news/2024/03/19/hong-kong-new-security-law-full-scale-assault-rights.

49. Joe Friesen, "Students Enrolled Online in China May Not Be Able to Access Course Content, Canadian Universities Warn," *Globe and Mail*,

Notes to Pages 216–220

September 11, 2020, https://www.theglobeandmail.com/canada/article-students-enrolled-online-in-china-may-not-be-able-to-access-course.

50. John Power, "National Security Law: Australian Universities Move to Protect Hong Kong Students," *South China Morning Post*, November 10, 2020, https://www.scmp.com/week-asia/politics/article/3109129/national-security-law-australian-universities-move-protect-hong.

51. Anna Patty, "Uni Warned to Avoid 'Unapproved Teachings' or Risk Losing Chinese Students," *Sydney Morning Herald*, September 15, 2020, https://www.smh.com.au/national/nsw/uni-warned-to-avoid-unapproved-teachings-or-risk-losing-chinese-students-20200915-p55vu5.html.

52. Kyle Mullins, "Dartmouth Encourages Faculty to Safeguard Students as Chinese Law Targets Free Speech Globally," *Dartmouth*, September 24, 2020, https://www.thedartmouth.com/article/2020/09/dartmouth-encourages-faculty-to-safeguard-students-as-chinese-law-targets-free-speech-globally.

53. Caleb Hampton, "Hong Kong Security Law Challenges Free Speech in U.S. Classrooms," *Davis Enterprise*, December 12, 2020, https://www.davisenterprise.com/news/hong-kong-security-law-challenges-free-speech-in-u-s-classrooms/article_dfcdc260-7812-5711-ac57-2ad05bb00618.html.

54. John Power, "National Security Law: Australian Universities Move to Protect Hong Kong Students," *South China Morning Post*, November 10, 2020, https://www.scmp.com/week-asia/politics/article/3109129/national-security-law-australian-universities-move-protect-hong.

55. Mark Choi [pseud.], "OPINION: How the Hong Kong Security Law Imperils All McMaster Students," *Silhouette*, August 19, 2020, https://thesil.ca/opinion-how-the-hong-kong-security-law-imperils-all-mcmaster-students.

56. "Spotlight on Speech Codes 2022," FIRE, accessed October 3, 2022, https://www.thefire.org/research-learn/spotlight-speech-codes-2022.

57. "Policies and Procedures Manual," College of the Holy Cross, November 1, 2005, https://www.holycross.edu/sites/default/files/files/its/pdf/use_of_information_technology_services_2014.pdf.

58. "Acceptable Use Policy," Tulane University, accessed October 3, 2022, https://it.tulane.edu/acceptable-use-policy.

59. "Computer Related Acceptable Use Policy," Kean University, accessed October 3, 2022, https://www.kean.edu/media/computer-related-acceptable-use-policy.

60. "Texas Christian University Tramples Student's Rights in Order to Appease Angry Internet Mob," *FIRE*, July 29, 2015, https://www.thefire.org/news/texas-christian-university-tramples-students-rights-order-appease-angry-internet-mob.

61. Will Creeley, "Revisiting Twitter Controversy, University of Rhode Island President Issues New Statement Acknowledging First Amendment," *FIRE*, December 28, 2012, https://www.thefire.org/news/revisiting-twitter-controversy-university-rhode-island-president-issues-new-statement.

62. "Albion College Student Under Investigation for 'ANTIFA and ISIS Hunting Permits' Joke," *FIRE*, December 13, 2017, https://www.thefire.org/news/albion-college-student-under-investigation-antifa-and-isis-hunting-permits-joke.

63. Sarah McLaughlin, "Cooper Medical School of Rowan University Revises Social Media Policy After Letter from FIRE," *FIRE*, October 6, 2017, https://www.thefire.org/news/cooper-medical-school-rowan-university-revises-social-media-policy-after-letter-fire.

64. Adam Goldstein, "Wake Forest's Investigation of 'Build a Wall' Instagram Post Chills Free Speech," *FIRE*, March 28, 2019, https://www.thefire.org/wake-forests-investigation-of-build-a-wall-instagram-post-chills-free-speech.

65. Adam Kissel, "East Stroudsburg University Suspends Innocent Professor for Weeks over Facebook Comments," *FIRE*, April 5, 2010, https://www.thefire.org/news/east-stroudsburg-university-suspends-innocent-professor-weeks-over-facebook-comments.

66. Sarah McLaughlin, "Drexel Professor Resigns After Months-Long Investigation, Exile from Campus," *FIRE*, December 29, 2017, https://www.thefire.org/news/drexel-professor-resigns-after-months-long-investigation-exile-campus.

67. Office of Public Affairs, US Department of Justice, "Eight Chinese Government Officials Charged with Directing Employee of a U.S. Telecommunications Company to Remove Chinese Dissidents from

Company's Platform," press release, April 17, 2023, www.justice.gov/opa/pr/five-individuals-charged-variously-stalking-harassing-and-spying-us-residents-behalf-prc-0.

68. Sarah McLaughlin, "Free Speech Coalition Warns Zoom: China's Censorship Requests Could Impact Online Teaching," *FIRE*, June 15, 2020, https://www.thefire.org/news/free-speech-coalition-warns-zoom-chinas-censorship-requests-could-impact-online-teaching.

69. Gabriel Greschler, "After Protest, Zoom Pulls Plug on San Francisco State Event with Leila Khaled," *Forward*, September 22, 2020, https://forward.com/news/454992/after-protest-zoom-pulls-plug-on-san-francisco-state-event-with-leila.

70. Leila Ettachfini, "'I Had to Be the Voice of Women': The First Female Hijacker Shares Her Story," *VICE*, August 4, 2016, https://www.vice.com/en/article/9k99k7/leila-khaled-first-female-hijacker-profile.

71. Greschler, "After Protest, Zoom Pulls Plug."

72. Lawfare Project, letter to Gregory Gonzalez, Counsel to the Assistant Attorney General for National Security, September 14, 2020, https://www.thefire.org/sites/default/files/2020/09/23122515/LP_Letter_to_Gonzalez_re_SFSU_2020_09_14.pdf.

73. Academic Council for Israel et al., "Letter to SFSU President Lynn Mahoney Concerning Upcoming Leila Khaled Event and Academic Freedom Abuse," September 17, 2020, https://www.thefire.org/sites/default/files/2020/09/23122412/86-Orgs-to-SFSU-Lynn-Mahony-9.17.20.pdf.

74. Rep. Doug Lamborn (@RepDLamborn), "Breaking: I sent a letter to @BetsyDeVosED," Twitter, September 22, 2020, https://twitter.com/RepDLamborn/status/1308454653202489348.

75. Alice Speri and Sam Biddle, "Zoom Censorship of Palestine Seminars Sparks Fight over Academic Freedom," *Intercept*, November 14, 2020, https://theintercept.com/2020/11/14/zoom-censorship-leila-khaled-palestine.

76. Adam Steinbaugh, "As Critics Call for Deplatforming, Defunding, and Prosecution over Leila Khaled Discussion, San Francisco State University President Gets It Right," *FIRE*, September 23, 2020, https://www.thefire.org/news/critics-call-deplatforming-defunding-and-prosecution-over-leila-khaled-discussion-san.

77. Sarah McLaughlin, "Pressure Grows on Universities to Address Zoom Academic Freedom Concerns," *FIRE*, February 3, 2021, https://www.thefire.org/news/pressure-grows-universities-address-zoom-academic-freedom-concerns.

78. Brian Soucek, Chair, University Committee on Academic Freedom, letter to Mary Gauvain re: censorship by Zoom and other private platforms, December 23, 2020, https://senate.universityofcalifornia.edu/_files/reports/mg-mb-zoom-terms.pdf.

79. "On Academic Freedom for Our Higher Education Users," Zoom, April 13, 2021, https://explore.zoom.us/docs/en-us/trust/academic-freedom.html.

80. Sharon Wrobel, "Zoom Registration for Upcoming Webinar with PFLP's Leila Khaled Now Removed from Platform," *Algemeiner*, April 21, 2021, https://www.algemeiner.com/2021/04/21/zoom-registration-for-upcoming-webinar-with-pflps-leila-khaled-now-removed-from-platform.

81. Mirka Martel and Julie Baer, "Spring 2022 Snapshot on International Educational Exchange," Institute of International Education, June 2022, https://www.iie.org/wp-content/uploads/2022/12/SpringSnapshot_Final.pdf.

82. Joanna Zajchowska, "Rektor Uniwersytetu w Białymstoku ogłasza zajęcia zdalne od stycznia. Powodem rosnące ceny prądu," *Gazeta*, October 4, 2022, https://wiadomosci.gazeta.pl/wiadomosci/7,114883,28984768,rektor-uniwersytetu-w-bialymstoku-oglasza-zajecia-zdalne-od.html.

83. Alicja Ptak, "Poland's Oldest University to Move Classes Online After Energy Bill Rises 700%," *Notes from Poland*, October 3, 2022, https://notesfrompoland.com/2022/10/03/polands-oldest-university-to-move-classes-online-after-energy-bill-rises-700.

Chapter 7. A Free World Needs Free Campuses

1. Aaron Terr, "University of Florida Task Force Recommends 'Strong Presumption' That Faculty Can Testify in State-Involved Litigation," *FIRE*, November 30, 2021, https://www.thefire.org/news/university-florida-task-force-recommends-strong-presumption-faculty-can-testify-state-involved.

2. Austin v. University of Florida Board of Trustees, 580 F. Supp. 3d 1137, 1145 (N.D. Fla. 2022).
3. Patrick Svitek, "Shelley Luther, Anti-Lockdown Activist and GOP Candidate, Said Chinese Students Should Be Banned from Texas Universities," *Texas Tribune*, January 7, 2022, https://www.texastribune.org/2022/01/07/shelley-luther-chinese-students-texas.
4. Alexandra Sternlicht, "Senator Tom Cotton Ramps Up Anti-China Rhetoric, Says Chinese Students Should Be Banned from U.S.," *Forbes*, April 26, 2020, https://www.forbes.com/sites/alexandrasternlicht/2020/04/26/senator-tom-cotton-ramps-up-anti-china-rhetoric-says-chinese-students-should-be-banned-from-us/?sh=7ede7c9f99a2.
5. Demetri Sevastopulo and Tom Mitchell, "US Considered Ban on Student Visas for Chinese Nationals," *Financial Times*, October 2, 2018, https://www.ft.com/content/fc413158-c5f1-11e8-82bf-ab93d0a9b321.
6. Proclamation No. 10043, 85 Fed. Reg. 34353 (May 29, 2020).
7. Humeyra Pamuk, "U.S. Revokes More than 1,000 Visas of Chinese Nationals, Citing Military Links," *Reuters*, September 9, 2020, https://www.reuters.com/article/us-usa-china-visas-students/u-s-revokes-more-than-1000-visas-of-chinese-nationals-citing-military-links-idUSKBN26039D.
8. Stuart Andersen, "Biden Keeps Costly Trump Visa Policy Denying Chinese Grad Students," *Forbes*, August 10, 2021, https://www.forbes.com/sites/stuartanderson/2021/08/10/biden-keeps-costly-trump-visa-policy-denying-chinese-grad-students/?sh=55c167363641.
9. Patricia Zengerle and Matt Spetalnick, "Exclusive: Fearing Espionage, U.S. Weighs Tighter Rules on Chinese Students," *Reuters*, November 29, 2018, https://www.reuters.com/article/us-usa-china-students-exclusive/exclusive-fearing-espionage-us-weighs-tighter-rules-on-chinese-students-idUSKCN1NY1HE.
10. Foundation for Individual Rights in Education, Pen America, National Coalition Against Censorship, Defending Rights & Dissent, and Electronic Frontier Foundation, "Coalition Letter to Secretary of State Michael Pompeo, February 11, 2019," https://www.thefire.org/research-learn/coalition-letter-secretary-state-michael-pompeo-february-11-2019.

11. Sandra E. Garcia, "U.S. Requiring Social Media Information from Visa Applicants," *New York Times*, June 2, 2019, https://www.nytimes.com/2019/06/02/us/us-visa-application-social-media.html.

12. Hannah Allam, "U.S. Denies Entry to Leader of Movement to Boycott Israel," *NPR*, April 11, 2019, https://www.npr.org/2019/04/11/712189791/u-s-denies-entry-to-leader-of-movement-to-boycott-israel.

13. Hanan Ashrawi (@DrHananAshrawi), "It is official! My US visa application has been rejected," Twitter, May 13, 2019, https://twitter.com/DrHananAshrawi/status/1127959832013824002.

14. Rachel Leingang, "9 Chinese ASU Students Detained at Los Angeles Airport, Denied Admission to US," *AZ Central*, August 30, 2019, https://www.azcentral.com/story/news/local/arizona-education/2019/08/30/chinese-students-arizona-state-university-detained-los-angeles-airport/2169610001.

15. Shera S. Avi-Yonah and Delano R. Franklin, "Incoming Harvard Freshman Deported After Visa Revoked," *Harvard Crimson*, August 27, 2019, https://www.thecrimson.com/article/2019/8/27/incoming-freshman-deported.

16. Shera S. Avi-Yonah and Delano R. Franklin, "Freshman Previously Denied Entry to the United States Arrives at Harvard," *Harvard Crimson*, September 3, 2019, https://www.thecrimson.com/article/2019/9/3/harvard-student-turned-away-arrives.

17. Allan Barry, "In a Boston Court, a Superstar of Science Falls to Earth," *New York Times*, December 21, 2021, https://www.nytimes.com/2021/12/21/science/charles-lieber.html.

18. Jamie Satterfield, "Trial Reveals Federal Agents Falsely Accused a UT Professor Born in China of Spying," *Knoxville News Sentinel*, June 13, 2021, https://www.knoxnews.com/story/news/crime/2021/06/14/federal-agents-falsely-accused-university-of-tennessee-professor-spying-china/7649378002.

19. Gang Chen, "I Was Arrested Under the DOJ's China Initiative. Congress Must Investigate the Program.," *Boston Globe*, January 21, 2022, https://www.bostonglobe.com/2022/01/21/opinion/i-was-arrested-under-dojs-china-initiative-congress-must-investigate-program.

20. MIT Faculty, letter to President L. Rafael Reif, January 21, 2021, https://fnl.mit.edu/wp-content/uploads/2021/01/Letter-to-Reif-in-support-of-Gang-Chen-2021-01-27.pdf.

21. Jeffrey Mervis, "Prosecutors Drop China Initiative Case Against MIT's Gang Chen," *Science*, January 20, 2022, https://www.science.org/content/article/united-states-drops-case-against-mit-s-gang-chen.

22. Katie Benner, "Justice Dept. to End Trump-Era Initiative to Deter Chinese Threats," *New York Times*, February 23, 2022, https://www.nytimes.com/2022/02/23/us/politics/china-trump-justice-department.html.

23. Jeffrey Mervis, "Controversial U.S. China Initiative Gets New Name, Tighter Focus on Industrial Espionage," *Science*, February 28, 2022, https://www.science.org/content/article/controversial-u-s-china-initiative-gets-new-name-tighter-focus-industrial-espionage.

24. Ken Dilanian, "FBI Director Defends Investigations of Chinese Academics in Front of University Audience," *NBC News*, December 2, 2022, https://www.nbcnews.com/politics/national-security/fbi-director-wray-defends-investigations-chinese-academics-rcna59864.

25. Will Creeley, "A Weird State Law Lets Virginians Sue Books. Politicians Are Using It to Dictate What We Can Read," *FIRE*, July 26, 2022, https://www.thefire.org/news/weird-state-law-lets-virginians-sue-books-politicians-are-using-it-dictate-what-we-can-read.

26. Will Creeley and Nadine Strossen, "That Facebook Post About Abortion Could Land You in Jail—If South Carolina Legislators Have Their Way," *FIRE*, July 29, 2022, https://www.thefire.org/news/facebook-post-about-abortion-could-land-you-jail-if-south-carolina-legislators-have-their-way.

27. Adam Steinbaugh (@adamsteinbaugh), "NEW: @HoodCountyTX Constable Chad Jordan says his office is conducting an 'active and pending criminal investigation,'" Twitter, May 20, 2022, https://twitter.com/adamsteinbaugh/status/1527693206674100226.

28. Cat Zakrzewski and Drew Harwell, "Buffalo Massacre Report Seeks to Punish Broadcasters of Homicide Live Streams," *Washington Post*, October 18, 2022, https://www.washingtonpost.com/technology/2022/10/18/buffalo-shooting-livestream-ny-attorney-general.

29. Tracy Qu, "Chinese Regulator Pushes for Broadcast Delay of All Online Concerts and Shows, Tightening Censorship of Live-Streamed

Content," *South China Morning Post*, September 27, 2022, https://www.scmp.com/tech/big-tech/article/3193960/chinese-regulator-pushes-broadcast-delay-all-online-concerts-and.

30. Aaron Terr, "Investigation Reveals Boise State Suspended Diversity Courses over Unsubstantiated Rumor," *FIRE*, May 25, 2021, https://www.thefire.org/news/investigation-reveals-boise-state-suspended-diversity-courses-over-unsubstantiated-rumor.

31. Graham Piro, "Chilling Effect Remains as Oklahoma's 'Divisive Concepts' Law Becomes Effective," *FIRE*, July 2, 2021, https://www.thefire.org/news/chilling-effect-remains-oklahomas-divisive-concepts-law-becomes-effective.

32. Adam Steinbaugh, "Doubling Down: Iowa State Again Insists New 'Critical Race Theory' Law Applies to Its Faculty and Classes," *FIRE*, July 29, 2021, https://www.thefire.org/news/doubling-down-iowa-state-again-insists-new-critical-race-theory-law-applies-its-faculty-and.

33. "Understanding House Bill 7 - Individual Freedom" (PowerPoint obtained through public records request, North Florida College, August 11, 2022), https://cdn.muckrock.com/foia_files/2022/08/19/HB7_Presentation.pptx.

34. Emmy Hughes and Hannah Reale, "Wesleyan Stops Pursuing Joint-Venture Campus in China," *Wesleyan Argus*, October 24, 2019, http://wesleyanargus.com/2019/10/24/wesleyan-stop-pursuing-joint-venture-campus-in-china.

35. Wagdy Sawahel, "Draft Law for Foreign Campuses 'Constrains Autonomy,'" *University World News*, September 9, 2022, https://www.universityworldnews.com/post.php?story=2022090908005012.

36. Kevin Draper, "The Alliance of LIV Golf and the PGA Tour: Here's What to Know," *New York Times*, June 7, 2023, https://www.nytimes.com/2023/06/07/sports/golf/pga-liv-golf-merger.html.

37. "Ministries of Education and Investment Sign MoU with Arizona State University and Centana Education Company," *Saudi Press Agency*, March 3, 2024, https://www.spa.gov.sa/en/N2057614.

38. Sarah Wood, "10 National Universities with the Biggest Endowments," *U.S. News & World Report*, September 13, 2022, https://www.usnews.com/education/best-colleges/the-short-list-college/articles/10-universities-with-the-biggest-endowments.

39. Ben Wittstein, "Colleges That Are Richer than Some Countries," *Stacker*, August 21, 2019, https://stacker.com/education/colleges-are-richer-some-countries.

40. Frances Mao, "Tiananmen: Hong Kong Students Hide Tiny 'Democracy Goddesses' on Campus," *BBC News*, June 4, 2022, https://www.bbc.com/news/world-asia-china-61679435.

41. Thaïs Chaigne, "Hong Kong Activists Create Digital Rendering of the 'Pillar of Shame' to Save It from Authorities," *France 24 Observers*, November 3, 2021, https://observers.france24.com/en/asia-pacific/20211105-hong-kong-3d-rendering-pillar-of-shame-tiananmen.

42. Jake Epstein, "The Creator of a Tiananmen Square Memorial Released the Copyright on His Sculpture So 3D Printers Can Annoy China," *Business Insider*, March 30, 2022, https://www.businessinsider.com/tiananmen-square-memorial-creator-released-printing-copyright-china-2022-3.

43. Alex Chow and Shui-yin Sharon Yam, "Hong Kong's Universities Have Fallen. There May Be No Turning Back," *New York Times*, November 24, 2021, https://www.nytimes.com/2021/11/24/opinion/hong-kong-university-china.html.

44. Robert Quinn, Janika Spannagel, and Ilyas Saliba, "Why University Rankings Must Include Academic Freedom," *University World News*, March 11, 2021, https://www.universityworldnews.com/post.php?story=20210311071016522.

45. Isaac Stanley-Becker and Drew Harwell, "How a Tiny Company with Few Rules Is Making Fake Images Go Mainstream," *Washington Post*, March 30, 2023, https://www.washingtonpost.com/technology/2023/03/30/midjourney-ai-image-generation-rules.

46. Sarah McLaughlin (@sarahemclaugh), "Carnegie Mellon's Graduate Student Assembly says Chinese students' pro-freedom messages were defaced," Twitter, December 3, 2022, https://x.com/sarahemclaugh/status/1599074420231847938.

47. Athenai Institute (@athenaiinst), "A Vigil Set Up by Chinese Students at UC Berkeley Was Burned and Vandalized Today," Twitter, December 1, 2022, https://twitter.com/athenaiinst/status/1598524703257370624.

48. Jimmy Quinn, "Who Punched a Protester Against China Lockdowns at Columbia University?," *National Review*, December 5, 2022,

https://www.nationalreview.com/corner/who-punched-a-protester-against-china-lockdowns-at-columbia-university.

49. US Attorney's Office, District of Massachusetts, "People's Republic of China Citizen Arrested for Stalking," press release, December 14, 2022, https://www.justice.gov/usao-ma/pr/peoples-republic-china-citizen-arrested-stalking.

Index

academic freedom, 152; at branch/joint campuses, 153–56, 158, 164, 168, 173, 176, 183–87, 192, 195; CIs and, 56, 58; constitutional right to, 104; in Hong Kong, 208, 229; in Hungary, 119; off-campus activities and, 229–30, 239; online learning and, 199, 215, 221; prioritizing international engagement over, 131, 132; sensitivity and, 84–94; student rights and, 175–77; in UAE, 186, 192; university ties with authoritarian governments and, 134; US government's violations of, 238–41; Zoom's statement on, 225–26. *See also* discussions, academic; expressive freedoms/rights; First Amendment; speech protections; speech restrictions; speech rights; speech suppression; values

Academic Freedom Index, 249

academics (scholars): adjunct professors, 98; administrators' protection of, 127; attacks on speech rights of, 89–90; blacklisting of, 69–70, 74; censorship of, 1–2, 74–78; CIs and, 52; criticism of administrators and, 167, 231; investigations of, 149–50, 235–38; lack of protection for, 241, 242; national security law and, 215, 247–48; off-campus activities of, 229–30, 239; refusal to be intimidated, 127–28; reported for political wrongdoing (*jubao*), 157–58; tenure, 98, 167, 231, 241; universities' relation with China and, 51; vague speech rules and, 71. *See also* academic freedom; retaliation; self-censorship; visa denials

activism/activists, 37, 151. *See also* dissidents; Hong Kong protests/activists

adjunct professors, 98

administrators: academics' willingness to criticize, 167, 231; in Australia, 147; authoritarian governments and, 12; barriers to free expression and, 47–48; on BRTs, 92–93; censorship and, 12, 30–32, 74–78, 85–94, 240; China and, 51, 124, 147, 148–49; constraints on, 4; CSSAs and, 27; in Europe, 124; exploitation of, 32; increase in, 97, 98–99; national security law and, 211; in New Zealand, 148–49; protection of academics from retaliation, 127; speech suppression by, 9, 84–94; student disputes and, 18–20, 22–23. *See also* apologies/statements; branch/joint campuses; corporations/businesses; expansion, of universities; partnerships; universities

Ajjawi, Ismail B., 234–35

Alexander, Shirley, 217

Alford, William P., 75

Allen-Ebrahimian, Bethany, 26, 27, 59

American Association of University Professors (AAUP), 52

Index

American Defense, Harvard Group, 43
American University, 82
America Second (Fish), 80
"Anaconda in the Chandelier, The" (Link), 71
anonymity, in academic discussions, 209–14, 248
anti-Semitism, 107–10
Apatow, Judd, 80
apologies/statements: dissidents and, 22; English- vs. Chinese-language versions, 15, 102, 146; for incorrect mentions of Hong Kong, Tibet, or Taiwan, 101–2, 103, 156; on international events/conflicts, 134; on social media, 35; by students, 35. *See also* brand; social media
Arizona State University, branch/joint campus in Saudi Arabia, 244–45
art, censorship of, 8–14, 67–68, 203–5; in Australia, 143–44; in democracies, 68; protecting brand and, 99–100
Asat, Rayhan, 27
Ashrawi, Hanan, 234
Asian communities, harassment of, 21, 23. *See also* hate crimes
Austell, David, 77
Australian Strategic Policy Institute, 114
Australian universities, 135, 142; brand protection at, 135, 140; China and, 135, 136, 142; CIs at, 138, 143; funding for, 136; Hong Kong protests and, 135, 137–42; joint educational management model, 136; national security law and, 216–17, 218; protests against ties to China at, 139; self-censorship in, 142
authoritarian governments/authoritarianism: branch/joint campuses and, 161, 194–95; on-campus, universities' role in, 241–43; combating, violating values to, 231; compliance of institutions and, 6; critical conversations about, on campus, 84; difficulty of speaking freely about, 1; higher education and, 47, 255–56; increase in, 189;

investigation of students discussing, 32; limitations of criticism against, 110; line between freedom and, 230; pressure of on corporations, 5, 252; pressure of on universities, 3, 252; and universities' global expansion, 2. *See also* censorship; expansion, of universities; partnerships; self-censorship; silence; unfree countries; *individual governments*
autonomy, institutional, 136

Badiucao, 8, 67–68
Bao Haining, 13
Barge, Gayle, 99
Barghouti, Omar, 234
Barnett, Robert, 68
Bazzi, Mohamad, 192
Belanger, Matthew, 169–71
Belt and Road Initiative, 9–10
Benney, Jonathan, 218
Bensel, Richard, 162, 163, 164, 165, 166–67, 196
Berkeley, UC, 64
bias, broad definition of, 92
Bias Response Teams (BRTs), 92–93
Biden, Joe, 232
Blackburn, Zach, 10–11
blacklisting, 69–70, 71, 74, 79. *See also* visa denials
Blinken, Antony, 165
Bogos, Kristina, 178–81
Bolton, John, 50
books: banned, 46; censorship of, 80–81, 171, 177, 238–39; outside of China, Chinese interference with, 121
Boycott, Divestment and Sanctions movement, 106, 234
Brady, Anne-Marie, 149
branch/joint campuses, 136, 155; academic costs of, 177; academic freedom and, 153–56, 158, 164, 168, 173, 176, 183–87, 192, 195; authoritarianism and, 161, 194–95; branding for unfree countries and, 181; censorship at, 170–71, 176, 177, 193; as Chinese universities, 161; control of, 166–71; courses required by

312

Index

Chinese government at, 168–69; decline of freedom in China and, 156–57, 180; directive against Western influence and, 154–55; discussion of sensitive issues in China and, 156; employment model and, 169–70, 172; expressive freedom at, 182–83, 250–51; failure of to protect local students, 189–92; failure of to protect students/employees, 178–81, 183–87; funding and, 164, 172, 185, 187, 243; government interference in campus events at, 174–75, 181–83; internet access at, 155, 171; lack of protection for whistleblowing at, 195; laws applicable to, 168, 169–70; local laws and, 174–75, 182–83, 242, 245; management of, CCP and, 173; mission of, 153–54, 156; monitoring of by home institution, 160; national security law and, 204; opposition to, 163–67; political/social climate in China and, 161; reassessment of, need for, 244; research at, 178–81; in Saudi Arabia, 244–45; self-censorship at, 170, 173, 177; silence and, 197; speech protections at, 176; speech repression and, 204; student groups at, 156; students' freedom at, 175–77; support from home institutions and, 179; surveillance at, 193; in UAE, 183–93; in unfree countries, 152–53, 174–75, 193–95; values vs. local laws and, 243; values vs. money and, 243; visas/immigration and, 178–81, 192. *See also* educational exchanges; engagement; expansion, of universities; partnerships; *individual institutions*

brand, 241; media policy and, 96; protecting, 83, 95, 97, 99–100, 101, 135; social media and, 100–101; trademark infringement, 97; unfree countries and, 181. *See also* apologies/statements; reputational damage

Brandeis University, 27–28

BRTs (Bias Response Teams), 92–93
Bullock, Mary Brown, 155
bureaucrats. *See* administrators; companies, global; consulates/embassies, Chinese; government, Chinese; institutions, global
bureaucrats, American, self-censorship by, 81
Bureau of Educational and Cultural Affairs, 41
businesses. *See* corporations/businesses

California, San Diego, University of (UCSD), 65–66
Cambridge, University of, 124–25, 187–89
campus discussions. *See* discussions, academic
campus speech codes, 89, 93–94, 241
Canada, 112–19; China's influence in, 112–19; CSSAs and, 218–19; national security law and, 218; political expression in, 114
Carnegie Mellon University (CMU), 18, 20–22, 194–95
Carrico, Kevin, 137, 218
Carter, Jimmy, 50
Castiglione, James A., 173
CCP (Chinese Communist Party). *See* government, Chinese
CCTV, 13
Cena, John, 101–2
censorship, online, 170. *See also* social media; Zoom
censorship, tacit, 77
censorship: of academics, 1–2, 72–78; administrators and, 12, 30–32, 74–78, 85–94, 240; at branch/joint campuses, 170–71, 176, 177, 193; in Chinese academic culture, 154; CIs and, 58–59; disruption of events as, 27; foreign governments and, 1–2, 4; global repercussions of, 3–4, 5–6; institutions' compliance and, 7–8; international students and, 1–2; lack of incentive to resist, 249; student dissidents and, 30; students and, 1–2,

Index

censorship (*cont.*) 23–24; by US government, 238–39. *See also* authoritarian governments/authoritarianism; Chinese Students and Scholars Association (CSSA); expressive freedoms/rights; sensitivity exploitation; speech restrictions; speech suppression

censors without borders, 3, 8, 113–14, 199, 200. *See also* authoritarian governments/authoritarianism; national security law (Hong Kong)

Center for Language Education and Cooperation, 53

Chang, Roxanne, 76

Chen, Bonnie, 112

Chen, Gang, 236–37, 238

Chen Guangcheng, 75

Chicago, University of (UChicago), 28, 57

Chikli, Amichai, 67

China: allowing discussions critical of, 28; Beijing Olympics (2022), 7, 8–14, 33, 254; Belt and Road Initiative, 9–10; cultural outreach and, 41–42; decline of freedom in, 156–57, 180; disputes about, among students, 18; protests in, 254. *See also* authoritarian governments/authoritarianism; government, Chinese; Hong Kong; human rights; international students; national security law (Hong Kong); Taiwan; Tibet; unfree countries

China Center, 166

China Initiative, 235–38

Chinese Communist Party (CCP), 44, 173. *See also* consulates/embassies, Chinese; government, Chinese

Chinese Cultural Association, at GW, 9

Chinese International Education Foundation (CIEF), 53

Chinese Language Council International (Hanban), 53, 55, 138. *See also* Confucius Institutes (CIs)

Chinese Overseas, The (Wang), 171

Chinese students. *See* Chinese Students and Scholars Association (CSSA); international students

Chinese Students and Scholars Association (CSSA): in Australia, 136–37; in Canada, 112–13, 118, 218–19; censorship by, 8–12, 24, 25, 28–30, 77, 137, 231–32; Chinese government and, 25, 26–27, 29; consulates/embassies and, 26, 113, 118, 128, 136–37; Dalai Lama invitations and, 65; dissidents and, 12, 39; harassment by, 34–35, 39, 116–17; original purpose of, 25; partnerships and, 165; payments to students by, 27; surveillance by, 25; in UK, 128, 129, 130

Chinese students/scholars, historical, 42–44

Chinese studies curriculum, 144

Chinese University of Hong Kong (CUHK), 201, 202, 204–5, 206, 246–47

Chiu, Joanna, 113

Chow, Alex, 247–48, 251

Chronicle of Higher Education, The, 76

Chyu, Minking, 158, 159

CIs (Confucious Institutes). *See* Confucius Institutes (CIs)

civil society, destruction of in Hong Kong, 201, 247. *See also* national security law (Hong Kong)

classes. *See* courses; curriculum

climate change, online learning and, 227

CMU (Carnegie Mellon University), 18, 20–22, 194–95

CMU-Africa, 194–95

code, speech. *See* speech codes/policies

Codling, Andrew, 148

Cohon, Jared, 195

Cold War, educational exchanges during, 45–46

Columbia University, 66–67, 76–77

companies, global. *See* corporations/businesses

compromises: expansion and, 152–53, 161, 195, 196; global institutions and, 253; values and, 152, 195, 196

concepts, divisive, 103–6, 110, 240

Index

Confucius Institutes (CIs), 51–63; academic freedom and, 56, 58; in Australia, 138, 143; censorship by, 58–59; closures of, 60–63, 118; courses taught by, 133; criticism of, 57–58, 133; described, 53; efforts of to control speech at universities, 54; funding from, 54; in Germany, 121; hiring practices of, 118–19; interference of with campus events, 56; in Ireland, 131, 133; in New Zealand, 149; in Portugal, 121; propagandistic goals of, 53–54; purpose of, 60; replacement of, 62–63; transparency and, 56; in UK, 130; universities' relationships with, 52, 54, 102; US government and, 52–53, 55–56

Confucius Institute US Center (CIUS), 61–62

Constitution, US, 89, 104, 106. *See also* First Amendment

consulates/embassies, Chinese: advice to Chinese students abroad, 77; in Australia, 136–37, 139, 143; in Canada, 116, 118; CSSAs and, 26, 27, 113, 118, 136–37; Dalai Lama invitations and, 49–50, 63–66; endorsement of threats, 150; Hong Kong protests and, 139; interference in campus politics/events, 63–66, 128–30, 143, 148; in New Zealand, 148; in UK, 128–30. *See also* government, Chinese

Cook, Steven, 66

Cornell University, 18–20, 244; engagement and, 162–63, 166; expansion of in China, 163–67, 196, 251; Global Cornell, 166

corporations/businesses: authoritarian governments' pressure on, 5, 252; blacklisting of, fear of, 79–80; compromises and, 253; cooperation with Chinese authorities, 38–39; stakeholder demands vs. expressive values and, 224; universities as, 83, 95, 97, 102, 241–42. *See also* apologies/statements; institutions, global; social media; tech companies/technology; Zoom

Cotton, Tom, 232

courses: Chinese influence on, 133, 144; enrolment in, international students and, 40, 70, 209–10, 212; fear of retaliation for taking, 145–46; national security law and, 209–10, 212; partnerships with China and, 145; required by Chinese government, at branch/joint campuses, 168–69

courts: attempts to silence academics and, 73; divisive concepts bill and, 105; off-campus activities and, 229–30, 239

COVID-19 pandemic: branch/joint campuses during, 171; censorship/free speech issues and, 5–6, 8, 37, 95–96, 202; higher education and, 135; lessons from, 227; restrictions in China, 36, 171, 254. *See also* online learning

critical race theory (CRT), 103–4, 106, 224, 240. *See also* divisive concepts

criticism, of government, 14, 28, 117

critics: exiled, targeting of, 3; peaceful, demands for protection from, 13. *See also* dissidents; Hong Kong protests/activists

Crowley, Tim, 132, 133

CRT (critical race theory), 103–4, 106, 224, 240. *See also* divisive concepts

CSSA (Chinese Students and Scholars Association). *See* Chinese Students and Scholars Association (CSSA)

Cuellar, Henry, 61

CUHK (Chinese University of Hong Kong), 201, 202, 204–5, 206, 246–47

cultural sensitivity, justification of censorship by, 4. *See also* sensitivity exploitation

culture learning centers, 57. *See also* Confucius Institutes (CIs)

curriculum, 144, 168. *See also* courses

customers, students as, 92

Dalai Lama, 49–50, 58–59, 63–66, 119, 143. *See also* Tibet

Index

Daniels, Mitch, 39
Davidson, Christopher M., 177
Davis, Miles, 99
Deeks, Andrew, 133, 134
Del Bono, Emilio, 67–68
democracy: art and, 68; educational exchanges and, 45, 47
Dennis, Everette E., 176
DeSantis, Ron, 109
disciplinary cases, speech-related, 90
discipline. *See* retaliation
discrimination, 29–30, 107. *See also* anti-Semitism; racism
discussions, academic. *See* discussions, academic
disruption, coordinated, 27, 28, 113
dissent: Chinese officials' fear of, 37; expressive freedom on campus and, 231; punishment of, 10
dissidents: administrators and, 39; apologies and, 22; censorship of by other students, 30; CIs and, 60; consequences for, 10, 17, 32–40; CSSA and, 12; families of, 11, 23, 33; harassment of, 39; punishment of, 191; self-exiled, 37. *See also* international students
diversity initiatives, 10. *See also* sensitivity exploitation
divisive concepts, 103–6, 110, 240. *See also* critical race theory (CRT); expression, controversial; political speech
Dixon, Jennifer, 149
DKU (Duke-Kunshan University), 153–56, 172, 251. *See also* branch/joint campuses
Duberstein, Andy, 223
Dukalskis, Alex, 131, 133, 134
Duke-Kunshan University (DKU), 153–56, 172, 251. *See also* branch/joint campuses
Duke University, 33, 153–56, 251
Durden, Lisa, 88–89

education, restriction and, 160
educational exchanges, 41–47, 107, 157, 161. *See also* branch/joint campuses; engagement; expansion, of universities; international students
educational models, cooperative, 136. *See also* branch/joint campuses
Education City, 174, 177. *See also* Qatar
Eisgruber, Christopher, 67
email, speech policies for, 220
Embassy, Chinese. *See* consulates/embassies, Chinese
Emerson College, 31–32
endowments, 246
engagement: academics' views of, 195–96; belief in benefits of, 157; guidelines for, 188–89; increased repression in China and, 162; liberalizing China, claims of, 161; local law and, 245; need to reassess programs, 244–45; prioritizing over academic freedom, 132; problems with, 156; in unfree countries, 242; ways of doing, 157, 160. *See also* branch/joint campuses; expansion, of universities
entertainment industry, 78–80, 162
European Association for Chinese Studies, 121
European universities: academic ties with China, 120–21; administrators' response to repression by China, 124; Chinese influence in, 119–34; financial relation with China, 124; as global institutions, 131–32; need for international students' tuition, 131; opposition to Chinese interference, 121. *See also individual countries*
exchange. *See* educational exchanges
expansion, of universities, 2; and ability to improve openness, 180; academic costs of, 177; academics' careers damaged by, 195; and authoritarian governments, 2; compromises and, 152–53, 161; effects of on US universities, 185; guidelines for international engagement and, 162–63; money and, 164, 196; opposition to, 185; toleration of human rights violations and, 196–97; into unfree countries,

Index

152–53, 161, 174–75, 193–95; values and, 195, 196. *See also* branch/joint campuses; educational exchanges; engagement; partnerships
expression, controversial, 103, 103
expression, political, 10, 14, 84, 107, 108, 110, 114, 137. *See also* divisive concepts; human rights
expressive freedoms/rights, 152, 221; barriers to, administrators and, 47–48; BRTs and, 92–93; on campus, dissent and, 231; endowments as shields for, 246; vs. financial ties with China, 102; foreign governments and, 1; sedition laws used against, 214–15; vs. suppression of unpopular speech, 86–94; universities' global reach and, 5; universities' promises of, 86; US government interference with, 238–41. *See also* academic freedom; censorship; discussions, academic; dissent; First Amendment; national security law; speech, online; speech protections; speech restrictions; speech rights; speech suppression; values

faculty. *See* academics (scholars)
Fairbank, Wilma, 41–43
Falun Gong, 54, 80, 114, 119, 143
Farahi, Dawood, 172
Faust, Drew, 75
FBI, 235–38
film industry, US, 78–80
Finkelstein, Claire, 109
FIRE (Foundation for Individual Rights and Expression), 1, 12, 89, 96, 97, 105, 182, 223, 244
First Amendment: anti-Semitism and, 107, 108; BRTs and, 92; campus speech codes and, 89, 93, 241; divisive concepts bills and, 106; legislative threats to, 238–41; public universities and, 85–86; social media and, 239. *See also* academic freedom; Constitution, US; discussions, academic; expressive freedoms/rights; speech protections; speech restrictions; speech rights; speech suppression; values
Fish, Eric, 44
Fish, Isaac Stone, 80
Fiskesjö, Magnus, 20
Florida, University of, 229–30, 239
Fordham University, 30–31
foreign policy, educational exchange and, 41–47
Foundation for Individual Rights and Expression (FIRE), 1, 12, 89, 96, 97, 105, 182, 223, 244
freedom, academic. *See* academic freedom
freedom: decline in, 6, 156–57, 180, 230, 245, 254; line between tyranny and, 230; universities' importance in building/maintaining, 230
free expression. *See* expressive freedoms/rights
Freeman, Kemper Jr., 100
Freeman, Miller, 99–100
free speech. *See* expressive freedoms/rights
Friedman, Eli, 163, 165–66
Fudan Hungary University, 120–21
Fulda, Andreas, 125–27
funding, universities', 247; and administrators' censorship of scholars, 78; in Australia, 136; branch/joint campuses and, 164, 172, 185, 187, 243; China and, 57, 124–26; CIs and, 54, 130; compromises vs. values and, 196; endowments, 246; federal, anti-Semitism and, 107; from foreign sources, 56–57, 60, 78; from international students' tuition, 4, 125, 126, 131, 242; loss of as retaliation, 66; partnerships and, 164; vs. speech rights, 60; in UK, 124–26, 130, 187; visa denials to international students and, 232

Galschiøt, Jens, 203, 204, 229, 246–47
Garfield, Jay, 63–64
Georgetown University, 224–25
Georgetown University in Qatar (GU-Q), 178

Index

George Washington University (GW), 8–14, 27, 64
Georgia, University of, 22–23
Germany, 45, 121
Gilligan, William, 31
Global China Connection, 64
Global Cornell, 166
Goldstein, Avery, 212
government, Chinese: CCP, 13, 44, 173; censoring critics of, 85; critical conversations about, on campus, 84; interference in off-campus events, 67–68. *See also* authoritarian governments/authoritarianism; Chinese Students and Scholars Association (CSSA); Confucius Institutes (CIs); consulates/embassies, Chinese; retaliation: by Chinese government
government, US: anti-Semitism and, 107–10; censorship by, 238–39; divisive concepts legislation, 103–6, 110, 240; interference in campus speech, 83, 103–10; Islamophobic speech and, 108–9; off-campus speech restrictions and, 238–41; punishment of political speech, 110; purpose of universities and, 84; restrictions on international students' admittance to US, 232–35; surveillance of international students, 233–35
Government Accountability Office (GAO), 55, 155
governments, foreign: censorship and, 1–2; challenges to speech protections, 50–51. *See also* authoritarian governments/authoritarianism; government, Chinese; *individual countries*
Great Firewall, 170. *See also* censorship, online
Green, David, 148
Greitens, Sheena Chestnut, 70
Grose, Timothy, 40, 70
Grundy, Tom, 216
Gu, Sulaiman, 22–23
GU-Q (Georgetown University in Qatar), 178

HAF (Hindu American Foundation), 72, 73
Haley, Nikki, 50
Hall, Matt, 18, 19
Hamilton, Andrew, 186
Hanban (Chinese Language Council International), 53, 55, 138. *See also* Confucius Institutes (CIs)
harassment: of academics, 150, 186; in China, 123–24; criticism of Chinese government described as, 29–30; by CSSAs, 116; on social media, 115, 255; vs. unprotected speech, 82–83. *See also* threats
Harvard Law School, 74–77, 81
Harvard University: administrators' interference in events at, 246; American Defense, Harvard Group, 43; earlier Chinese students and, 43; endowment of, 246; foreign funding for, 56–57
hate crimes, 23
Haywood, Art, 109
Heaslip, Audra, 95
Hedges, Matthew, 183–87, 189, 191, 192
Henderson, Jeffrey, 128
Hessler, Peter, 157–60
higher education: authoritarianism's effects and, 47; China's role in, 2, 3; sudden move to online learning, 198–99. *See also* universities
Hikvision, 171
Himbara, David, 195
Hindu American Foundation (HAF), 72, 73
Hindu nationalism, 72–73
Høj, Peter, 138
Holz, Carsten, 206
Hong Kong, 5, 76, 146; apologies for incorrect mentions of, 101–2, 103; demise of academic freedom in, 229; destruction of civil society in, 201, 247; Law, 28–29; Morey's tweet about, 14–17; "one country, two systems" agreement, 129; online learning in, 206–7; student unions, 201; UK universities and, 128–30; as warning for global academia, 247.

Index

See also China; Hong Kong protests/ activists; international students; national security law (Hong Kong)
Hong Kong, University of (HKU), 201, 203–4, 207
Hong Kong Baptist University, 201, 205
Hong Kong Polytechnic University, 201
Hong Kong protests/activists, 129–30; attempts to intimidate, 200; Australian universities and, 135, 137–42; branch/joint campuses management and, 173; in Canada, 114, 118; China's efforts to stifle, 199; mass scale of, 200–201; Pavlou and, 137–42, 150, 151; sedition laws used against, 214; threats against, 139; world-wide, 111. *See also* national security law
Hong Kong's Polytechnic University, 205–6
Hong Kong University of Science and Technology, 206–7
Horsley, Jamie P., 53
Hu, Anming, 236, 238
Huang Xueqin, Sophia, 123–24, 125
Huawei, 124, 188
Humanitarian China, 38
human rights, 7, 165; branch/joint campuses and, 161, 165–66, 196–97; China's attempts to silence activists abroad and, 29; China's record on, growing awareness of, 29; CIs' efforts to suppress discussion of, 54; COVID-19 in China and, 36; deflecting attention from, 181; support of, as attack on business interests, 16. *See also* expression, political; Uyghur crisis; Xinjiang
Human Rights Watch, 142, 143, 146
Hungary, 119–21

IHRA (International Holocaust Remembrance Alliance), 107, 108
image, protecting, vs. values, 97. *See also* brand
immigration. *See* visa denials
India, 72, 80
Indiana University, 69
industries. *See* corporations/businesses
institutions, global, 253; compliance with authoritarianism, 6; exported censorship and, 7–8; international consequences for, 79–80; response to critics of authoritarianism, 14–17; self-censorship by, 81; universities as, 2, 5, 111, 131; values vs. money in, 16–17. *See also* apologies/statements; branch/joint campuses; corporations/businesses; engagement; expansion, of universities; partnerships; universities
intellectual freedom, 229. *See also* academic freedom
International Holocaust Remembrance Alliance (IHRA), 107, 108
international students: expected to follow party line while abroad, 39–40, 77; families of, 3, 11, 23, 33, 34, 35, 36, 113, 121–22, 130, 143; harassment of other students, 255; history of, 40–48; imprisonment of, 35–36; lack of protection for, 4, 191; monitoring of by home government, 39–40; number of, 17; repercussions for, 32–40; required to follow laws of home country, 39–40; restrictions on admittance to US, 232–35; targeting of, 4. *See also* Chinese Students and Scholars Association (CSSA); dissidents; educational exchanges
internet, 155, 170, 171, 220, 250. *See also* online learning; social media; speech, online
In the Name of Confucius (documentary), 143
Ireland, 130–34
Irish Institute for Chinese Studies, 133
Islamophobia, 84–85, 108–9
Israel, 18, 31, 67, 106, 107, 109–10, 234

James, LeBron, 15
James, Letitia, 239
Jiang Jianjun, 77
Johns Hopkins University, 29
Johns Hopkins University–Nanjing University Center for Chinese and American Studies, 156

Index

joint campus arrangements. *See* branch/joint campuses; partnerships
joint education arrangements, 136, 158. *See also* branch/joint campuses
Jones, Suzanne, 95
journalists, student, 251
jubao, 157–58
Justice Department, 235–38
Justus & Karin Rosenberg Foundation, 108

Kachani, Soulaymane, 77
Kagame, Paul, 194–95
Kao, Kinen, 20
Karacsony, Gergely, 120
Kaulin, Oleg, 46
Kaushik, Divyansh, 21, 22
Kazakhstan, 39–40
Kean, John Jr., 173
Kean University, 171–73
Kendzior, Sarah, 98
Kennesaw State University, 52
Keshavarzian, Arang, 192–93
Khaled, Leila, 222–24, 225, 226
Khashoggi, Jamal, 189, 245
Khoo, Lester, 148
Kodak, 102
Kong, Zhihao, 37–39
Kratz, Dennis, 52

Lam, Carrie, 205
LaMay, Craig, 175
Lamborn, Doug, 223
language education programs/language learning centers, 57, 62. *See also* Confucius Institutes (CIs)
Larson, Satyel, 67
Law, Nathan, 28–29
law enforcement, 10, 92–93, 100
laws, Chinese, 74
leadership, university. *See* administrators
Lee, Ching Kwan, 248
legislators. *See* government, US
Lehman, Jeffrey S., 168, 169
Lhamo, Chemi, 115, 116–17, 150, 151
libraries, 238–39
Lieber, Charles, 235

Liebowitz, Ron, 28
Lin, Anastasia, 129
Link, Perry, 71
Liu, Meiru, 58
Liu Yunshan, 54
Livingston, James, 88
Lloyd-Damnjanovic, Anastasya, 23, 63
Lodato, Mark, 103
López Prater, Erika, 84–85
Luo Daiqing, 35–36
Luo Qijuan, 59, 60
Luther, Shelley, 232
Lynum, KJ, 31

Made in Hollywood, Censored by Beijing (PEN America), 78
Ma Huateng, 166
"Marie" (CUHK academic), 205
Markov, Sergei, 46
Marlin, Nancy, 52
Maryland, University of, 34
Mashrou' Leila, 174–75
Massachusetts Institute of Technology (MIT), 49, 50
Mayer Brown, 203
McCaul, Michael, 61
McCormack, Derek, 148
media policy, 96, 124
migrant workers, 178, 180, 193
Miller, Fayneese, 84
Miller, Stephen, 232
Mills, Nicolaus, 97
Millward, James, 69–70
Minhaj, Hasan, 80
Minnesota, University of, 35
Minsky, Lauren, 186
MIT (Massachusetts Institute of Technology), 49, 50
Morey, Daryl, 14
Morgan, Stephen, 160
Morris, Barry, 52
movie industry, 78–80, 162
Munroe, Anthony, 88–89

Nathan, Andrew J., 71
National Association of Scholars (NAS), 54–55, 59, 62

Index

National Basketball Association (NBA), 14–17
National Congress of the Chinese Communist Party (CCP), 13. *See also* government, Chinese
National Defense Authorization Act, 61
national security, US, 235–38
national security law (Hong Kong), 74; academic freedom and, 208; academics and, 200, 208, 215, 217, 247–48; anonymity and, 209–14; branch/joint campuses and, 204; classroom modifications and, 210–15; courses and, 209–10, 212; criticism prohibited by, 202; fear caused by, 217–19; global application of, 74, 200, 208; international students and, 207–8, 217–19; mandatory national security education and, 205–6; online learning and, 206–7; rapidity of implementation, 205; self-censorship and, 208, 211–12, 213, 216–17, 248; student unions and, 200, 207; Tiananmen Square massacre memorials and, 202–5, 229–30; UK and, 216; used with other repressive laws, 214–15; vagueness of, 199; Zoom and, 213
Neitzey, Christina, 73
New York University (NYU), 29, 192, 251; funding from China, 57; NYU Abu Dhabi, 185–86; NYU Shanghai, 167–71, 172
New Zealand, 147–50
Nolan, Peter, 125
North Carolina State University, 58–59
Northwestern University, in Qatar (NU-Q), 174–77
Notre Dame vs. the Klan, 87–88
Nottingham Ningbo China, University of (UNNC), 160–61
NU-Q (Northwestern University, in Qatar), 174–77
NurMuhammad, Rizwangul, 18, 19

Obama, Barack, 50
Office of Equity & Title IX. *See* harassment
Olsen, Matthew G., 237
Olympics, Beijing (2022), 7, 8–14, 33, 254
Omar, Ilhan, 108–9
"one China principle," 121. *See also* Taiwan
"one country, two systems," 129. *See also* Hong Kong
online learning, 199; academic freedom and, 199, 215, 221; anonymity and, 209–14; classroom modifications and, 210–15; corporations' power over, 224; expressive freedoms/rights and, 199, 219, 221; future of, 226–28; in Hong Kong, 206–7; international students and, 207–8; national security law and, 206–7; new threats from, 219; prevalence of, 226–27; sudden move to, 198–99; surveillance and, 219; technology for, 171; threats of to academic freedom, 215; Zoom and, 221–26. *See also* COVID-19 pandemic; surveillance; Zoom
online speech, 220–21. *See also* campus discussions; social media; speech restrictions; Zoom
Orbán, Viktor, 119. *See also* Hungary

Palestine, 18, 31, 97, 109–10
Palestinians, 234. *See also* Khaled, Leila
pandemics, 227. *See also* COVID-19 pandemic; online learning
Panyi, Szabolcz, 120
papers, student, 91
partnerships: authoritarian governments/authoritarianism and, 63, 134, 230; censorship and, 1–2; with human rights offenders, 166–67, 230; in Hungary, 120–21; increasing repression and, 164; institutional autonomy and, 136; loss of, 35, 66; opposition to, 163–67; protection of, 83; replacing CIs, 62–63; suspension of, 163; universities' need to reconsider, 249. *See also* branch/joint campuses; expansion, of universities; institutions, global

Index

Patrick, Dan, 104
Pavlou, Drew, 137–42, 150, 151
Peace Corps, 157, 160
Pearson, Elaine, 146
Peking University, 163–67
PEN America, 66–67, 78
Pennsylvania, University of (Penn), 29, 57
People for the Ethical Treatment of Animals (PETA), 86–87, 101
People's Republic of China (PRC). *See* China; consulates/embassies, Chinese; government, Chinese
Perdue, Peter C., 69
Perry, Ralph Barton, 43
PETA (People for the Ethical Treatment of Animals), 86–87, 101
Peterson, Rachelle, 59
Phansey, Asheen, 98
Phillips, Michael, 96
phones, surveillance and, 210, 233–35. *See also* social media
Pittsburgh, University of, 157–60
policy, speech. *See* speech codes/policies
political speech, 10, 14, 84, 108, 110, 114, 137. *See also* academic freedom; discussions, academic; divisive concepts; expressive freedoms/rights; First Amendment; human rights; speech protections; speech restrictions; speech rights; speech suppression
Pollack-Pelzner, Daniel, 99
Pompeo, Michael, 165, 232
Portugal, universities in, 121
PRC (People's Republic of China). *See* China; consulates/embassies, Chinese; government, Chinese
press, purpose of, 251
press, student, 91, 154, 164, 182, 186, 251
Price, Vincent, 153
Princeton University, 55, 67, 246
professors. *See* academics
professors, adjunct, 98
propaganda. *See* Confucius Institutes (CIs)
ProPublica, 39

protest(s): in China, 254; repression of, branch/joint campuses and, 204. *See also* Hong Kong protests/activists
punishment. *See* retaliation
Purdue University, 37

Qatar: Education City, 174, 177; funding from, 57; migrant workers in, 178; NU-Q, 174–77
Qatar Foundation, 174, 175
Qatar National Research Fund, 176

racism, 21–22, 23, 117, 133, 136, 235–37. *See also* sensitivity exploitation
repression, increase in, 162, 199, 245
repression, transnational, 250
reputational damage, 88. *See also* brand
research: at branch/joint campuses, 178–81; in unfree countries, 183–87. *See also* academics; visa denials
retaliation, 68, 122; by administrators, 75–77; by Chinese government, 65–66, 68, 69–71; fear of, 145–46; by Indian government, 72–74; protection from, 127; research-related, 69–71; self-censorship and, 126; for students' actions, 122; in UK, 126–28. *See also* visa denials
Richmond, Yale, 45, 46
Right to Maim, The (Larson), 67
Rochester, University of, 24
Rodrigues, Ray, 109
Rose-Hulman Institute of Technology, 40
Ross, Andrew, 193
Rubio, Marco, 12, 52, 61
Rusesabagina, Paul, 194
Russia, 3; censorship of American films, 79; invasion of Ukraine, 18, 134, 196; investigation of academics and, 237; UCD's internationalization and, 134
Rwanda, 194–95

Saccamano, Neil, 163
Sahlins, Marshall, 57
Sampson, Keith, 87
San Diego State, 52

322

Index

San Francisco State University (SFSU), 222–23, 226
Saudi Arabia, 3, 80; branch/joint campuses in, 244–45; censorship of American films, 79; funding from, 57; Khashoggi execution and, 189, 245
Savannah State University, 59–60
Schakowsky, Jan, 108
scholars. *See* academics (scholars)
SCUPI (Sichuan University–Pittsburgh Institute), 157–60
sedition laws, in Hong Kong, 214–15
self-censorship, 71–72; in American institutions, 81; in Australian universities, 142; at branch/joint campuses, 170, 173, 177; CIs and, 58; in entertainment industry, 80; equivalence to veto power, 212; financial relationships and, 78; financial ties to China and, 126; by institutions, 77; by international students in Australia, 142–43; national security law and, 208, 211–12, 213, 216–17, 248; retaliation and, 126; in UK universities, 126–28; uncertainty/vagueness about rights and, 159; visa applications and, 233–34; Zoom and, 216–17. *See also* silence
sensitivity, 84–94
sensitivity exploitation, 4–5, 83, 117, 241; among students, 18; attempts to prevent criticism of China and, 29–30; at Australian universities, 135; deflecting conversations about China and, 22–23; described, 14; off-campus, 67–68; speech policies and, 93–94; at UK universities, 129
Sexton, John, 192
Sherman, Brad, 97
Sichuan University–Pittsburgh Institute (SCUPI), 157–60
silence: academics' careers and, 231; branch/joint campuses and, 197; lack of understanding of authoritarian governments and, 151. *See also* self-censorship
Simon, Denis, 156

Slotkin, Elissa, 18, 19
Smith College, 63
Smith Finley, Jo, 127
social media, 98, 146; attacks on academics on, 159; blacklisted words, 100–101; brand protection and, 100–101; censors without borders and, 113–14; Chinese, censorship of, 154; Chinese threats to European students and, 122–23; First Amendment and, 239; harassment on, 35, 115, 255; hiding replies, 31–32; of international students, 113–14; organization of demonstrations on, 130; protection on, 250; punishment for posts on, 30–31, 35–36, 143; removal of events from platforms, 226; retaliation against academics and, 72–73; sedition laws and, 214; speech policies for, 220; surveillance of, 233–35; threats to families of international students, 143; universities' investigations of, 140, 141. *See also* apologies/statements; corporations/businesses; speech, online; tech companies/technology; WeChat; Weibo; Zoom
soft power, China's, 53. *See also* Confucius Institutes (CIs)
Sony, 79
South Asia Scholar Activist Collective, 73
Southern California, University of, 57
Soviet Union, 45–46
Spain, universities in, 121
speech, freedom of. *See* academic freedom; discussions, academic; expressive freedoms/rights; First Amendment; speech protections; speech restrictions; speech rights; values
speech, online, 220–21. *See also* campus discussions; social media; speech restrictions; Zoom
speech, political, 10, 14, 84, 107, 108, 110, 114, 137. *See also* divisive concepts; human rights

323

Index

speech codes/policies, 89, 93–94, 220, 241
speech perceived as offensive, 83, 89
speech protections, 152; administrators and, 91; at American universities, 50–51; at branch/joint campuses, 176; BRTs and, 92; foreign governments' challenges to, 50–51; vs. funding partnerships, 60; vs. revenue from international students, 242; Title VI and, 107. *See also* academic freedom; expressive freedoms/rights; First Amendment; values
speech restrictions, 3, 105, 219–20, 238–41, 253–54. *See also* censorship
speech rights, 89–90, 94, 231, 246–51, 254. *See also* academic freedom; discussions, academic; expressive freedoms/rights; First Amendment; speech protections; speech restrictions; speech suppression; values
speech suppression, 5, 9, 84–94. *See also* censorship; expressive freedoms/rights; speech restrictions
Sperling, Elliot, 69
Stanford University, 55, 57, 246
statements/apologies. *See* apologies/statements; brand
Stern, Kenneth, 108
student governments, 91, 115–17
student groups/organizations, 86–87, 156, 231–32. *See also* Chinese Students and Scholars Association (CSSA)
students, Chinese international: control over, 136; disappearance of, 123–24; loyalty pledges required of, 121; number of, 17. *See also* Chinese Students and Scholars Association (CSSA); international students
students, international. *See* international students
surveillance: at branch/joint campuses, 179, 193; by Chinese government, at GW, 13–14; ease of, 44; by home government, 39–40; of international students, 117, 230, 233–35; by other students, 20, 25, 117; of phones/social media, 233–35; technology for, 166, 171; Zoom and, 207. *See also* online learning
Susskind, Alex, 163
Sweden, universities in, 121–22
Switzerland, universities in, 122–23

Taiwan: apologies for incorrect mentions of, 101–2, 103; and Chinese interference in European universities, 121; CIs' efforts to suppress discussion of, 54; consular complaints about events regarding, 64; language education programs, 62; "one China principle," 121; potential invasion of, 196. *See also* China
Tang, Chris, 5
Tang, Rose, 76
Tanyolacar, Serhat, 100
Tatum, Mark, 16
teaching, online. *See* online learning
tech companies/technology, 166, 171, 223, 224. *See also* corporations/businesses; online learning; social media; surveillance; Zoom
Tencent, 166
Teng Biao, 75–77
tenure, 98, 167, 231, 241
Texas at Dallas, University of, 52
threats: against academics, in New Zealand, 150; endorsed by consulates, 150; against Hong Kong protestors, 140; lack of action against, 116. *See also* harassment
Tiananmen Papers, The (Link and Nathan), 71
Tiananmen Square massacre, 30–31, 44, 76, 173
Tiananmen Square massacre memorials, 37–39, 148, 202–5, 221, 225, 229–30, 246–47
Tibet, 49; apologies for incorrect mentions of, 101–2, 103, 156; censorship by students and, 24, 54, 115–17; student events regarding, 33–34; Students for a Free Tibet, 76. *See also* China; Dalai Lama

Index

Tibetans, in Canada, Chinese repression and, 114–19
Title VI of Civil Rights Act, 107
Tohti, Ilham, 69
Tong, Austin, 30–31
Tonra, Ben, 134
Toope, Stephen, 188
transnational repression, 250
Truex, Rory, 70, 211–12, 213
Trump, Donald, 21, 50, 61, 107, 232, 235–38
Truschke, Audrey, 72
Tsai, Joe, 15
Turdush, Rukiye, 112
Turkey, 66–67
tyranny, 230. *See also* authoritarian governments/authoritarianism

U, Eddy, 208–10, 215
UAE (United Arab Emirates), 183–93
UAE-Cambridge Innovation Institute, 187–89
UK-China Global Issues Dialogue Centre at Jesus College, 124–25
Ukraine, Russian invasion of, 18, 134, 196
unfree countries, expansion into, 152–53, 161. *See also* authoritarian governments/authoritarianism; branch/joint campuses; *individual countries*
United Arab Emirates (UAE), 2, 57, 183–93
United Front Work Department, 114
United Kingdom, Hong Kong and, 129
United Kingdom universities, 123–30; branch/joint campuses in China, 160–61; Chinese interference in, 128; funding of, 124–26, 130; Hong Kong and, 128–30; national security law and, 216; retaliation against academics in, 126–28; self-censorship at, 126–28; UK-China Global Issues Dialogue Centre at Jesus College, 124–25. *See also individual colleges*
universities: authoritarian governments' pressure on, 3, 252; changed by engagement with China, 162–67;

First Amendment and, 85–86; free expression and, 1; importance of in creating free societies, 230; open and free, need for, 255; protecting, 238; purpose of, 84, 224; role of in growth of authoritarianism, 241–43. *See also* academics; administrators; branch/joint campuses; European universities; institutions, global; *individual countries; individual universities*
University Alliance of the Silk Road, 9
University College Dublin (UCD), 131–34
Uyghur crisis: Campaign for Uyghurs, 76; CSSAs and, 24, 27; discussion about repressed at UK universities, 125; and enrolment in classes, 40; professors forbidden to talk about, 173; retaliation for speaking about, 127; student disputes about, 18–20; technology used in, 166, 171; Tohti, 69; toleration of, expansion and, 165, 196; Turdush, 112; unfamiliarity with, 94. *See also* human rights; Xinjiang
Uyghurs: acknowledgment of oppression of, 22; in Canada, Chinese repression and, 114; discrimination against, 165; unwillingness to speak honestly, 137. *See also* Xinjiang

Valdez, Jessica R., 207
values: vs. bottom line, 16–17; branch/joint campuses and, 243; vs. brand protection, 97, 135; compromises and, 152, 195, 196; vs. demands of stakeholders, 224; vs. expansion, 195, 196; vs. financial ties with China, 102; vs. local laws of branch/joint campuses, 243; vs. money, 16–17, 243; violating, to combat authoritarianism, 231. *See also* academic freedom; expressive freedoms/rights; speech protections
Vest, Charles M., 50
Virginia Commonwealth University, 177

Index

visa denials, 68, 69, 71; blacklisting and, 70; branch/joint campuses and, 178–81, 192; to international students, 232–35; national security law and, 208; self-censorship and, 71–72; UK academics and, 126; viewpoint-based reasoning for, 234–35
VPN access, 155, 171

Wack, Patrick, 102
Walker, Mark E., 105, 229–30, 239
Wang, Grace, 33–34
Wang, William, 19
Wang Gungwu, 171
Wang Jianbing, 123–24
Washington University in St. Louis, 9
Wasserstrom, Jeffrey, 213–15
Waters, Dacen, 22
WeChat, 26, 27, 102, 115, 130. *See also* social media
Weibo, 35. *See also* social media
Wenzhou-Kean University, 172–73
Wesleyan University, 244
West, Jordan S., 10
whistleblowing, lack of protection for, 195
White Paper movement, 36
Wiemer, Calla, 69
Wisconsin-Madison, University of, 64
Wolford, Wendy, 165
Woodrow Wilson International Center for Scholars, 23, 63
Wong, Joshua, 29
Wray, Christopher, 237
Wrighton, Mark S., 9–10, 11, 12–13
Wuhan University, 153. *See also* Duke-Kunshan University (DKU)

Xia, Ming, 68–69
Xiaolei Wu, 255
Xiao Yewen, 148
Xi Jinping, 114, 254. *See also* government, Chinese
Xi Jinping—The Most Powerful Man in the World (Aust and Geiges), 121

Xinjiang: blacklisting of academics and, 69–70; CIs' efforts to suppress discussion of, 54; discussion about repressed at UK universities, 125; embassy complaints about campus events regarding, 64; fire in, 254, 255; NBA and, 16; retaliation for speaking about, 21, 127; student disputes about, 18–20; surveillance in, 166, 171; threats against critics of, 139. *See also* human rights; Uyghur crisis
Xinjiang: China's Muslim Borderland, 69–70
Xu Jie, 139

Yale University, 57, 246
Yang Shuping, 34–35
Yiu, Jack, 138
Yu Lizhong, 168
Yuzhin, Boris, 46

Zhang, Jinrey, 36–37, 41
Zhang Ming, 154
Zhang Sheng, 13
Zhou, Jake, 128
Zhou Fengsuo, 38
Zhu Lihan, 34–35
Zoellner, Tom, 193–95
Zoom, 209, 221–26; cooperation with Chinese authorities, 38–39, 221–22; demands of stakeholders and, 224; freedom of speech/academic freedom and, 225–26; Khaled event and, 222–24, 226; national security law and, 213; power to determine campus discussions, 223; protecting identities on, 211; removal of events from platform, 226; self-censorship and, 216–17; surveillance and, 207; terms of service, 225; Tiananmen Square massacre memorials and, 38–39. *See also* corporations/businesses; online learning; speech, online

Browse more books from HOPKINS PRESS

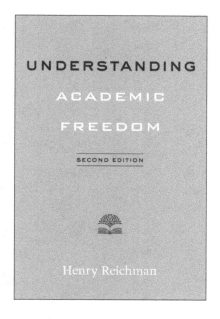

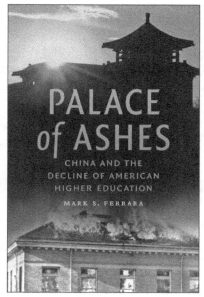

JOHNS HOPKINS UNIVERSITY PRESS | PRESS.JHU.EDU